Kicking SaaS

101 Founders on What it Takes to Launch a Software as a Service

Interviews by Kelsey Yarnell

All rights reserved.
Kicking SaaS Content LLC, February 2022

Imagine it is 2003. You are working on a $250K project. You send an email to the customer with an attached contract. The customer has to print it, sign it, and send it back to you. It takes 48-72 hours, based on the situation.

DocuSign was born to solve this problem.

Today, in the same situation, you open DocuSign, attach your contract, add signature blocks, and send it to the customer. The customer opens the link, does a digital signature, and *voila*! The contract is signed, and both parties receive a signed contract.

This was all done via a Contract Management SaaS platform running on the Cloud Infrastructure.

The story of DocuSign inspired me to become a SaaS entrepreneur. SaaS allows me to automate and simplify complex, repeatable workflows–and achieve incredible, repeatable results. Today, I have automated event marketing processes to help SaaS founders to do co-sell marketing with Cloud hyperscalers.

As a SaaS founder and Fortune1000 Next Entrepreneur, I've always loved building SaaS solutions that leverage Cloud and AI. I have been blessed to help 5,000+ companies embark on their Cloud journey by helping them to build SaaS solutions. I have also architected the Women in Cloud Accelerator, which helps female tech founders co-sell their SaaS solution with Microsoft to win enterprise opportunities via marketplaces.

Why am I passionate about SaaS? The size of the opportunity. According to Fortune Market Insights, the global software as a service (SaaS) market size was $113.82 billion in 2020. The market is expected to grow from USD $130.69 billion in 2021 to $716.52 billion in 2028 at a CAGR of 27.5% during the 2021-2028 period.

I've had to overcome logistical, financial, and emotional challenges on my SaaS journey. From the beginning, I wish I had access to 100+ SaaS founders who could have helped me answer critical questions like:

How do you acquire customers?

How do you succeed as a non-technical founder?

How do you develop the proper KPI's?

When Kelsey told me about her upcoming book on what it takes for founders to launch a SaaS solution, I was intrigued and excited. Every day I meet and engage with SaaS founders who are constantly looking for the silver bullet to build a $1M ARR SaaS business to secure funding, win customers, and achieve great things in the world.

The magic sauce for the founders in *Kicking SaaS* was that they dared to go after their dreams of solving complex problems, being coachable, building an audience before developing a solution, pivoting fast to stay relevant, partnering with the right companies, and making a positive impact in the world.

Kelsey's book shows how 101 founders are launching and growing their SaaS businesses. On the way, they have gathered valuable lessons that can help you fail less and win more every day on your own SaaS journey.

This book is a must-read book for anyone willing to learn, experiment, and bring innovative SaaS solutions to the 21st Century.

Chaitra Vedullapalli

Co-Founder & CMO, Meylah

Co-Founder & President, Women In Cloud

INTRODUCTION

Over the last 12 months, I've interviewed 100+ people who have launched SaaS businesses.

Some of these founders have a decade-plus experience and have started multiple businesses. Others are first-time founders who are just a couple years in. Some of them have seen crazy growth, and others have struggled to pinpoint the real problem that their customers are experiencing. Some are technically skilled; others are pivoting into tech from an entirely different industry.

All of them have made mistakes.

All of them have learned valuable lessons.

And all of them are eager to share the good advice they wish they knew before.

You might have heard it said that SaaS is a marathon, not a sprint.

I want to help you run that marathon more quickly, with fewer sprained ankles and less chafing.

To make this book simpler, I've divided it into six categories of founders. Feel free to flip to the section that's most relevant to you, and skip all the others (or read every single interview, if you're that kind of person).

If you want to niche down even more, use the indexes of key terms and industries to look for interviews that relate to a specific topic–like building an MVP, finding a co-founder, or bootstrapping.

My one request? Don't put this book down before you have at least one *aha!* moment–the kind of moment that can save you from making a costly mistake, wasting time, or losing your sanity over SaaS.

There have been plenty of entrepreneurs who have gone before you. Let them pack down the path and cut the air for you.

– *Kelsey*

INDEX OF KEY TOPICS

AI – 38, 52, 54, 71, 74, 77, 147, 205, 258
Bootstrapping – 49, 57, 61, 64, 65, 115, 133, 138, 152, 192, 2833, 245, 254, 269, 276
Calm company – 61, 120, 126
Chicken or the egg – 22, 95, 164, 175, 212, 258, 272
Company culture – 120, 142, 184
Customer acquisition – 9, 16, 35, 46, 49, 52, 83, 95, 106, 109, 135, 138, 155, 164, 169, 172, 181, 189, 192, 201, 223, 231, 235, 237, 272
Customer discovery – 38, 61, 87, 99, 103, 112, 138, 195, 251, 272
Development – 2, 29, 41, 43, 46, 59, 74, 77, 81, 84, 92, 155, 157, 169, 187, 227, 240, 247, 260, 267, 282
Distribution – 83, 95, 155, 195, 223, 231, 282
Enterprise sales – 9, 157, 160
Female founder – 9, 29, 38, 46, 52, 68, 74, 178, 181, 216, 221
Fundraising – 12, 16, 26, 29, 32, 38, 61, 71, 78, 92, 103, 115, 123, 130, 133, 164, 192, 199, 218, 221, 227, 269
Hiring – 22, 29, 120, 135, 138, 145, 187, 223, 258, 284
Iteration – 95, 109, 112, 184, 269, 276
Marketplace – 43, 65, 123, 258, 260, 272, 282
Metrics – 26, 164, 172, 223, 284
Mindset – 5, 16, 19, 26, 29, 35, 41, 59, 68, 83, 86, 112, 126, 133, 135, 142, 145, 147, 152, 157, 160, 172, 175, 178, 181, 184, 187, 227, 233, 240, 242, 245, 247, 251, 256, 264, 267, 269
MVP – 7, 12, 22, 26, 29, 43, 59, 78, 84, 92, 112, 130, 169, 181, 189, 192, 212, 221, 237, 262
No-code – 95, 218, 267, 272, 276, 278
Non-technical founder – 2, 12, 29, 32, 35, 38, 46, 49, 54, 61, 84, 95, 221, 227, 235
Pricing – 49, 106, 109, 120, 199, 216, 233, 245
Product/market fit – 7, 19, 41, 57, 77, 99, 145, 254
Resources – 87, 147, 160, 216, 247, 249
Side hustle – 95, 210, 240
Team – 32, 43, 65, 123, 142, 145, 227
Time management – 7, 12, 19, 242, 262
Top up/bottom down – 115, 205
Validation – 49, 54, 74, 78, 103, 106, 123, 195, 212, 221, 242, 251, 254
Virality – 95, 223, 231
Work-life balance – 86, 120, 126, 147, 169, 175, 235, 242

INDEX OF INDUSTRIES

Brewing/restaurant – 7
Civics/legislation – 78
Customer experience – 189, 192
Customer support – 195
Cybersecurity – 9
E-commerce – 210
EdTech – 164, 221
Education – 260
Employee insight – 54
Estate planning – 112
Fintech PropTech – 282
Freelancing software – 61
Future of Work – 133, 231
Human resources – 187, 242
Identity Confirmation – 256
Insurance – 26, 76
Interior design – 45
Manufacturing – 43, 86
Marketing – 22, 35, 52, 57, 95, 99, 106, 126, 142, 145, 178, 233, 247, 272
Medtech – 41, 68, 71, 74
Mobile service – 32
News media and content – 82
No-code – 267
Oil and gas – 59
Outdoor recreation – 12
Pet care – 175
Podcasting – 218
Project management – 126, 169
Property management – 19, 282
Real estate – 5, 49, 184, 227
SEO – 235
Shipping/heavy equipment – 2
Social media – 251, 264
Social/Lifestyle/Community – 87
Software development – 216
Team communication – 16
Technical writing – 240

Telephony – 157
Time analytics – 133
Travel – 262
Website management – 120

TABLE OF CONTENTS

PART 1
THE MAVERICKS
*Founders who went rogue, changed their careers,
and started a SaaS with minimal experience* 1

PART 2
THE GUIDES
*Founders who know the ropes…and are
willing to share their expertise and wisdom* 91

PART 3
OVERACHIEVERS
Founders who keep starting SaaS companies 168

PART 4
THE LONE RANGERS
Founders who are going it alone 215

PART 5
NO-CODE HEROES
*Founders who believe that building a
SaaS doesn't have to mean coding* 266

PART 6
REFOUNDERS
*Founders who are giving fresh starts to
existing SaaS companies* 281

PART 1

THE MAVERICKS

Founders who went rogue, changed their careers, and started a SaaS with minimal experience

#1

Dusty LaValley

Title: Founder & CEO, Trusted Dispatch

Value proposition: Trusted Dispatch expedites heavy shipping through a broker-free digital platform

Industry: Shipping, trucking, heavy equipment

Keywords: Co-founder, development, non-technical founder

How did you get into tech?

I was a professional rodeo athlete for many years. I traveled all across North America and made good money, but for the most part, I had very little knowledge of how the business world operated—especially technology. After 15 years, my career was winding down, and I started to think, *I've often wanted to do something major and run a business*. The only thing that I had was the guts to go for it. Five years ago, I was literally sitting around having a few cocktails one night with my brother and my brother-in-law when I decided to start a business and spun up an idea.

But I got a big giant slap in the face, a wakeup call, when I realized how challenging it is to run a business. Running a business is somewhat like a professional career in sports. It takes you several years of learning, perfecting, practicing, and making sacrifices. You do the same things over and over, but you keep your vision and your competitiveness. You don't just stop. You continue to go for it, and you do whatever you have to do to succeed.

How did you arrive from that original business plan to running a SaaS today?

The journey has been interesting because the initial business model was very different from Trusted Dispatch. One year in, I did a major pivot that led me to recognize that the trucking industry is very inefficient. We have these semi-trucks that are rolling down the highway empty, always looking for extra loads. Traditionally, they're getting paid to go from A to B, drop off the product, turn around, and come back to home base empty.

For many years I simply listened to my users in the industry and let them tell me what was needed as a solution to the problems. I just continued to build. Eventually, I felt myself getting pulled into being a traditional low broker. I was taking lots of phone calls, writing down lots of notes, sitting on many, many emails, and managing touch points and interactions with every single transaction that I was trying to fulfill. It was extremely frustrating. I started thinking, *There's got to be some technology or software that can make this better for me.* That's when I started looking into tech. My website developer spun up an online system where I could publish load sites and communicate to customers without a phone call. That was phase one of a validation process for me, although I didn't really know what I was doing at the time.

At what point did you decide to become more intentional with going digital?

I realized that there was something there, and that I had to get this thing fully automated. That's also when things got really challenging for me. Being from this small town up in northern Alberta (Canada), there are zero tech resources available. I just began using Facebook to look for insight from any of my connections. Sure enough, I got hooked up with a development group in Boulder, Colorado. Unfortunately, they did a really horrible job and it was many months over the timeline and many tens of thousands of dollars over budget. I took it upon myself to blueprint everything on my own. I just drew it all out on paper.

The same development group looked it over and said, "That's a very simple application and we can spin it up in a couple months for around $10k." To be honest with you, what we have today is very similar to what I had originally blueprinted.

Was it smooth sailing from then on?

Not really. Next thing you know, a year later and we're tens of thousands of dollars over budget. It was also a really bad time for me personally and for the business. But at the end of the day, I finally had some kind of a product that allowed me to start networking with the right people. I moved to a bigger city—Calgary—where there are least some tech resources. Then I got lucky. I met the right person to partner with, and he's now my CTO. We've been together for two years now and we've been through some highs and lows. But he was excited about what I was doing, and had some background in the industry. He took six months to re-create Trusted Dispatch into what it is today.

From there, we've spent some time fine tuning and perfecting the process. Installing the UX lens allows us to watch users anonymously and identify problems immediately. I'll never forget the day that we installed that. I remember asking, "Why the hell is that user clicking over there? Why did he do that?" It doesn't matter. We just have to adjust things. And that has made a giant difference. Now, we're starting to scale and business is going really well.

What kinds of advice would you give to founders without a technical background?

Step one, you've got to validate your idea. It doesn't matter if you think you have a good idea or not, or if your friends think you have a good idea. Step two is that you've got to immerse yourself in the right ecosystems and network. I've had really bad experiences and bad luck with outsourcing. Finding the right person to partner with is going to take some luck. Because you're going to have to get along. Your partner has got to want to invest their sweat equity into the business, and get passionate about this opportunity as well. Once you've got a partner, then you can hit step three: start building and listen to your customers. Listen to people who don't know you, and aren't influenced by you.

How have you approached funding?

I've been self-funded until this point. But we have great, consistent marketing metrics, and we're at a point where we're ready for our Series A round. Three years ago, I had never even heard of a pitch deck. But now, I've been to Silicon Valley, had a few offers, and made some great connections. In my off time, I've been working on a deck and a financial model and projections.

I'm passionate about my business. People have told me that when I start talking about this opportunity, I light up. It's not fabricated. I wholeheartedly believe in what we're doing and in the opportunity in this market. Let's say we make $300-$400 per transaction—times that by 10k and it's pretty easy to get excited.

TAKEAWAYS:

- Find potential customers that will give you honest feedback (i.e. not your friends).
- Be tenacious. The journey can take years.

- Immerse yourself in the right ecosystems and networks—especially if you're new to tech.

#2
Eddy Boccara

Title: Co-founder & CEO, Corofy

Value proposition: Provides real estate brokerages with the highest quality market and human capital intelligence

Industry: Real estate

Keywords: Customer success, data, mindset

What is Corofy?

Corofy is a brokerage intelligence platform. We pull, aggregate, and analyze data from multiple public sources. We make that information accessible and digestible to real estate brokerages—their employers—through our platform where they can identify the top performers and access competitive intelligence. We make it really easy to get in touch with the best agents in the market.

How did you identify this as a problem?

Real estate is competitive and brokerages compete for salespeople in order to generate revenue. Before founding Corofy, I was responsible for running a brokerage, hiring agents, and training them. I just felt like there was no dedicated platform for me to connect with talent. My time wasn't optimized and it slowed down our growth.

Are you a technical founder?

I'm a non-technical founder. I have one technical co-founder.

What kind of expertise do you bring to the table?

A deep understanding of the brokerage business.

What advice would you give to a SaaS founder for generating growth?

I can't stress enough how important it is to actually listen to customers to really understand their pains.

What's been the biggest challenge so far of building Corofy?

The biggest challenge was to help customers build new habits. This industry can be a little old school and old fashioned. So it's been a challenge to create an adoption process. We've focused a lot on customer success and customer support. Once customers adopt the technology–and experience the benefits–they learn that they can't live without it.

Do you have any other advice for founders who are building something in an industry that's a little old-school?

Be an expert of the problem you're solving. I think too many founders get into a specific industry without having the right background. If you want to solve a problem, you need to have been bothered by it for a while.

What sort of mindset do you need to be a founder?

You have to be obsessed. One of my advisors told me that that being obsessed is the greatest skill you have in the early days, until you really prove product/market fit. Be obsessed with customer success. Building a good product is great, but it's not enough. Relentlessly providing your customers with the support they need to achieve their goals is what will set you apart from your competition.

How do you manage a co-founder relationship?

In the early days, everybody is doing a little bit of everything. But the sooner you figure out who manages what part of the business, the better.

TAKEAWAYS

- The problem you're solving should be a problem that's bothered you for a while.
- Get obsessed with customer success.
- Figure out which co-founder is managing which part of the business.

# 3

Pulkit Agrawal

Title: Founder & CEO, The 5th Ingredient, Beer30

Value proposition: Beer30 helps brewers leverage data to save time, improve quality, and increase sales

Industry: Brewing, Restaurant

Keywords: MVP, product/market fit, time management

How did you get into the brewery business?

I studied mechanical engineering at Harvard University, and was then recruited to come to San Diego and work as a Process Engineer at Ballast Point Brewing. I focused on packaging equipment, kegging, bottling, and canning. Then I helped launch nitrogen brewed brands for Ballast Point and bulk production.

In October 2017, I started The 5th Ingredient. The first four ingredients in beer are water, grains, hops, and yeast. The fifth is data.

As I hit up potential clients, I realized that most brewers still use paper logs, spreadsheets, and whiteboards for data, which makes it pretty difficult to run analysis. That's when I came up with the concept for Beer30.

After getting feedback from a few early adopters, I launched our Alpha version in early 2018, with the first paying customer in May 2018. The team and the product have been scaling and growing organically ever since.

How did you get feedback and test viability?

In the beginning of 2018, I told myself I had five months to test market fit for Beer30. So I approached a couple brewery owners and brewery friends in San Diego and asked them to check out the product. I continued to meet up with them, collecting feedback and building out the product. In April 2018, I went to the national Craft Brewers Conference, where I showed Beer30 to 110 brewery employees across 70 breweries. I asked them simple questions, like, "Do you like it? Would you use it?"

The response was overwhelmingly like, "Yeah, this is really cool. It's nowhere near what I need, but at least I like where you're headed." I got my first customer and realized that this was something people would pay for.

Get feedback on what your intended customers like and dislike about your product, and keep on updating the software until you can prove that somebody is going to pay for it. Someone may tell you they love your platform, but when you ask them if they're willing to pay for it, it changes the entire conversation.

You should also have a couple industry-specific contacts who are interested in the product enough to give you true feedback on it. If you don't have those contacts, that indicates there's no clear product/market fit or you haven't found your target ideal customer.

How did you land on a timeline for testing viability?

The important thing is to put a legitimate timeline on when you think you're going to have an MVP up and running, even if it seems arbitrary. Use external events like conferences to hold yourself accountable to your timelines and product launch. I told myself five months because my lease was expiring, but people will spend one to three years just building something out. I wanted to make sure there was traction before I wasted that much time.

Give yourself a true deadline and hold to it. Be honest. Are you hitting your goals and setting proper metrics?

Any final advice for founders?

As a founder, you're not working a 9 to 5. You're only being held accountable to yourself. That being said, it's super important to be time-sensitive.

From the start of Beer30, I've kept track of an entire workflow of how I'm spending my hours. Actually, all our team members and developers block out their time to see how many hours they're working on things that make an impact for the company.

At the minimum I should be working "40 hours" per week because that's the standard workweek by definition. But I average about 70 hours a week.

So that's one thing that I love telling other entrepreneurs. Document your hours. Don't just guess what you're doing. Manage expectations, don't overcommit. Be diligent, meticulous, and vigilant...all the time.

TAKEAWAYS:

- Go to industry tradeshows and events to get validation from potential customers.
- Don't just ask, "Do you like it?" Ask, "Would you pay for it?"
- Find at least two industry contacts who will give you honest feedback throughout development.
- Hold yourself to your own timelines, even if they feel arbitrary.
- Document your hours to determine how you are actually spending your time.

Daniela Applegate

Title: Cofounder & VP of Marketing, rThreat

Value proposition: rThreat is a breach and attack emulation platform that challenges your cyber defenses using real world and custom threats in a secure environment. Think of rThreat as your live fire exercise for cyber attacks

Industry: Cybersecurity

Keywords: Customer acquisition, female founder, enterprise sales

What is rThreat?

rThreat is a breach and attack emulation platform with built-in threat intelligence. We run security assessments for your company by using real malicious scripts or malware in a secure testing environment. The goal is to see how effective your cyber defenses are in preventing cyber attacks from infiltrating your network.

If you're a big enterprise company, you can easily spend a million dollars a year on security software. But companies often get a rude awakening when they're actually hacked–or they see our demo. When we emulate a real attack, they realize that their tools don't work.

Just because you have big name brands that everyone touts as the "best in the industry" doesn't mean you're going to be safe.

How did you get involved in rThreat?

Jesus Garcia, our original founder, started rThreat back in 2018 as a passion project. He had been working in cybersecurity for over 10 years for some big corporations. In March of 2020, he reached out to me and said, "I have this great idea, but I'm not a business person. I'm an engineer. But I think we can take this to the next level. Would you join me as a founder?"

Why did he reach out to you?

I graduated with a degree in digital design from Seattle University in 2015, so I had come from the creative world in branding and graphic design marketing. For a while I worked in e-learning and curriculum development. I've always been interested in tech, but I didn't know about cybersecurity. It's been a learning curve, but I wouldn't change it for anything.

How did you help rThreat get off the ground?

When I entered, Jesus was bootstrapping it out of his own salary. The product itself was approaching the Beta stage, but he hadn't done anything on the business side. That's where I came in to help. I started our social media pages and developed our brand and our visuals marketing collateral, and got it ready to pitch to both investors and to potential clients.

What have you learned from the pitching process?

Cybersecurity takes a specific approach. You're not buying a pair of $50 shoes. You're buying a product that costs $50k a year or more. There's definitely a greater emphasis on building trust with potential clients. Promoting your own thought leadership and creating content that shows that you know the space are key.

What kind of advice can you give to companies who are wanting to start a subscription with a larger price tag?

Articulate both your value proposition and also what makes you different from the competition (if you have competition). One of the questions that we get is, "Why are you better than competitors who have been around 5+ years?" Be able to give an answer to that and also show, if possible, data that supports why you are better or why you are the more cost-effective option with more features.

Any other advice for SaaS companies who are entering this enterprise space?

Reach out to your network and see where you can make connections with enterprise companies. Warm intros always make the sales process easier because your referral is coming from a trusted source versus cold emailing or cold calling.

It's good to have people on your team who come from that world because they already have those connections. They understand the space better.

You mentioned thought leadership. Any advice on how to gain traction with that?

Don't be afraid to start out small. It might feel weird because you have an audience of five people and you're trying to act like an industry leader. But a "fake it till you make it" approach will take you a long way. Believe in yourself and put out educational content that isn't always geared towards trying to sell something. Being a trusted source establishes your legitimacy, especially when starting out and being a brand new company.

What kinds of advice can you give to other Latin founders?

Something that we're really proud of here at rThreat is that we're a completely Latin founded company. My mom is from Mexico City, and I grew up speaking Spanish fluently. My entire family is still in Mexico. The CEO Hugo Sanchez is from Morelia, Mexico. And of course, we have Jesus, who lives in Mexico City. He was born and raised there. It's also rare to have a woman on the founding team, especially in cybersecurity. Not only are we trying to disrupt the industry through our product, but through our team and our company culture. We are a diverse group of people, both in professional backgrounds and in who we are as human beings.

There are a lot of VCs out there now who are wanting to invest in people of color and women. If you are a woman or minority founder in tech, look for that when you're starting out that fundraising process.

Community is also really big in tech and cybersecurity. I've joined several groups of women and people of color in cybersecurity. Coming in without a cybersecurity background, I felt intimidated. When you're in meetings with partners or doing sales, nine times out of 10, it's just white men. I discovered that communities exist to support women and people of color. Seek out community and people who are like you in the industry who can provide support. I belong in cybersecurity because I had this group of people cheering me on.

TAKEAWAYS

- Create content that shows you know your space; it will help you build trust with potential customers (and don't be afraid if you have a super small audience at first).
- Get data and proof that show you are better than the competition.
- When it comes to enterprise sales, be creative about leveraging your network for warm intros.
- If you find yourself as a minority in the tech space, seek out community who are like you and who can support you.

#5

Lanford Holloway

Title: Founder & CEO, Terrastride Inc.

Value proposition: Allows users to create and share the best hunting maps possible

Industry: Outdoor recreation

Keywords: Freemium, fundraising, MVP, non-technical founder, time management

What is HuntStand?

　　HuntStand is a hunting and land management piece of software. It's the most popular hunting app in the country. We have a couple million active and engaged users on the app. It's monetized through selling ad space as well as through a freemium model. The app is free, but there is a premium product for $25 per year that unlocks additional features.

What problem does HuntStand help solve, and how did you identify that problem?

I'm a hunter myself. After graduating from Emory University in 2006, I moved back home to Colombia, South Carolina. I was hunting on a piece of land that I knew well, but that I hadn't been on in a couple of years. I was frustrated because I didn't know where anything was on the property, including the stand. There was a new trail and the property was being cut, and all these things had changed.

Finally I found the stand. As I got up there, I was playing on my phone, looking at Google Maps and thinking about how the satellite imagery for this piece of land was outdated. That's when I got the idea to create a tool that allows people to overlay a personalized annotation layer, and to share that map layer with their friends. You would always know where you were on a property. You would know exactly where this trail went and how close one stand was to another. For a hunter, that helps out in a thousand different ways, including safety.

Was there nothing else on the market that offered this?

It turned out there was a company that was doing something relatively similar. But we were looking at the problem in a very different way. Incidentally, we actually acquired them last year.

How did you monetize the tool?

Recently, an investor asked me, "What's the sales process like? Do we have people that are calling potential customers?" I said, "It's $25 bucks a year. We can't afford to have a team member call to get someone on board."

For Huntstand, marketing equals sales. We market the app and get people into the ecosystem for free to start. But there are enough reminders saying, *If you're willing to pay, you can unlock these additional features.* Then we sell ad space and we make about a dollar per year per user.

When we launched the app, we knew we wouldn't try to monetize it for a couple of years. My strategy was to create a piece of software, make it good and free, and build a large user base. Then we gradually add features into the premium tier to get people to upgrade and pay for the app. Of course, there was expected friction. People told us we were getting greedy. Of course, we tactfully responded that this isn't free for us to do.

How did you go from idea to execution?

I was excited about the idea, but I didn't have a great way to draw it up. One night I used Microsoft Paint to snip little components from a Google image search and paste them into what a social mapping website might look like. I had a few pages that sat in a drawer for a couple of years while I worked a different job.

I went to business school, and there was a business plan competition in the first year. I told my group, "You might not like this, but I have an idea for this hunting piece of software." There was a girl from California in my group–a good friend of mine–who was totally against it. But the more we talked about it, the more she agreed that it was a solid proposal. We refined what I had made and pitched it in a five minute presentation. It won first place. Not a huge deal, but I did start thinking that it was nice to have third party validation of the concept.

After graduating, my classmates were getting jobs that were paying them actual money. I was starting this company and paying myself a thousand bucks a month after having just been in school for two years.

Incidentally, one of our first investors was Teddy Turner–not Ted Turner–but his son, Teddy. We had interviewed around forty hunters or land managers on what problems they faced, and we got connected with one of the Turners' land managers. When I called Teddy, it went straight to voicemail. A couple of months later, I tried again. He answered the phone and said, "If you want to drive to Charleston, I can give you fifteen minutes." We talked for three hours, and he gave me a check. It wasn't huge, but it was some of our first money.

How did you build the MVP?

It sounds crazy, but I went to the School of Computing Engineering at University of South Carolina. I basically said, "I'm a business school grad student and I'd like to find some folks who can help me build this. Who's really good?"

I got a few names, took them out for coffee, and showed them this terrible-looking PowerPoint. I told them, "I can give you something you can stick on your resume if you can help me create the MVP. I'll also give you some company equity." They all said yes.

Did you raise any other investment?

We had another investor who gave us $50k, which ended up being nothing compared to what we ultimately needed. But when you're starting, that seems like a fortune. Of course, it was helpful. The story was this: We had an Android app that was coming along, and I wanted to launch the product at the end of 2013. But we needed money to hire somebody who could write for iOS.

I went to an investor and gave a very impassioned speech about how I was quite confident this was going to work, and that we could get about 40k downloads of the app prior to the end of the year. He responded, "I will give you $25k, as personal debt to you. However, if you reach that threshold that you just told me about, I'll invest another $25k under X valuation."

I was a poor grad school student. The thought of going into a lot of personal debt on top of not making any money was scary. But I had just finished telling him I was sure it would work. I did some soul searching and went back and said, "Okay, I'll take the deal."

In November of 2013, we got 65k downloads in 45 days. HuntStand was at the top of charts for both Google and Apple for Sports categories. There still wasn't any revenue coming in, but it did get a lot easier to raise money. The message was, *Look at what we accomplished with nearly nothing. Imagine what we could do if we actually had some resources.*

What's the best piece of advice you've received?

A professor in business school said that if you consider everything that must fall into place for you to be successful, you will never try. There are so many potential pitfalls that you start to believe that it will be impossible to succeed.

Instead, look at things within a two-week window. Establish short-term goals and work on them as hard as you can in two-week chunks. It makes things much more digestible.

Any final thoughts on fear/risk-taking?

There was an article in *The Atlantic* that said that the greatest fear of the millennial generation is the fear of failure. With HuntStand, I had to come to terms with the idea that if I did this, I would attach my name to it. It might fail, and people might say, "That was the stupidest thing ever." But I had to embrace that risk.

There's a badge of honor in failure. If you fail, well, you can get three job offers. You started this thing. It didn't work, but you proved that you can execute.

TAKEAWAYS

- Create short-term goals that you can accomplish in two weeks.
- Failure isn't a dead end.

Jordan Walker

Title: Co-founder, Yac

Value proposition: Asynchronous meetings & messaging for remote teams

Industry: Team communication

Keywords: Customer acquisition, fundraising, mindset

What is Yac?

We are an asynchronous meeting platform designed to help you reduce the amount of unnecessary calls in your life. Text lets you get ideas across quickly and asynchronously, but with no room for complex ideas. Video calls let you express your ideas as they are, but require scheduling a meeting and being there at the same time. We want to offer a "happy medium" between both.

In a world in which hundreds of hours are burned on calls and people let their messengers descend into chaos, Yac is here to help you have goal-oriented and focused conversations on the things that actually matter.

We're seeing teams on Yac save hundreds of hours in meeting time and over $7,000 per employee, annually. Our users tell us how happy they are to be saving time during the workday and it never gets old hearing. The data speaks for itself as we're pioneering the future of meetings and collaboration.

How did you identify this as a problem to be solved?

Prior to Yac, my cofounders and I ran a design agency. During that time, the team became more remote. Our director of design moved to Mississippi. We hired someone in New Jersey. We had folks move to the UK. One of our developers wanted to travel the world with his girlfriend. As we grew this way, we realized there is no great way to send high-quality updates among people in that remote environment. We also realized that it was often inconvenient to ask remote workers to hop on a phone call—especially when they're in totally different time zones. As we grew this way, we realized we had no way of sending high-quality updates, and planning calls across time zones had become nearly impossible.

There was no happy medium to communicate among teams, and we wanted to build something ourselves. In 2018, Product Hunt had their first Makers Festival, and we decided to enter. We built a very scrappy version of Yac in four days across Thanksgiving break. Long story short, we ended up winning the Makers Festival, and beating out the competition, which was insane. We were the no-name folks out of Orlando,Florida building with remote-first in mind, before being remote was the "cool" thing to do. Through that, we got a list of about 3,000 people in just a few weeks from Google, Spotify, CVS, Barstool Sports, and more. We're like, *There's probably something to this thing. Let's just put a little more time and effort into it.* We did that for a couple of months before my co-founder Justin connected with Adam Draper on Twitter. He wanted to fund us, then brought in Betaworks Ventures, and we've been rocking ever since.

What kind of challenges have you encountered since that initial surge of growth?

Every startup has to be able to answer the question, *How do we convince somebody to pay for this thing?* That's a very difficult task. I don't think there's one cookie cutter answer for it. Our focus is on delivering value to the customer over and above the price of their subscription to Yac. Meeting owners need decisions to be made, and meeting participants want to get back to work on the tasks that matter to their KPIs. We want to ensure that meetings are effective and efficient, and have a signal-to-noise ratio.

If you raise some VC, you're going to get a lot of "follow on" interest from VC. While it may seem like a good idea to take on money, if you get too comfortable early on, there's no incentive to go figure out your strategy or product/market fit. Instead of handling the growth, founders can potentially become more focused on raising money which is a scary situation to be in.

As a multi-time founder, what entrepreneurial qualities do people need to succeed?

You have to be internally driven and resilient. Nobody is going to lay out the plan for you, and say, "Go do this thing and you will be successful." You have to get after it every day. You have to be resilient because sometimes–especially when trying to raise VC money–you'll get a lot of "no's." People won't believe in you. You'll get customers who misunderstand your product. That's on you. Because it's your product, your company, your idea. People tend to underestimate how difficult it can be to handle the negativity that gets thrown at you every day. Even following the successful fundraising, I still have to stay chill when people react strongly to our product positively or negatively.

What solutions have you found to finding your first customer?

One thing I'm doing now is iterating around what the best experience is for a new user or customer. We want to make people feel like this is the best experience in the entire world and they're getting something so valuable they have to pay for it. We've found a lot of success doing that.

What is one of the most common mistakes you see other SaaS founders making?

People get scared that someone else is going to steal their idea. They're too private with their information. That's a huge mistake. You should talk about what you're doing. You should talk to customers. You should talk to others to understand what features and what requirements people want. Because if you keep it to yourself, how are you ever going to scale and build it? Eventually you have to go talk to a VC about it. You have to go get a customer, and you have to hire people.

One thing worth mentioning here as well on the note of being timid is this idea that your pitch deck should be *highly* shareable. This means not having it password-protected, behind closed doors, or limiting who has access to it. VCs talk. They share decks and information. If your deck gets passed around and there's friction in accessing it, you're taking opportunity off the table for you and your business – from both a fundraising and networking perspective.

What I always tell founders is that at the end of the day, ideas are meaningless. It's always about execution. I guarantee that somebody else in the world has the same idea as you. Just go do it better than everyone else.

TAKEAWAYS

- Beware of this danger: Focusing more on raising money in the early stages than focusing on product/market fit or strategy.
- Don't be too protective of your pitch deck; make sure it's shareable and accessible to other VCs.
- Execution matters more than ideas.

#7

Damian Esparza

Title: Founder, SmartProperty

Value proposition: Helps property managers with planning and forecasting

Industry: Property management

Keywords: Fundraising, mindset, product/market fit

Why SaaS?

The beautiful thing about SaaS is it's almost like an annuity. You acquire a customer and you have a decent product. You don't have to reacquire that customer next year. Just keep a high lifetime value, and provide enough value to this customer on an ongoing basis. The cost of acquisition doesn't go up. Customers keep renewing and your growth keeps doubling.

What's your background?

I studied philosophy at Boston College. I worked in the movie business. I worked in investment banking. I worked in politics. I worked for the Bishop of San Diego. And now I'm in SaaS. You don't have to have an engineering degree to be in SaaS. You have to have fortitude.

You have to have to be able to connect dots and you've got to be able to see patterns. You've got to be a critical thinker.

Look at Steve Jobs. Some of the most successful guys didn't have an engineering background. They were able to understand the psychology of the market, to see around corners. They were able to see gaps before they actually happened. That's part of seeing those patterns and gaining a macro understanding of things.

What makes an early entrepreneur successful?

You can't simply seek the approval of investors. You've got to have an internal compass. I've gone mad trying to seek approval from investors. That's the way to either run out of cash or waste your time, or both. The job of the entrepreneur is to set a date for your vision, and then decide how you plan to get to that vision.

Successful entrepreneurs have learned that they have credits and debits. The credits are equity; the debits are failures. But ultimately, you turn the failures into assets. To be an entrepreneur, you have to accept failure as part of the journey.

This is something I never thought I would say, but the best advice I've received is to start with something small that you're not going to have to lose a lot on. That's a good way to get comfortable with failing. I want my companies to fail in an iterative, fast way, so they ultimately get to whatever the answer needs to be. They really understand this up in Silicon Valley.

A decade ago, if you would have told me that it would take us this long to get where we need to be, I don't know if I would have said I would do it.

Ultimately, it's about fortitude. I've done an Ironman. I've done other things where I had to go deep and believe in myself, and believe that I would get out to the other side.

What does it look like to fail fast?

You can't aim for perfection. We built this capital planning software. COVID hit last year and I was like, *What the f*ck are we going to do?* We had spent three months trying to get the attention of Angel investors, when I should have been focusing on acquiring customers and learning product market fit. We didn't even get any money. I decided to focus on sales, and COVID literally hit that same week.

It sucked. Mike Tyson says that everyone has a plan until they get punched in the face. I felt like a loser, but I decided, okay, we're just going to build this software product.

We knew that our ideal market did not want to do the job our software does, but we hadn't been able to find a repeatable sales model. So we went back to the drawing board. There was a lot of surrender in that. Our thesis wasn't working. We did user research, and basically ended up asking, what are these property managers doing? What do they need? What we came up with was planning software, or basically forecasting software, which says what you should do as a property manager and how you should manage your property.

Using PowerPoint, we built something and sent it to about 30 customers and prospects. Once we got enough validation from our current customers and evidence from prospects, I said, "Let's go." We shipped the product a couple weeks ago, and we're getting traction.

Why do you think you initially failed?

There wasn't a product/market fit. We thought we were going to build this maintenance management system, but people told me it was too much work. So we shifted two or three times and now we're there.

I don't think anyone nails product/market fit the first time, even though they didn't really say that. If you don't have product/market fit but you have customers, then talk to those customers and figure out how to get them to engage more.

After you talk to your customers, then come up with some mockups, show it to as many as you can, get that validation, and then build. You have to shrink that into a very short period of time.

What kinds of advice would you give to entrepreneurs who don't yet have an idea?

Trying to catch a market is kind of like chasing a butterfly. You've got to see things before the market is actually happening. Look at the observable world. Look all around you; there are so many things that need to be better. It's about awareness. Meditate, learn how to be still, learn how to be aware of who you are, and learn how to be aware of the world around you. Realize that the world's going by like a freeway. We can step out of that reality, observe it, and not just react to it. What are your "shower moments"—the moments of epiphany you have when you're not thinking about much else?

Before we started Smart Property in 2017, I got asked to work for the Bishop of San Diego, doing fundraising and helping Catholic education. I'm a big believer in Catholic education. It changed my life. So I was really successful at that. When I left that position, I had to ask, *Why was I so successful over there, but I can't be successful for my own venture?*

I had a "Come to Jesus moment" with myself. I realized that I had negative thinking. The words we use about ourselves are very important. I started to change my thinking about myself and my successes. That was a pivotal moment. It helped accelerate my own growth and then the growth of Smart Property.

You have to be fully aligned with the universe to find success in SaaS. If I wasn't having fun, I wouldn't do this. SaaS is hard. You have to get used to delayed gratification. It's a long journey. You have to have the fortitude and that sense of peace with who you are.

TAKEAWAYS

- Start with something small that you're not going to lose a lot on.
- Fail fast and don't aim for perfection.
- If you don't have an idea yet, learn how to be still and observe.
- Get used to delayed gratification.
- Learn how to dig deep—you need fortitude, an internal compass, and a sense of peace with yourself to make it for the long haul.

Galin Kozarov

Title: Founder & CEO, Pixai

Value proposition: Reduces cost and efforts by automating document creation and personalization

Industry: Marketing

Keywords: Chicken or the egg, hiring, MVP, prioritization

What is Pixai?

Pixai is cloud-based software that automates the customization and personalization process of all corporate and product documents. This includes Product Sheets, Technical Guides, and User Manuals in any format—PDF, Microsite, Email, Presentation, Spec Sheet, etc. Pixai's unique personalization content management capabilities allow for product information to be intelligently segmented into contextual topics and stored in a central database.

Employees can use these existing topics to mix, build, and deliver customized product information instantly, reducing the time, cost, and complexity of creating documents.

How did you identify this as a problem to be solved?

In my previous job, I was sitting in between the product development team and the sales team. It was my responsibility to communicate the value proposition of our product to our "go to market" team. In the span of one year, we created 200-400 materials that we kept in a portal. What we learned is that we didn't really need new pieces; we needed to repurpose pieces. For example, salespeople would come to us and say, "We have this white paper and it's great for the communication industry, but I'm talking to someone in the health care industry and there are a couple of things we need to change." We soon realized that 80% of the requests that we got were not to generate new content, but just to edit the existing content. That created a lot of overhead in our marketing team. In sales, that matters. If you don't send content to a prospective customer overnight, you might delay the sales process. I knew there had to be a better way—so I quit my job and for the past three years I've been focusing on developing the platform.

What was the process of building an MVP like?

It was kind of a two-step ideation and validation process. The ideation phase was me just trying to solve a marketing bottleneck issue and saying, "How can we leverage technology to automate the creation of sales and marketing materials?" We tested that a little bit and we got very positive feedback. Our workload decreased substantially.

The validation phase began when I quit my job. I spoke to about 40 companies trying to quantify the problem. One of the learnings was that it takes an average of about three hours for a salesperson to build a sales pitch. That means that during these three hours that salesperson is not picking up the phone and making phone calls. But the majority of the wasted time is spent on changing the font, changing the colors, looking for the right images. That's assuming salespeople are working from master decks. We can decrease that time to 20 minutes through automation processes. So we were able to quantify the value of our product.

The true validation of the product came when we actually started working with customers. Today, we work with customers with all different use cases, not only in the sales enablement space. Many of our customers are manufacturers that help digitize their product manuals and optimize their document creation processes. In this phase, we've actually been able to slightly pivot and expand the use cases of the software.

What's been one of the most challenging parts about validation?

There have been many, but two come to mind. One of them is the chicken or the egg problem. We need to have the product in order to sell it. But we want our development roadmap to be driven by real customers. How do we play this balancing act between building the features that we know our customers want, but at the same time being able to sell the product without the feature?

The second challenge is building the team. This is something that I completely underestimated. Coming into the company, I felt that I had sufficient experience in working with people and forming teams. I had done some of that in my previous company. So I thought, *That's not something I've done in the past. I can probably do it fairly well.* But honestly, finding customers for us is probably easier than finding the right people.

What have you learned in the process of trying to put together the right team?

We're still in the early stages of our startup, so this is strictly an opinion. But in my opinion, soft skills are probably more important. Are you a hustler? Are you a risk-taker? Do you have a startup mentality? If I had to put a number on it, I'd say the first three to five people on the team should have the startup mentality, which means that you can tolerate risk. By definition, a startup is a high risk venture. Let's say that you're a developer. Are you ready to put in an 80 hour-week, bust your ass, and write a thousand lines of code, only to scratch it all the following week and start over again and be excited about the new course?

Have you always been an entrepreneur?

I don't think of myself as an entrepreneur. I think of myself as a problem-solver. I stumbled upon a problem that I'm incredibly passionate about solving. And in that journey, I can pick my job. Do I want to be the CEO, the CMO, or the developer? I know that as the company grows, that will change, but while we're a small team, we can work on things that likely we wouldn't have had the flexibility to work on at more established companies.

More importantly, and more broadly, in this journey we can dictate our trajectory, and we have an opportunity to leave our own footprint on this world. And if done right, hopefully, we leave this world in a better place than we found it.

What would you say to an aspiring SaaS founder?

I cannot emphasize enough that it's 1% inspiration and 99% perspiration. Working 24/7 is what made the difference between us giving up on this idea and overcoming the tough periods in 2018 and 2019. There are reasons that many startups fail that are outside of the founders' control. Maybe it wasn't the right timing or it wasn't the right kind of business model. But when we're talking about the things that we can control, the business is going to give you back whatever you put into it. If you treat the business as a hobby, if you have a day job, and if you like to take vacations and you like to spend your time on things that matter to you outside of your startup, the startup is going to give the same amount of care back to you.

We all have 168 hours in a week. How are we going to spend those 168 hours? There's nobody stopping me from being at the beach right now. These small decisions make or break the success of a business.

TAKEAWAYS

- Look for team members that are risk-takers.
- Your business will give you back what you put into it. Are you willing to put in the work, and give up your free time?

#9

Jon Corrin

Title: Founder & CEO, XILO

Value proposition: Sales and quoting automation for insurance agencies

Industry: Insurance

Keywords: Fundraising, metrics, mindset, MVP, sales

What is XILO?

My co-founder used to be an independent insurance agent, and later inherited his dad's agency. I was a software engineer. We started XILO because we noticed that a lot of digital insurance agencies were popping up, but no one was building technology to help the mom and pop insurance agencies. Simply put, we're trying to take that same technology that digital insurance agencies are using and give it to retail agencies so they can continue to thrive in their market for the next 10 years.

Can you tell me about developing the MVP?

My co-founder was inheriting an insurance agency. Our MVP development was really built around his business. We built a slide deck and pitched it to his dad. We said, "Here's what we want to do for your agency."

We started working inside of his agency to construct what we thought would be the ultimate shopping experience for a customer. Once that was figured out, we decided to go out and sell it. And we just fell flat on our faces. So we tried to give it away for free and still fell flat on our faces. That's when we brought in Taylor (Cavanah, see page 175). Taylor showed us a couple of different sales methodologies that helped us create a natural sales process. We finally started selling at the end of 2018, going into 2019.

Why did you fall flat on your faces at first?

We didn't have the right strategy in place. We would have phone calls with agencies to discuss what we're doing. There would be no form of demonstration. We tried to use different tactics from random learnings in other places, and it never worked. No one took us seriously. We did get a few people to sign up for a free trial, but they never ended up using it. It wasn't a successful experience.

The real pivot was that we put a process in place. We spent time constructing a sales demonstration where we came in as experts, and showed customers where their problems were. Basically, we were rationally drowning them in their inefficiencies. Then we would tell them how our solution would help them overcome the challenges that we had discussed. That was when we started seeing people interested in the product.

Can you expand on the idea of "rationally drowning people in their inefficiencies"?

We often deal with agencies who are salespeople themselves. Sometimes they won't admit that they have a problem. You have to prove it to them. You need to know how to ask them about their processes, and then tell them how those processes don't line up with those of a modern agency, and how customers aren't going to accept that kind of process. This is called "the challenger sale." It's the idea of getting people to a point where they cannot ignore the challenges that you're bringing to the surface.

What's it been like to raise funding?

We are not the company that went out and had a really exciting idea and pitched it really well, and someone invested in us. Every step of the way we got a "prove it to me," even when we thought we had a lot of proof that what we were doing was great.

We went out to raise our Pre-Seed in October 2019. At that point, we already had somewhere around $80,000. It wasn't a lot, but it was enough, and we had a repeatable sales model behind it. We had a ton of happy customers. Even at this stage, investors were saying, "Prove it to us. You need to do X, Y and Z." It was challenging because at the time, we weren't paying ourselves. We were basically running our savings dry. We weren't making enough money to really do anything with the capital. It was difficult because we really needed to raise funds just to have a comfortable lifestyle and to hire people to help us out.

That's been one of the biggest challenges and we continue to face that challenge. No matter how much further along we are than other startups in certain stages, it seems like we're inexperienced founders. The reality is that we are first-time founders who are younger and who don't come from Google or Harvard. We have to prove out a lot more.

What kinds of metrics are important for you to show to investors?

Some investors are so smart, you can tell them three parameters and they will have calculations about what metrics you need to focus on the most and where you're going to have difficulties down the line. We got that insight during our Pre-Seed. The biggest thing that the investors have always been hyper focused on when we were raising funds was obviously growth rate–UARR, but also churn and ACB. That's because we have a smaller, more niche market of about 40,000 independent agencies and 80,000 captive agencies, but we're focusing on independent. ACB and churn are super important. And because we're going after SMB's, it's important that we start raising ACB even more so that we can take advantage of that smaller, more niche market.

There are things that investors will give us pushback on and then we just make those the top metrics that we want to improve.

Were there any metrics where you saw extremely significant growth?

Churn. A lot of SMB SaaS companies will deal with high churn, and it's because you're dealing with smaller businesses that don't have don't have the finances to pay for certain products. You're also dealing with people who are more likely to shop around. Our churn was somewhere around 3% loss month over month at one point. Because of that, we were getting pushback.

We took a look at the current process we had that would prevent churn or make customers happy, and we realized that we were doing very reactive account management. If somebody had a problem, we solved that problem. If we never figured out that they have a problem, we never solved it. So we changed to a proactive model where we track users based on product usage, the activity of this person, or bugs they ran into that they may not have known about. We receive alerts based on that kind of activity, and then we follow up with customers to make sure they're happy. That reduced churn to almost 1% month over month.

How do you stay resilient enough to persevere through the ups and downs of being an entrepreneur?

To sustain yourself, you have to be really healthy. I drink a gallon of water every day. I try to eat as healthy as I can. I exercise and meditate daily, read books, go through a traditional self development path. I don't drink a lot of caffeine, so I'm not overly anxious all the time. That helps tremendously because as an entrepreneur, you can get burnt out really fast from anxiety.

To move forward, you'll want to maintain homeostasis and a sense of fulfillment through the ups and downs. As everyone says, it's going to take a lot longer than you think. There are going to be a lot of challenges that you have to navigate. It's an incredibly hard occupation to take on your own. My recommendation for everyone is to try to be as healthy as possible, because that will help you persist over a long period of time.

TAKEAWAYS

- Be prepared to show prospects their own inefficiencies.
- SMB SaaS businesses will face higher rates of churn. Take a proactive, not reactive, approach to customer problems.
- To make it for the long haul, you need to stay healthy.

Allie Knull

Title: Founder & CEO, ResumeFree™

Value proposition: Matches employers and candidates based on data points rather than resumes

Industry: Hiring, recruitment

Keywords: Development, female founder, fundraising, mindset, MVP, non-technical founder

What's special about ResumeFree™?

ResumeFree™ matches employers and candidates on over two hundred data points. Not one of those data points comes from a resume.

What's your professional background?

I've been doing professional recruitment on many sides of the table for 20 years, either directly as the hiring manager or as the recruiter. I've worked with companies to help them hire their first person, and I've worked with companies with 80,000+ employees. I am a Certified Professional in Human Resources (CPHR) and a Registered Professional Recruiter (RPR). My education start was a Bachelor of Science with focus in Biochemistry, and minors in the social sciences. Turns out I love data and even more, I love the social sciences!

What was the "aha" moment that helped you realize there was a problem with recruitment?

For me, it was more of a slow burn that stemmed from my role with high volume recruitment. I was dealing with hundreds of thousands of candidates. Over a single year, I would actively have anywhere between 25-35 different requisitions. I recognized that we were hiring a specific type of person based on some keywords. But I also realized that there were people who had their titles changed, and were getting excluded from search.

The other problem is that when you're using a resumé as the only determining factor as to whether somebody is going to be a good fit for the role or not, you are excluding people that may have English as a second language. You're excluding people that could be in a different market space. You're excluding people that maybe have reskilled or up-skilled, or who have had a different career and are now returning to the industry. There are untapped talents that are applying for these roles that aren't getting them because we're too short sighted to see that keyword searches aren't working anymore.

A lot of the tech right now for the recruitment industry is just aiming to parse through resumés faster. We don't need to look through resumés faster. We need a better way to do it. That's when I asked the question, "Could we do this without a resumé?"

Typically, it takes about four months to fill a vacancy. Our first hire out of beta, the company hired within 13 days.

How did you build your MVP?

I'm not a technical founder, so I started off by piecing together a few free tools to build an MVP. One of the tools was a portal for the assessment that we've licensed. One of them was an online survey component. The other one was the GoDaddy Website with the wordpress page to control postings and applications.

I basically created everything through these enhanced experience products that were created for other purposes. I stitched them together to create a client journey as well as a candidate journey. That got a really great response and gave me the confidence to start building.

How did you approach development as a non-technical founder?

I talked to four different software development firms in my city. Going into a space that is predominantly male with predominantly male clients was a head spin. I had to be more aggressive than I would normally have in an interaction with a client or vendor. I would say, "No, this is what I want. This is how I envision it. This is what I want you to do. How much would that cost me?" I had quotes from $45k all the way up to $250k. But I didn't have $50k burning a hole in my pocket, let alone a quarter of a million dollars.

So, I had to start looking at building a business plan, showing my market research, and going into banks and applying for grants. In my neck of the woods, there's a loan for people under forty and there's a loan for women entrepreneurs. But I was going in as a technology entrepreneur. They had no idea what the hell I was talking about. So if I wasn't trying to argue against one thing, I was trying to argue against another thing. It really tested my resiliency muscle, which I flex a lot these days. At the time, I could have counted on two hands the number of female tech founders I knew. So I joined Women in Cloud, which is run by Microsoft. It's a phenomenal group of ladies with a mixture of women who are technical founders and non-technical founders.

What advice would you give to a female founder?

Don't give up. What you're doing is going to take a little bit more hustle. It always feels like you're sinking so much money at the very beginning. But if you get sound financial projections out there and you've really tested your market, don't give up.

Fall in love with the problem, not the product, because your product might change. You might have the best purple sock knitter in the world. But if people don't want purple socks, your product isn't going to work. You're going to have to pivot.

When are founders most tempted to give up?

A lot of people give up because of money. Your product is going to be pre-revenue for a long time. Sit tight and see what you can do to make it. Set small milestones and make sure you hit them, because it could be a long time before it actually feels like true success. But if you keep putting in effort, it could be that you're almost at the goal line.

Where are you on the journey of funding and revenue?

We are no longer pre-revenue. We have contracts coming in from three different countries, and we're looking to expand into deeper markets. We've had our Friends and Family round, and we're getting ready to go after some venture capital in the future, after hitting a few more milestones.

We're always asking, "What's the next step and how can we get there?" The thing that I always keep in mind though is that "sales solves all problems." One of my mentors says to focus on your sales and everything else will come.

TAKEAWAYS:

- Fall in love with the problem, not the product.
- Be patient. You may be pre-revenue for longer than you think.
- Set small milestones as markers of success. That will help you to feel encouraged and motivated, especially in the beginning.

Leigh Hunt

Title: Founder & CEO, FreeMo
Value proposition: Allows brands to provide free cell phone service
Industry: Mobile service
Keywords: Fundraising, non-technical founder, team

What's the elevator pitch for FreeMo?

FreeMo is a platform that allows brands to launch their own ad-subsidized mobile phone service. We've also got our own B2C cell phone service—Beast Mobile—which is licensed by FreeMo.

Is anyone else doing free cell service?

Nope.

How did you get to where you are today?

I started this company about six years ago. We raised about a million dollars over approximately a three-year span, built the product, and then brought our first company on board and built out their platform. They decided not to launch for whatever reason. Then we launched with a couple of different companies that failed at their rollout. So we decided to launch our own brand and figure it out ourselves.

Now, we've got two companies—FreeMo and BeastMobile. I'm the CEO of both.

How are you marketing your product to consumers?

We have very specific customers that we're targeting from a business to consumer standpoint. FreeMo, for example, targets college students or community college students—anybody that has some type of limited income.

BeastMobile, which I launched with Marshawn Lynch, has a different demographic. So those two services look different from an advertising standpoint.

How did you get into mobile?

I've spent 20+ years in the mobile phone business in every capacity you could possibly think of. But I'm not a technical founder. My first CTO was one of the big back-end database engineers for Credit Suisse Bank. He built out the complete framework of our tech stack. Once that was completed, I brought on a new CTO that is now in charge of all of our monetizing the data that we collect. He had a company that had 10 million daily active users, and was making a ton of money with Google advertising before selling the company. I brought him on to guide us through onboarding massive amounts of customers and then being able to monetize that customer base.

How did you learn to put the right team together?

As a non-technical founder, I've had to learn to trust my CTO. If you're an entrepreneur, it's really hard to give up control. I let him pick our tech team, because I trusted his judgment. That's turned out well. Today, we still have guys on with us that have been with us from day one.

What have been the biggest challenges of getting into SaaS?

I think the biggest challenge was trying to understand who our first customer was. The cell phone business is interesting in and of itself, because you have big carriers. Why would you want to leave them to go to somebody else? You do have all of these players in the game that are using larger carriers, towers, and networks to launch their own niche market–like T-Mobile, Cricket, and Metro. There are probably 100+ other cell phone companies out there looking to set themselves apart.

When we launched our team, it was pretty much all engineers. We focused on raising money for the company and we focused on building up the tech, not the team. Once we were close to launch, I got on phone calls and emails and started hitting up different people that I thought would want to get on board with this. That's when we landed our first customer.

What challenges have you faced in terms of fundraising?

It depends on where you're raising money from. The Friends and Family Round is easy, for the most part. They believe in you. But when you get into the next level, it's different. We're trying to raise $2 million right now, and we're dealing with wealthy individuals and wealthy companies who don't know me. They're like, "What's the opportunity and what's my exit? What's my return on this investment?" They don't give a shit about anything else.

Then they'll ask, "Who are you and who are your team and can you pull this off?" That was hard for me, because I was the sole founder of my company and big money and big investors hate that. So I brought on a co-founder.

Honestly, trying to start a company, run a company, and raise money at the same time is almost impossible.

Do you think technical founders sometimes lack the expertise or knowledge that they need in the industry they're entering?

Yes, 100%. It's tougher for technical founders, in all honesty, because they're not salesmen. You've got to be able to sell what you have, not only to customers but to investors. Then there's the flip side–everybody has an idea, but can they build it?

For technical founders, my advice is to bring on a founder as soon as you possibly can. Find somebody that doesn't need money right away, somebody that can bring that whole marketing piece, including the pitch and presentation piece, to the table.

What's your #1 advice to SaaS founders?

Fill a niche, get a great co-founder, build out great tech, and continually ask your customers what they like and what they hate, and just keep moving.

TAKEAWAYS

- If you're a technical founder, find a co-founder that can help you sell your product.

#12

Bethany Stachenfeld

Title: Co-founder & CEO, Sendspark

Value proposition: Create personalized video messages to connect with customers

Industry: B2B marketing

Keywords: Customer acquisition, mindset, non-technical founder

What is SendSpark?

Sendspark is for B2B companies who want to create personalized video messages to connect with customers. They can use Sendspark to record introductions, tutorials, demo support videos, really any kind of quick shareable content.

How did you identify this as a problem?

For the last five years, I've worked at different B2B startups as head of marketing. At my last company, I came to this point where I had two monitors up. On one of them, I was unsubscribing from emails. On the other one, I was writing marketing emails. I was sending out content I don't even like receiving.

My coworker Brandon, a product designer, and I started to ask the question, "How do we communicate with people normally?" You see a lot of Snapchat and Tik-Tok and FaceTime. We came up with Sendspark as a professional way for marketers and salespeople to use video for all of their communication.

We were both leaving our jobs at the time, so we decided to go all in on Sendspark. Worst case scenario, everything would fail and we would just get jobs again. Two years later, and we're working on building out a lot more capabilities, especially on the analytics, management, and team collaboration side. But we have a strong product. We have over 10,000 users at companies all around the world.

What has customer acquisition looked like for you?

There are basic things everyone can do. Super early, you can beg your friends to use your product. After your launch, AppSumo's a great option for getting feedback.

I'm also a huge fan of content. You can invest in content and it just keeps on building.

What does team look like at Sendspark?

My background is in marketing, and my co-founder's background is in product design. The clear gap is that there's no technical co-founder. A lot of people might say, *I'm not technical, can I start a company?* The answer is, of course. Unless you have a giant founding team, there are always going to be gaps. But you want to know what your strengths are and lean into those. For us, that's marketing. A lot of people who start tech companies lack the marketing experience that they need to actually acquire customers.

Then you're going to have to hire out for the things that you can't do.

How have you had to pivot your product over time?

We've had to change a lot over time, especially in determining who the right customer is. Since my background is in email marketing, I thought this would be amazing for marketers. We quickly discovered that marketers often don't want to be the ones in front of a camera. We had pretty low adoption at first. We ended up pivoting to focus more on sales and support teams who are sending hundreds of emails a day.

We haven't lost our marketing focus. But we also think about how marketing and sales and customer support work together. We've got to think about who will actually use the product.

What do you know now that you wish you had known two years ago?

As a first-time founder, you're always trying to learn a lot because everything you do is new. Something to keep in mind is that people are often trying to sell you something. When people sell you something, they do that by making you feel like you have a need. Maybe people are trying to convince you that you should hire them, or that you should take their investment money, or that you should take their course or whatever it is.

There are also things that have worked for other people that might not work for you, because their company or team looks different than yours. The bottom line is that you have to know what your strengths are and not just do what everyone else says you should be doing.

Don't get distracted. Learn from customers, the people paying you money, not all the people who are telling you what you should be doing.

What does it look like for you to stay motivated?

Enjoy what you're doing. As soon as it stops being fun, I take a break. Make sure that you love the customers and you think that their problems are interesting. Everything's going to be fun from there.

TAKEAWAYS

- There are always going to be gaps on your team. Leverage your strengths and hire out for the rest.

- Your target users may not be who you think they are. Be willing to pivot.

- Learn first from those who are paying you (your customers) – not necessarily from those who are trying to sell you something.

#13

Pradnya Desh

Title: Co-founder & CEO, Advocat AI

Value proposition: Makes legal research and drafting faster and more efficient with artificial intelligence

Industry: Legal

Keywords: AI, customer discovery, fundraising, non-technical founder, female founder

What is Advocat AI?

We do conversation-driven legal research and drafting for large enterprise companies.

How did you identify this as a problem?

I'm an attorney. I worked in house with the government for many years. After that, I launched a small law firm, where I was expecting the private sector to be way more efficient than government. While it is, legal is still really a mess. Legal is very manual. Attorneys do very specific, careful, and time-consuming work. As a result, people who need legal documents get frustrated with how long it takes. When it's billed by the hour, they're also frustrated with how expensive it is. It's a problem I was surprised to find.

So I set out to solve it, and pretty quickly found that AI was the solution. The process that attorneys do is very manual. There's no way that a person can speed up that process and still maintain quality.

What was it like to go from being an attorney to running a legal-related SaaS?

I had to learn everything from scratch. I knew how to be an attorney, but I did not know how to be a tech CEO. I read lots of books. I went to as many seminars as I could, and was in a few accelerators. I just absorbed information as much as I could, which worked. Actually, I'm still in that process. That sort of knowledge is absolutely accessible–but it started with knowing that I didn't have it.

For example, I had never raised funds for a company before. How do you raise a seed round? What does that look like? Who do you go to? I had to learn that from scratch right at the beginning. My first 50 pitches or so were really terrible. After that, they started to get pretty good. At around 110 pitches, we raised $1.3 million. So I got to see that process and the journey. In the beginning it's tough, but as you pass through the gate, it works great. I'm hoping to find that exact same thing as we progress.

Can you tell me about the pitching process?

At first, I didn't really know what it was that the investors needed to hear. I had the format down, but not the meat. Getting feedback from investors really helped me to shape that. So that's what I'm expecting now, in the stage of customer acquisition. There are going to be things that customers don't like and then we'll get feedback and we'll make it better.

What's it like to be a female founder in SaaS?

I knew that only 2.2% of VC funding goes to female-founded companies. I knew it was going to be hard. But I think that in anybody's fundraising journey, you should start with that mindset.

I have to say, it wasn't as hard as I thought it was going to be. Maybe because I was prepared for a challenge. But it did take a long time. We started raising right towards the end of 2020. In the end, I don't know why it took so long. Was it the pandemic? Was it being a female founder? Was it being a founder of color? It could be any of the above, but it could also have been that our company was not ready for funding it and we were a little too early in the process.

All I know is that around March of 2021, it all started clicking. It was really tough until it wasn't. Months of nothing, and then one month, $1.3 million.

How did you reach your target market?

Early on, I wanted to make sure that I wasn't building a product only for me because I have a particular way that I like working. Everybody does. I knew a lot about the space, but I also did not want to think that I already knew the answers before actually going out and testing. I was mindful of that.

One of the things that surprised me is that I went out thinking that this product would be good for the whole legal market. I tested it really broadly with a lot of different attorneys in different practice areas, as well as different types of legal practices. I found out quickly that law firms did not like what I was doing, because we make legal quicker, and they bill by the hour. That being said, some of these law firms—including my friends—were pretty hostile to what we are doing. So I went broader. We found in-house counsel to have a completely different response. These are attorneys who are paid on salary and we were helping them to get their job done quicker.

What would you say to another non-technical founder who wanted to start a SaaS for their industry?

Test, test, test. You can even test before you have the product. Don't spend a whole lot of engineering dollars building something, only to find out that it's terrible. We tested on PowerPoint and drawings and ideas before spending a lot of investment dollars on something that shouldn't have been built.

If you had to do it all over again, would you start a SaaS?

Absolutely. The fact that we're making the industry more efficient makes people more efficient, which makes the world more efficient. That's the way I see it, because people interfacing with the law and interfacing with the rule of law is important. It's what protects everybody. So we're starting the road to making it all work better.

TAKEAWAYS

- Learning to pitch to investors is a process. Get feedback, and implement.
- Test everything—even before you've built a product. Don't waste your money on building something that shouldn't have been built!

#14

Ajit Viswanathan

Title: Founder & CEO, Doctible

Value proposition: Automates front office tasks for dental and healthcare practices and helps build better patient relationships

Industry: Medtech, healthcare, dental care

Keywords: Development, mindset, product/market fit

What is Doctible?

We are a platform that helps dental practices and other medical practices be efficient and profitable by leveraging technology. Through automating front office tasks, staff can focus on patient care first.

How did you identify this as a problem?

We've gone through three different permutations at this point, but they've all started in health care. Our initial premise was to provide a technology that allows patients to negotiate with their doctor and to see if they can reduce the bill. But there wasn't product/market fit. We went through multiple pivots and talked to different practitioners. Over the last four years, the product has taken shape as a result of customer feedback.

How have you tackled the challenge of building a compliant SaaS in healthcare?

Healthcare adds a layer of complexity because we're dealing with what's called Protected Health Information, or PHI. It's not as simple as going on Amazon and spinning up a database. We have to have an extra layer of security behind the scenes and train our staff as well. It adds not just complexity, but cost.

When did you realize that you had hit the mark with your product?

We realized we hit the mark when we could call someone and say, "Here's the problem we can solve. Is that something you would be willing to pay for?" and they would take out their credit card and pay for it. When we could see that we provided value to the initial group of practices, we knew we had hit the next level.

We've been very fortunate to add a new product to the suite every year for the last five years. Even today, when we launch new products, we don't spend months and months of effort building our products. What we do instead is spend four to six weeks designing something. We show the wire frames to a customer advisory group. From there, we build the product and go to market. By now, we understand what the market entails and what the problems are. We know that when we launch a product, it will be fairly successful. But back in the day we had to plan and then test, and then sometimes, fail.

There's definitely been grunt work needed to get to the point where now we have a good understanding of our customers. We needed to go through years two, three, and four to get to where we are now.

Is there any final advice you would give to SaaS founders in healthcare?

The first thing is security. Setting that aside, the challenge in healthcare is often the sales engine to get product/market fit. Typically, people go in and spend a lot of time and effort building the most extensive platform, but if you can't get it to market and can't get it to speed, then it becomes extremely hard because all you have is a great product that no one uses.

Look at the lens of how you can get this product in the hands of your customers as soon as possible, and then ask questions. What do they like? What don't they like? Why is churn happening? The answer to your product stickiness lies with your user base.

In healthcare, you've got to have automation and integrations that work. You can't afford to build products that look good on a UI, but add more workflow into a practice. It doesn't matter how easy it is— it's one more thing added to the plate. Staff are not going to remember to open up your cool SaaS dashboard to type in some information. Without integration with their source of record, typically EHR, the product becomes dead on arrival. You might get a few people really excited about using it, but that will be a very small base. You'll see that usage drops off significantly. So the mission is critical to not add more work for the staff.

It's amazing how referral effects come through when customers are happy. We get inbound leads every day from people—and we don't even have to advertise, because our customers are a small community of dentists and doctors. But to get to that level, you've got to push that boulder uphill.

It's a pretty hard struggle, and typically, many founders feel discouraged doing that uphill journey. But once you've got the first 500 customers, you've got a product that will start rolling. That's when it's time to pay attention to your engagement stats, your churn stats, your new acquisition cost of sales. Because then it can be a scalable business.

Don't get too dogmatic on what you think the market needs. Listen to the market and build a product that customers love. At the end of the day, everything else will happen if you build a product that customers love.

TAKEAWAYS

- If you're building a healthcare SaaS, focus on integrations and automation. Your customers won't use your product if it adds to their workflow.

- Once you've hit 500 customers, you've built a scalable business. Start paying more attention to metrics like churn and cost of acquisition.

#15

Mitchell Eaton

Title: Co-founder & CEO, Prototype Hubs

Value proposition: Automates the manufacturing RFQ process and connects customers with local and global manufacturers

Industry: Manufacturing, Software, AI

Keywords: Development, marketplace, MVP, team

What was the problem that you were trying to solve by creating Prototype Hubs?

We're a two-sided marketplace, so we actually solve two problems at once.

The first problem is that when a manufacturer receives a request for a quote, they often rely on a manual time consuming process— either pen and paper, or Excel spreadsheets. It takes them a couple hours just to put the quote together. Often, manufacturers never hear back from customers, who have often found someone cheaper in the meantime. So, manufacturers waste time putting together quotes that don't get a high return.

The second problem is on the customer side. Potential customers will send out a bunch of RFQ's to different manufacturers, but they don't really know who can produce what they're looking for. And they won't even get a response from every manufacturer. Customers spend a lot of time on this process—researching, sending out emails to different manufacturers, and waiting to hear back.

Prototype Hubs saves time and labor for both parties by automating the RFQ process and connecting customers with manufacturers.

How did you identify this problem?

I've worked in industry as a design engineer, a manufacturing engineer, and a mechanical engineer. I've experienced both sides of the problem—as someone putting together a quote, and as someone sourcing a quote.

Was software development something you could tackle with a background in mechanical engineering?

Yes and no. I do enjoy complex problems, whether that's coding or something to do with mechanical design. Going into it, I didn't know exactly what coding language to use, or how to host it online. That's where putting the right team together came into play. I needed not only software engineers, but people who understood machine learning and who are proficient in their skill sets and who know what they're actually good at.

Assembling the right team is half the battle. Without my team, I don't think that it would be possible to be where we're at today.

What surprised you about building your product?

I was wrong about the timeline for what I thought was achievable. Software takes time to develop. Nothing happens overnight. So it was a bit of an adjustment. At first, I thought, *I have this idea. Why can't we just implement it and get it done?* The problem is that you end up having to overcome a lot of obstacles, one at a time, just to achieve a single goal.

Have you found any solutions that helped speed up the timeline?

Planning is a huge factor to success. Find developers who can identify some of the unforeseen obstacles or circumstances and plan ahead.

What does running a SaaS business full-time allow you to do now that you weren't able to do as an employee?

Having freedom is huge for me. As long as I have an Internet connection, I can work from anywhere I want. I can even do a lot of work from my phone. I can also set my own schedule. If I want to work at midnight, I can work at midnight. The people that I'm working with often have the same mentality. So, we'll have working sessions between 8 PM and midnight, just because we want to do it that way. If I want to spend the day mountain biking and start work at 2 PM, I can do that too.

At the same time, running a business takes more out of you than going to work for somebody else and then coming home and leaving your work at work.

Any final advice for someone wanting to start a SaaS business?

Get validation. A lot of people have ideas and some have really good ideas that could take off right away, but make sure it's going to work first. If your MVP doesn't fly, keep making changes. Finally, don't ever give up!

TAKEAWAYS

- Find developers and team members who can identify hurdles and challenges in advance. Planning for future problems will speed up your timeline for development.

Andrea Orrego

Title: Co-founder, Atelier

Value proposition: Allows non-professional interior designers to design and conceptualize interior spaces in a sustainable way

Industry: Interior design

Keywords: Customer acquisition, development, female founder, non-technical founder

What is Atelier?

Atelier is an interior design app for the savvy regular user, which means they don't have any technical skills, but they want to design their space. This app allows them to visualize their ideas in space that is scaled to their actual room size and drag and drop elements like paint, flooring, and furniture. Once they're ready and happy with their design, they purchase everything directly through the app. The app connects them with the makers and artisans who create the furniture, wallpaper, etc. through a marketplace.

Atelier creates a synergy of interaction, and also advances a more sustainable way of approaching manufacturing and home improvement.

How did you identify this as a problem to be solved?

I'm a third generation architect by trade. I have been working in the residential field for the last six years, and I started identifying this strand within my clients. My clients are more of a high-end clientele, which means there tends to not be a limited budget. But they don't want to hire an interior designer; they wanted to try their own ideas and create their own spaces. As an architect in charge of the project, I have ended up creating 3D models for them, putting together spreadsheets, and sourcing things just so that they could experience all their thoughts visually. I realized if there were a tool that was simple enough for them to use, then they wouldn't need to be paying ridiculous amounts of money for extra hours of labor for me to create a 3-D model.

I set out to investigate this idea, and surveyed over 300 women who were interested in interior design. I realized that this was a real problem. A lot of people struggle with making a decision because they don't know if what they see online is going to be good quality, if it's going to look good in their space, or even if it's even going to fit. I decided to create an app to simplify the process.

How did you get the app developed?

I didn't even know what the process of creating a digital product was, especially software. I put an ad on Craigslist saying that I was looking for an engineer that could help me develop this, not really knowing what it meant to develop an app. I had over 200 responses. After talking to a bunch of different developers, I understood I needed to have a budget. At that point, it was either hire a firm or an independent developer, or find my own team. I found a developer back home in Peru who could put together a first version of this idea. He ended up becoming my co-founder.

Now we have five co-founders—two software engineers, a graphic designer who's helped us with the brand and marketing, a furniture display specialist, and myself.

How have you approached customer acquisition?

It's been a fun journey. We ended up finding out along the way that there was a lot more demand for Atelier than we thought there would be. A lot of our customers have come to us organically, searching for apps like ours in the App Store. The first initial group, the early adopters, however, came through outreach. I went on Facebook groups that were focused on interior design, and sometimes mentor them through the design process before bringing them over to the platform or signing them up for the email list. We also ran Facebook and Instagram ads.

Have there been any unexpected challenges to the process, other than the initial task of development?

Nailing down what the product should do and how it should interact with the client has been the biggest challenge so far. We invested a lot of time, money, and effort trying to put together our platform, just to realize that populating the library of products in 3D models was going to be a significant investment that we couldn't afford. We had to pivot and create a new platform with flat images of products. It also took a lot of work to create the library, but that interaction platform ended up being too simple for what the user was looking for. We landed at a solution that blends both interfaces.

We needed to create a product that wasn't just simple to use, but also useful. That was our main goal. We didn't want customers to come into our space and say, *I can design a space that looks cool on a screen, but does that help me when I want to put together my actual space?*

That's been the challenge that led us to pause the product last year and take it out of the market. We've been developing the next version, and we're going to release it in a few months, but it was a challenge to nail down the user experience. I think we're very close, and we're very happy with what's coming up.

What has the journey been like for you personally?

It's been tough, especially as a first time founder, a Latina, and an immigrant. I didn't have the network. I didn't belong in the tech industry. Ever since we started building, I've been learning not just how to run the company, but how to do the fundraising process, how to get the resources that we need.

Feeling like I belong has been tough, too. Every room that I walked into, I was the only person that looked like me. If there were other women, they had been part of the industry for many years. They were typically older, and ended up being great connections. But it was hard to find peer support for a long time.

I think I'm a much better entrepreneur because of it, because I had to overcome so much so early on.

Can you speak more to the experience of being a Latina tech founder?

The hardest bias to overcome as a Latina founder is that we need to prove ourselves to be worthy. When you're first seen, you're not seen as a strong profile. Every time I've been able to pitch, though, I've surprised people. I'm not a charity case or a token to have as part of their network. It's rewarding to feel that I'm actually performing better than some of the stereotypes that people usually invest in. But at the same time, I wish that wasn't the case. I wish more women could just have that initial door opening.

Being resilient is going to be harder than you think. If you think it's going to be hard, it's going to be 10 times harder than that. If you are in love with your product, make sure that you're in love with your users. Make sure that what you're doing is not just for yourself, but for a greater good. That's going to help you keep going.

TAKEAWAYS

- Make sure your product isn't just easy to use, but also useful. It should deliver real value to your users!
- Fall in love with your users.

#17
David Beitz

Title: Co-founder, Planned Grocery

Value proposition: Provides access to data on planned grocery store sites, improving site selection and market planning

Industry: Retail Real Estate

Keywords: Bootstrapping, customer acquisition, pricing, non-technical founder, validation

What is Planned Grocery?

Planned Grocery helps shopping center owners, grocery retailers, and other relevant groups know about planned grocery retail locations before they even start construction. Whole Foods, for example, is a client, and Regency Centers, which owns many grocery anchored centers across the U.S. Another client is CBRE Capital Markets Group, which uses our data to help buy and sell shopping centers and to understand the market a little bit better. All this data is in a platform that displays everything on a map. We also have an API data feed that goes into other applications, basically other GIS mapping systems.

We partner with Esri–Environmental Systems Research Institute, to help us with mapping.

What's your professional background?

I worked for a shopping center developer for about 14 years. I was working in geographic information systems and did a lot of research on new locations. I had the idea to start a company that was based on location research and marketing. I started that about eight years ago with George Daigh, who I worked with at the previous company. About two years into working in that area, we came up with this idea to track planned grocery locations. We spent two years working on that database just to see if it was possible. We had interns, and we worked on the business on the side. After two years, we started showing it to different developers and grocers and it took off from there.

Did you have any concerns about leaving your previous job and starting your own company?

We always felt like there'd be a market for what we did. I do think it's really wise to save up some money before getting started. That first year you might not make very much. You have to prepare for that. And if you're not technical, you need a technical co-founder. Both George and I were technical to a certain degree, but we can't actually code and do the stuff that our now technical co-founder Todd Atkins— who had also worked with us at the previous company—can.

Are you bootstrapping or raising money?

We are bootstrapped, but I've got a lot of friends that have raised money. There are advantages both ways. If you raise money, you can grow faster. You can create a moat around you. But you spend a lot more time focused on your financials and updating your investors, who are always kind of wondering when the exit is going to be.

Having a technical co-founder is really important if you're bootstrapping because they can keep working on your MVP without spending crazy amounts of money. Meanwhile, you can focus more on getting customers, on marketing, on operations, finances, everything else.

What's been the biggest challenge so far about running Planned Grocery?

Getting customers to sign up for the platform. We have about 50 companies using the platform and it's grown every year since we've been a business. But the whole sales process is a huge challenge. I'm learning that having a great sales person makes a huge difference. If you have the skill to adapt and carry on conversations and close a sale at the same time, it's amazing. It's a superpower that I do not have.

What did it look like for you to test out Planned Grocery?

We started off by showing our MVP to some different real estate developers. They would give us feedback like, "It'd be nice if you had property owner information," or "A traffic count would be super helpful." We would get this kind of feedback along the way and incorporate new details into the platform, iterate a new version.

Has starting a SaaS company been harder than you thought it would be?

I'm glad we did it. Things are going well, and we're excited. When you're in services, you're only going to be so successful based on the amount of time you have in the day, unless you can charge thousands of dollars per hour, which most of us can't. That's why we really like the idea of building the product, because we could double our clients overnight without doubling our workload. That's the beauty of SaaS.

The hard part is figuring out where you're going to take it to the next level. How do you get acquired? Do you raise money? You get to a point where you have to do something to keep it going. Now, for example, we've got 50 companies that are dependent on us for the service and we're figuring out how to keep it growing.

What's been one of the linchpins of your success so far?

Listening to customers is huge. In some cases, we've turned around client requests the same day. For example, a client will ask for a print function, and a few hours later, they'll reload the app and suddenly, it's there. Most of the data companies are hard to deal with. It's hard to find somebody on the phone, it's hard to get good pricing, it's hard to get any kind of person to respond. The fact that we're hypersensitive to what customers need makes a big difference.

What's one mistake that you see SaaS companies making?

Early on, people are afraid to charge too much for their product. You're not in the business of ripping people off, but you have to charge enough to keep the thing going. You need to be fair about your prices. And if you're a data product, come up with a solution that has a nationwide scope. People get confused if your product is limited to certain cities or states.

A while back, we got to meet with the president of Esri. He said, "There are three things that you have to remember when you're starting a business. You have to be able to get the work, do the work, and get paid for the work. That's why you charge three times more than you think you're worth."

TAKEAWAYS

- Save up—you probably won't make any money for at least a year.

- A technical co-founder means you can make changes to your MVP without going way over budget.
- Listen to customers, and respond to requests quickly. It will set you apart from the competition.
- Charge three times more than you think you're worth.

#18

Kate Bradley Chernis

Title: Co-founder & CEO, Lately

Value proposition: Automates content creation

Industry: AI/Marketing

Keywords: AI, customer acquisition, female founder

What is Lately?

Lately uses AI to learn any brand voice and then turn longform video, audio or text into dozens of social posts it already knows will get you the highest possible engagement.

It works like this: you give us access to all your social channels, we study your analytics, and we look for the keywords, phrases and sentence structures that get you the highest engagement (what people like, comment on, and share). We then build a writing model based on this information that we update in real time every day AND give you the opportunity to steer the AI all along the way. After all, AI *must* be guided. It's only a robot!

Once we've created the writing model, it's time for you to feed the beast and ingest any longform piece of content video, audio or text. In the case of video or audio, we will then transcribe into text. Next, Lately's AI studies the words from that text and applies the writing model. In the case of video, we also clip it into dozens or even hundreds of miniature videos. The end result is a series of social posts made up of the coolest quotes that the AI *already knows* will get you the highest engagement.

What's your professional background?

I used to be a rock 'n' roll dj. My last gig was broadcasting to 20 million listeners a day for Sirius/XM. My superpower is turning listeners into fans, aka customers, into evangelists. I did this using what I learned about how the neuroscience of music works. Get this: each time your brain listens to a new song, it must instantly access every song you've ever heard. In that moment, nostalgia, memory and emotion (the essential factors of trust) all rush forth, as the brain looks for familiar touch points so it knows where to index that new song in the library of the memory of your brain. Now, every voice is like a song. It has a frequency; it has a note. When you write text, the person reading the text on the other side hears your voice in their head. So it's the onus of the author to give the reader familiar touch points in writing and trigger nostalgia, memory, and emotion–queueing trust, the baseline for any sale.

Fast forward a few years later when I owned a marketing agency and my first client was Walmart. The Walmart project was unique. It was a collaborative campaign that included Bank of America, AT&T, and all their respective franchises. Also on board were the National Disability Institute, United Way Worldwide, and the IRS–about 20,000 participants in all. Walmart owned a piece of software that was designed to help lift the poor out of poverty through federal income tax credits and financial empowerment education. The idea was that everyone would work together to help promote it. But this was 2011. The cloud didn't really exist yet. There was no easy way to collaborate. We had to invent it. So I built a spreadsheet system to unite us, and my spreadsheet system ended up getting the project 130% ROI YoY for three years.

What's it like to be a female founder?

Hard. Hard as hell. Female founders only get 2% of all venture capital funding. That means I have to work 98% harder than a white dude every damn day. The whole industry makes a big deal of how they are changing this and yet it remains unchanged. Even female investors discriminate against female founders. According to Pitch Book, it's not only the funding, but even the median valuation for female-founded companies drags behind by about 6 million on average. Yet female founded companies outperform their male counterparts by huge swaths when it comes to exit values.

What would you say about customer acquisition?

We only use Lately for all of our lead generation. Nothing else. No cold calls. No cold emails. No paid ads. 100% organic. And we have a 98% sales conversion, because the AI is so smart at learning what our targets want to read, watch and hear.

Any specific advice for female founders?

One, if you don't have the courage to stand up for yourself in the moment, don't get down on yourself about that. It's okay. That's what happens to all of us so often. Because we are genuinely shocked at what's happening so that in the moment, it's impossible to react the way you might imagine you should. Just acknowledge what happened and share with others. Don't blame yourself. I know, that's hard to do. My default is to always first examine everything possible that I've must've done to cause xyz – what I've done wrong. But we've done nothing wrong. Bullies are bullies, whether it's sexual harassment or someone just trying to do "gotcha" on you. Do your best to silently give them the middle finger and move on.

TAKEAWAYS

- For female founders: Don't get down on yourself if you fail to stand up for yourself when you should.

Paola Ortega

Title: Founder, Air

Value proposition: Real time data-driven insights on employee engagement

Industry: Employee insight

Keywords: AI, non-technical founder, validation

What is the elevator pitch for Air?

Air is a SaaS model survey product that helps companies understand in real time what their employees want or need. Specifically, it's designed to intervene when the company is adapting to something new – like COVID-19. Employers need more information than ever about working from home vs. working in the office. They're asking questions like, "If I send my people to their houses, what do they need? Do they need Internet? Do they need someone to take care of their children? Do they need a chair to sit down on?"

A business consulting process takes too long to collect this information. Employers need this insight in real time. Air started as a way to gather insight to respond to that specific change, but now it's evolved to include other changing conditions, such as an emerging acquisition process, a change of CEO, or a change of product portfolio.

What's your professional background?

I'm a psychologist, and my co-founder has a background in marketing. We worked together in business consulting for many years. When COVID hit, we realized the need for internal insights in real time and the kind of data that would require. My partner's husband has a data science company and overheard us talking about this one day. He was like, "Oh, that's so easy! All that's needed is an algorithm – in other words, AI." That's when the three of us decided to start a joint venture with his company.

Have either you or your co-founder worked in a corporate setting, where Air might be used?

Yes, both of us have. I worked in HR and marketing at Coca Cola, where I learned how a huge company cares about their employees, cares about how they work, and cares about employee engagement and career development. My co-founder worked at Interbrand and Ogilvy. We met in a business consultancy in Mexico with less than 15 employees, where there were long hour work shifts and a ton of responsibility. We came from huge global companies to a situation where sometimes we'd spend the night in the office. So we have perspectives and learnings from both sides of the spectrum.

What has surprised you about validation?

It's funny because we thought we were just going to have the web page and "by art and magic," people would say, "This is awesome," click *buy*, and we were going to become rich. Obviously, that didn't happen. We started asking, "How do we make this business work long term?" That's when the service changed 180 degrees to respond to any kind of external change – not just COVID-19. Companies are living organisms and are constantly suffering changes, not only external but internal. Companies merge, get acquired, and get new CEO's. Vision, culture, values, and ways of working change, and that shakes people up. We're defining this new product that helps companies understand how employees need to adapt.

Right now, we're doing some trial and error before we invest a lot of money into the product or look for foreign investment. We want to make sure the algorithm is solid. We've given free trials to four different companies because we really wanted feedback.

When you're close to the product yourself, you don't see the obvious. For example, a user might say, "Where should I click? Here or there?" For us, it might be obvious that it's a specific button. But it might not be as obvious for a user. There's a phrase to describe that in Spanish: *taller de ceguera*, or "workshop blindness."

What has been one of the hardest things about starting a SaaS company?

Honestly, I had no idea what SaaS was. That was the first big issue.

The second big issue was that SaaS is a completely different language for us. It's very hard for a psychologist and a marketing specialist to speak the same language as the people who are developing the software because we design it and they develop it. How do we take what we have in our heads and translate it to the people who are programming? That has been really challenging for us and for them. Maybe we want the type to be bigger, or to change the color of a circle, but they're like, "You have no idea what you're asking of me." Or it's the other way around. It's like they're talking to us in French, we speak Latin, and we think we're both speaking English.

We've actually found a translator to help us with that aspect of communication. She speaks both "languages," and she's been a great asset.

What's been the most important lesson of your journey so far?

Be ready to end up with a completely different product than you first imagined. Stay strict with your purpose, but be ready to surrender the rest!

TAKEAWAYS

- Don't let yourself be blinded by being too close to your product. Be willing to change and pivot if needed.

#20
Kevin Yun

Title: Founder, GrowSurf
Value proposition: Develops referral marketing for tech startups
Industry: Marketing
Keywords: Bootstrapping, product/market fit

What is GrowSurf?

We are referral software for tech startups. There are already a lot of platforms out there for referral marketing—but before GrowSurf, there wasn't anything that acted as a self-serve platform for startups. Most tools are either too lightweight or way too enterprise for our target customers.

How did you identify this problem?

In 2015, I found myself looking for referral software for a specific project. I found that nobody was really doing referral marketing the way I thought it should be done.

To be honest, we had a really bad product in the beginning. At that point, GrowSurf wasn't a full time thing. It was just a project that we had launched, hoping it would be useful and valuable to customers. But we didn't have a lot of customers and we didn't keep the customers we did have because the product was bad. So we hunkered down and spent a year revamping things. That's what it took to shift focus and create a successful platform. In a really saturated market, this was going to be super risky. We ended up getting lucky and seeing success. But we were also persistent.

Why would you say your product was "bad"?

In the beginning, we compromised a lot. It just wasn't the product that we wanted. The vision was there, but we couldn't connect the dots.

Are you raising money, or bootstrapping?

We're bootstrapping 100%. It takes a lot of time and effort, but I had previously sold a web and mobile design education company, so I was able to start working full time on GrowSurf before it was bringing in revenue.

What was your biggest mental hurdle in starting a SaaS?

It was hard because we started everything from scratch. I didn't have a network or a community in SaaS. I didn't have a lot of concrete experience in building a software tool, other than a bit of web development. Now I was teaching myself to build a large-scale SaaS business that could, on the structural end, support millions of requests on a monthly basis.

In the end, it's all a numbers game. If things are looking good, and the numbers are working, then you know you're on the right track.

What's the most important thing a SaaS founder needs to know, starting out?

You've got to know who the customer is, and be willing to talk to them. You can't know what people need without actually talking to them. If you get into a cycle where you're not talking to customers, that can get dangerous. It's dogma in the startup world, but it's easy to fall out of that habit and think that you're fine – but you're not.

You've also got to niche down. We started off too broad. But there's a catch-22 there. I don't know if we would have had our first customers if we had targeted only tech startups from the beginning. We started out with a seed idea, threw it out to the world, and saw who grabbed on. That's how we eventually niched down. Ultimately, the easier you can make it for a specific party to choose your product, the better. Your market is smaller, but when it hits, it really hits.

TAKEAWAYS

- Keep talking to customers and getting feedback, even when you're doing well.
- Niche down and make it easy for specific customers to want your product.

#21

Brandon Ambrose

Title: Founder & CEO, EZ Ops

Value proposition: Equips operations teams to focus on top priorities in order to produce the world's cleanest and most profitable hydrocarbons

Industry: Oil and gas

Keywords: Development, mindset, MVP

What is EZ Ops?

EZ Ops allows blue collar workers to perform at their best.

We're in the oil and gas industry. Our platform consolidates and synthesizes data, and then provides data-driven directions so that every action that workers take aligns with corporate goals. EZ Ops takes the cognitive load off workers.

How did you identify this as a problem to be solved?

I started a services company in 2008. I was basically trying to transplant my brain into all of my guys, but there were limitations around that. To find a solution to solve that, I started developing an internal platform in 2015. In 2019, EZ Ops became its own company, and we started licensing it to producers.

There have been others who tried to solve the same problem, but purely with computers. I realized that if we could allow computers to do what computers do well, and allow people to add that human intuition component, that would provide the optimal outcome.

How did you approach development?

I brought on a developer to the team. We used our own development team for 90% of the development and outsourced the other 10%.

If you had to do development again, what would you do differently?

We were a bit narrow minded. We were only leveraging the talents that we had in house, which caused a lot of refactoring after.

If I had to do it again, I would have one really experienced person on the team that was comfortable leveraging outsourced people. That way, you could get the best talent working on a contract basis on specific aspects of the business–and one person with a very high level understanding and the ability to manage offshore people with specialized talents and traits.

How did you build an MVP and validate your product?

We did that wrong, too. We built it as a solution for ourselves, and then we got lucky in that it fit the problem of the industry. In hindsight, we should have been validating with at least five or six main clients to make sure that we were building a solution that was going to fit the market.

Where are you now in terms of growth?

We incorporated in September of 2019. We grew to $10k in MRR over the first year and then we saw 300% growth in 2020. We're on target for 300% growth again in 2021. So we're right around $1M in ARR. Now we're figuring out how we're going to get to 300% in 2022.

Have there been any unexpected challenges of of building this product?

You're constantly learning. In retrospect, we were horribly wrong in how we went about building the platform. I've learned so much even over the last year. I'm excited that a year from now, I'll look back and realize that I know nothing today.

What would you say to another SaaS founder in manufacturing/ operations?

Get lots of money. There's a lot of opportunity, but it's probably the slowest industry to change. There's been so much money that has been made in this industry that people might think, *If it's not broken, why fix it?* That makes sales slow.

In a way, you're teaching the market. Make sure you have lots of resources that you don't run out of before you've accomplished that goal.

What kind of mindset do you need to maintain to make it for the long haul?

First, you don't know anything. Second, don't reinvent the wheel. Get over your ego and make sure that you're truly listening and learning from as many resources as you can. It's very costly to make these mistakes yourself. Learn from other people that have done exactly what you're doing.

TAKEAWAYS

- "Teaching the market" takes time – and money.
- Do yourself a favor and learn from others' mistakes before making them yourself.

#22, #23
Samantha Anderl & Andrea Wildt

Title: Co-founders, Harlow

Value proposition: Helps freelancers manage their day-to-day operations and get paid

Industry: Freelancing software

Keywords: Bootstrapping, calm company, co-founder, customer discovery, fundraising, non-technical founder, prioritization

How do you work together as founders?

A: Samantha and I both have very strong go-to-market experience. We do a lot of things in partnership with each other. Samantha takes the lead right now on our marketing strategy, and I'm taking the lead on the product side so that there's a key owner. That being said, we're both present in all of these conversations right now.

S: We did all of the fundraising together.

That feels less conventional than the traditional co-founder relationship.

S: We know that at some point along the journey, we will fall into more traditional roles. We have been working together for eight years now, and we have this really good partnership. We complement each other. There are no egos involved. Naturally, one of us usually steps up to lead one thing or another, while the other person falls into a support role. That can shift from week to week, depending on our priorities.

How did you meet each other?

A: We worked at an email marketing company called Campaign Monitor. Samantha worked for me.

S: I was Andrea's first hire.

A: I became the CMO of Campaign Monitor and Samantha ran the self-service side of the business. When we both left, we founded a boutique consulting company, focusing on demand generation for very early stage SaaS companies. Eventually, we started to feel like we wanted to do this for ourselves. We wanted to move into the product space. Building a product to support freelancers felt natural to us, given that we have essentially been freelancers ourselves for the last three and a half years.

What is Harlow?

S: Harlow was built specifically for the "white collar solopreneur," such as a designer, a content writer, a social media consultant, or any other type of business consultant. It's focused on making that person's day-to-day life easier by providing a layer of organization, helping them keep their clients, tasks, and projects managed, and helping them get paid on time. Harlow brings everything into one place, so that their day-to-day can be less scattered.

Did you experience this problem yourselves?

A: Yes, absolutely. Then, we went out and we conducted a bunch of freelancer interviews. What we heard over and over from freelancers is that they struggle with some of the basics of running their business. It boiled down to answering questions like, "Where do I manage my tasks? How do I prioritize my day-to-day? How do I make sure I get paid on time?"

How did you find freelancers for your early discovery calls?

S: Andrea and I have a large network of freelancers who we worked with while running our own boutique agency. When we were at Campaign Monitor, we worked with a network of freelancers who supported the business. For the first round of interviews, we reached out to 20 of our pals and went through questions like "How do you run your business? What tools do you use?" Once we collected all the information, we worked with a product consultant who helped us figure out the overlapping issues.

Tell me about the process of bringing in a product consultant.

S: Because Andrea and I work together so much, sometimes our perspectives start to align. As we're building Harlow, we're bringing on freelancers and others with different perspectives to challenge us and make sure we're looking at the whole story.

A: The product consultant was able to distill all of these interviews and break them down into themes. We had an assumption, but seeing it visually helped us figure out where to focus. He also helped us with some very early wireframes and ideas around how we might structure Harlow.

As non-technical founders, how did you approach development?

A: Because we're going a nontraditional route for funding, we don't have the money to bring on a technical founder. We need to get a product to market and get that early feedback from customers before we invest heavily in full-time employees. That's why we made the decision to go with an outsourced agency. We've actually seen that there are a lot of other companies that do that. Slack's MVP was outsourced. So was Calendly's.

What kind of advice would you give on demand generation?

S: One of the things that Andrea and I are doing differently is that we're launching our go-to market activities at the same time that we're building the product. Right now, we are working on establishing a community of freelancers, starting to engage with the audience, and building brand awareness. We're trying to avoid the "lull" after launch by putting into place programs like content and engaging our community on social early on.

What are some of the mistakes that founders make when it comes to prioritization?

S: As humans, we tend to focus on our strengths. Andrea and I could absolutely focus more on marketing as a priority than our product. But we know that we need to prioritize both.

What's your approach to funding?

A: We're currently bootstrapping, but we did raise a little over a million dollars from a Friends and Family round. Our intent is not to go raise traditional VC funds at a later date. At the beginning of this journey, we sat down, built a five-year model, and asked, "What's it going to take to build this business? What are our ultimate goals for this business? How much money do we need to actually build it?" At first, we thought we needed a couple hundred thousand dollars. Then we realized we probably need a million dollars to launch.

We talked to some of our friends who had experience in or with VC and angel investing who helped us focus on what we truly wanted to build. Samantha and I want to maintain autonomy and control of Harlow. For us, that meant maintaining a lot of the ownership of the company. That's part of the reason we decided not to go the traditional VC route.

S: We also want to build a calm company. When we start hiring internally – or even as we start to hire freelancers – we want to respect people's boundaries and work-life balance. Andrea and I strive for balance in our lives. We want to keep that as a core part of our business ethos. We are building Harlow to help freelancers organize their day-to-day, so that they can have better work-life balance and be more streamlined in what they do. We also want future employees of Harlow to feel that way too.

A: We also want to build a company that's really strong and profitable. Running a calm company doesn't mean that we're not going to work our butts off. We just want to do it our way.

Any final advice for SaaS founders?

A: Pick your co-founder wisely.

S: We are extremely lucky that we have been working together for the past eight years. It makes it more fun–and easier–to build something with somebody that you respect and that you've built a relationship with.

A: You want somebody that you can have the hard conversations with. It's a really long, bumpy path. Make sure that you've got a really solid partner along the way.

TAKEAWAYS

- Launch your go-to market activities while you build your product.
- Pick your co-founder wisely. Make sure it's someone with whom you can have hard conversations.

#24

Jose Sanchez

Title: Founder & CEO, Ecogistix

Value proposition: Shrinks the supply chain between farmers to buyers and manages the transportation; "Shrinking the Supply Chain from Farm to Fork"

Industry: Agrotechnology

Keywords: Bootstrapping, chicken or the egg, marketplace, team

How did "shrinking the supply chain" for farmers become a problem you wanted to solve?

I've been very lucky. I really got my education when I worked at Walmart.com. I worked on the technical side, but I wanted to learn something on the business side – I didn't even care what it was. I put my feelers out and found that Walmart really needed someone with a technical background to help support their supply chain systems. That's when I learned the systemic parts of supply chain and procurement, every step of how something gets from your online shopping cart to your doorstep.

In 2010, I moved out here to Discovery Bay. All of a sudden, I was surrounded by a bunch of farmers. I went around talking to them, trying to figure out what their problems were and how I might be able to help. Quite a few of them told me that they had a problem getting carriers to actually move their orders. These are small to medium sized farmers. They don't have a bunch of resources or teams of people to help. So, they were spending way too much time on the phone, trying to find slices of time to talk to carriers and make sure everything was being moved. Along with the industry changing to support product traceability and leverage blockchain. Once I learned that the produce on the shelf at your local store has seven to 10 touch points between resellers before it arrives at your store, I knew we could improve this.

That's when I decided to leverage my supply chain systems and operations background to solve this problem.

So I developed something that functions a lot like the "eCommerce warehousing." I basically took the supply chain warehouse systems and put them on top of the farm. We built a system to be able to digitize a farm, to create a unique trackable bar code that includes their GTIN for every case label. Farmers would know exactly the yields of their farm, who packed the case and how much inventory they have so it can surface up to a marketplace directly. That includes a transportation management system that will match a carrier to deliver their orders to the farmer's customers and push data to the buyer's blockchain if required.

Who gets to benefit from using your product, in addition to farmers?

One of the beneficiaries would be the buyers. Restaurants, hospitals, and businesses that serve food to their employees have a problem with sourcing. They can get food, but they have to go through a bunch of middlemen and a lot of fraud happens. Our platform allows those buyers to purchase directly from farmers, almost like an eBay. And if they have a large order, then multiple farmers can meet that need by aggregating their volume and shipping it directly to the buyer.

How are you funding Ecogistix?

We've been bootstrapping since our launch in 2017. No funding; we're basically paying for it out of pocket. Right now, we're focusing on reaching farmers and getting them into the marketplace. These farmers typically make super slim margins–about 4%. On our platform, they can make 25-40% margins.

Have you faced any challenges reaching potential users?

When we first talked to carriers about our business, they wanted to know that there were farmers on the platform first. And farmers wanted to know that there were carriers on the platform first. So that was a real challenge – getting buy-in from both parties at the same time. To solve that problem, we made a pivot and began creating tools for farmers, getting involved in their daily processes and getting hooked into their operations. We've added value to the platform, offering not only carriers, but traceability and the ability to see inventory in real time.

Did you have any fears or concerns as a first-time founder?

I feel pretty confident about our tools because I've built similar tools in the e-commerce industry. The bigger fear was about persuading farmers to pull the trigger and spend the money on the platform. That's still the toughest part about the business. One of the bright sides of the pandemic, however, has been that farmers are a lot more interested in getting on the platform after having their supply chains broken by COVID-19. They don't want to rely on middlemen anymore.

The other challenge is that a lot of farmers don't have WiFi. A lot of them pack out in the fields and there's not even a cellular network. How does a SaaS cloud-based platform work when there is no network connectivity? Another challenge is that they also need a special printer to print these shipping labels.

We're really trying to level up these farmers in terms of their technology. It's a learning curve for the farmer. That being said, we are told that our tool is super simple to use. Our users can usually learn it within five minutes, which is awesome.

How have you brought together the right team for Ecogistix?

You've got to pick a team of people that you're not going to have to chase to do the work. They've got to be passionate about the problem you are trying to solve and the product that supports the solution. There will be people who just see the glamor of an early stage startup and see what it could be. But you have to find the people who are willing to put in the sweat equity until you actually get to a point of success.

I would say finding a team is one of the toughest parts of SaaS. On that note, you have to not only be able to sell your product to investors or customers, but to a team that is basically working for equity alone in the beginning. You've got to have vision. You've got to be able to sell people on what you're doing, and believe in your product.

TAKEAWAYS

- Find team members who are just as passionate as you are about the problem, and willing to put in the sweat equity.

#25

Tammy McMiller

Title: Co-founder & CEO, Plan Heal

Value proposition: Automates remote patient monitoring to help populations gain key information on their health and have more engaging conversations with their medical care providers for better health outcomes and cost savings.

Industry: Medtech

Keywords: Co-founder, female founder, mindset

What is Plan Heal?

We scale and automate remote patient monitoring to help health care organizations, insurers, and large employers take care of their populations. Here's why we are committed to delivering this population health service: More than 10 million people in America right now have a disease and don't even know it. Plan Heal is here to help those organizations find a better way to monitor the holistic health of people and give them access to quality health information that they can act upon for better health outcomes. This ultimately decreases healthcare costs that, as of date, amount to more than $3T USD-in which $55B is Plan Heal's target serviceable market.

How did you identify this as a problem?

I identified this as a problem based on personal experiences with friends and family members and through doing more research and learning about what's happening in the health care sector. Today in America, more than six million people have a sexually transmitted infection, and half of those people don't even know it. What does that mean? Women who are in their childbearing years are experiencing challenges conceiving and carrying babies for the whole term. A lot of those women don't know that they have a sexually transmitted infection that's jeopardizing the health of their uterus.

People have this notion that if they drink, water, sleep, and exercise, they'll stay healthy. But there are so many other things going on with your health. We're using technology to help inform people so that they have a better view of their holistic health, and so that they can partner with health care providers to get better outcomes.

What's your professional background?

My professional background is in enterprise data. During my corporate career, I helped Fortune 100 companies get into new markets by leveraging enterprise data insights. That included identifying ways to acquire new customers, to retain existing customers, and to build products to best service those customers.

Are you a technical founder?

I'm a hybrid. I have technical knowledge and I have business knowledge. That was originally my claim to fame in corporate America and that I now use to advance the Plan Heal mission.

How involved were you in the development of your product?

I oversaw the coding and development of our product. I identified the vision for the product and I identified the architecture for the cloud. Then I hired team members to bring that to life.

Where are you in the process of launching Plan Heal?

We completed our beta testing and are in discussions to launch pilots with a few of our ideal enterprise customers.

What have you learned in beta?

People really appreciate having a better understanding of their health and engaging with their doctors. More than 80% of our users reported that they had a more engaging conversation with their doctor about their health because of Plan Heal. More than 90% of those people received preventative health tests and screenings that they would not have received otherwise.

What sort of challenges have you experienced as a female founder, and as a female founder of color?

The challenges didn't only start with me founding a company. In my corporate career, I led domestic and international teams of mainly men, and that was challenging at times. But being a founder, the challenges double. You don't have the team, the budget, or the name recognition of being at a bigger company.

The primary challenge is that there is a bias on women as founders and even more-so for women of color because there aren't a lot of us doing this – especially in the medtech space. Because of this, you don't always get the invitations to join the conversations and pitches to win the business or receive the funding. It's been very challenging, but we received some good news today. Plan Heal will be featured on the Nasdaq Tower as an emerging tech startup. So we're excited about that. The little wins empower us to keep going.

Do you have a co-founder?

Yes. My co-founder, Eric McMiller II, is the CIO. His job is to protect the data. In the past, he has worked with the NSA and the Department of Defense with their cybersecurity strategy. Now, he's brought that experience over to us to help us protect the data that people share with us. This is a foundational role for the company as we are essentially trusted with large volumes of people's personal health data. We take this undertaking very seriously. I'm the CEO. I identify the right types of partners and future services for growth and then keep the vision for the years ahead. How can we prepare for the future? On a day-to-day basis, I look at what types of data points we're collecting and how we're going to use those data points to continuously provide deeper health insights.

How do you maintain the right kind of mindset to be a founder?

You have to believe that you've been called to do whatever you're doing.

You're going to experience weariness, loneliness, and rejection. Maybe people won't take you seriously. Team members might drop off. Partners might leave. And maybe all of that happens in one month. If you don't feel that you've been called to do this, you won't have the resolve or the strength to get through to the next day. Millions of people could have a better quality of life because of Plan Heal. That's why I get out of bed every day.

Any final advice for SaaS founders?

Surround yourself with people who are technically talented and that believe in the mission; otherwise, they won't hang around for the tough times. When I say surround yourself with technical people, that doesn't just mean people that know how to build a product. They need to think outside the box of what's in front of them. I challenge my team everyday to look at new ways to leverage technology. For example, at Plan Heal, a data point is just not a data point. A data point is something you can use to understand what it is happening at this moment with a person's health. Data can help identify what's going to happen with a person's health in the future. There's always more to any data story.

And lastly, but most importantly, founders have to surround themselves with people who are smart, know their discipline, and are go-getters.

TAKEAWAYS

- When you believe that you're called to your business, you can persist through the ups and downs.
- Surround yourself with people who think outside the box and believe in your mission.

#26

Alexander Börve

Title: Founder, First Derm - Autoderm API

Value proposition: Allows users to address skin concerns with AI-powered algorithm

Industry: Telemedicine

Keywords: AI, fundraising

How did you come up with the idea for First Derm?

My ex-girlfriend was a dermatologist. We used to go to dinner parties together, and people would always ask her questions about skin concerns—"Does this mole look okay?" or "What's this rash?"– things like that. That's when I came up with the idea of "on-demand dermatology" through texting an image to a dermatology platform.

I started doing research for First Derm in 2009. Fast-forward to now, and we've collected hundreds of thousands of smartphone images of different skin concerns that have been diagnosed by dermatologists. We use these images and diagnoses to create machine learning models that can predict skin concerns.

Using the machine learning models, we have then built an API called Autoderm that can be used by other platforms to predict skin diseases.

Why have you focused on building an API?

If we do a source model, we don't spend anything on marketing. A regular mobile app might cost you ten to twenty dollars (many times a lot more) in marketing costs for one download, but a source model means that other platforms absorb the costs of acquiring customers. That allows me to focus on improving our artificial intelligence model every few months instead of worrying about the high costs of acquiring customers.

What's your professional background?

I was a medical doctor–an orthopedic surgeon–in Sweden. In 2013, I came to UC Berkeley to get my PhD. Being in the Bay Area, I "of course" had to start a tech company like everyone else. The problem with building a team in the Bay Area, however, is that it might be easy to find people, but it's expensive to pay them…especially if you don't raise a couple million dollars to get started. I raised a small round of money from angel investors, but then I wasn't able to raise a bigger round.

As an entrepreneur, you make a choice. You can either struggle, or you can find a place where you can live off whatever money you make from your business and where you can find cheap labor. That's why I'm back to Europe – in Spain.

As far as my technical background, I don't know any coding, but I can recognize good coding vs. bad coding from working with developers. I'm good at testing things, and I do

have an eye for products. I understand how things should work. That was the great thing about the Bay Area. You can run a new app by your friends, and they're great at giving informed, instant feedback. You can't do that in many other places. You might run an app by someone at a dinner party, and they'll tell you it's great and get right back to eating.

So, there are major pro's *and* con's to living in the Bay Area.

Yeah. Now they say that you can never really start a company in the Bay Area. Instead, you should start a company somewhere else, and then when you get traction, move to the Bay Area. Build your network and get connected to investors. I think that's true. I met one of my investors in a bar and she wrote me a check for $100k the next day in Starbucks. Those kinds of things still do happen in the Bay Area.

For example, in the Midwest your investors might have to consider that $100k for a while and get assurance from friends that it is a good investment. They might have to discuss the decision first with a partner or wife. But in the Bay Area, they know time is money.

How are you setting yourself apart from competitors?

I'm not a dermatologist, but I am a doctor. I understand dermatology and the healthcare system. I have a feeling of what is coming and what is important. Right now, we're not focusing so much on skin cancer as we are on sexually transmitted diseases. Around 30% of our image database is of genitals with some kind of dermatology issue. This is great, because if you're 17 or 18 years old, and you don't want to talk to your parents or go to the doctor, you can take a photo yourself, run it through the AI anonymously, and we can suggest what it can be.

What's been one of the challenges about using AI in your platform?

Within two or three years, artificial intelligence will be better than actual dermatologists at diagnosing these images. But the problem with that is that patients aren't as happy when they know AI is reading their images instead of a human being. About 40% of health care is the placebo effect. If you have a fever, for example, just going to the doctor's office can make you feel better, because someone with know-how and empathy has listened to you.

There's an expression that says that artificial intelligence will not substitute for doctors, but doctors who use artificial intelligence will substitute doctors who don't use artificial intelligence. Artificial intelligence will help doctors make better, faster, and more secure diagnoses and find the correct treatment faster.

That's not to say there hasn't been a lot of pushback. In 2013, I had world-renowned dermatologists, professors, and advisors on my team. My co-founder and I told them, we're going into artificial intelligence, and they told us, "It's not going to work. Give up on this idea. Just focus on what you're doing now with telehealth." So that's what we did. Then, three or four years ago, someone from Stanford published something about skin cancer detection and deep learning. All of a sudden there was interest from the dermatologists. Now, I move more on my own intuition. The dermatologists are still on board, but

I do not ask them advice in regards to AI. I read more on the subject myself and follow what science has published or where bigger tech companies are moving.

TAKEAWAYS

- Consider a source model; it effectively removes the need for marketing.
- You don't need to move to the Bay Area to start a tech company, but you should know that raising money may be more difficult elsewhere.

#27

Donna Conroy

Title: Co-founder & CEO, SciMar ONE

Value proposition: The SDE is a drug development platform expediting delivery of safe and effective innovations using disease-specific clinical data powered by AI

Industry: Healthcare

Keywords: AI, development, female founder, validation

What's your professional background, Donna?

I'm a microbiologist who transitioned to sales and then marketing in pharma for several years. I launched three large products into the pharmaceutical arena, one of which made $1.2 billion. After I had my first kid, I started my own gig. What I've been doing ever since is using scientific data to help pharmaceutical companies develop drugs better, faster, safer and more efficiently.

In the last year, my team and I began to take some of our smaller technology solutions and figure out a way to build them into a multi tenant solution – i.e., a SaaS solution. Now, our platform not only expedites the delivery of safe and effective drugs, vaccines and diagnostics, but also strives to get scientific data and accurate information out to other relevant stakeholders in the healthcare industry.

Tell me about your journey as a female founder, and as a mom.

Before starting SciMar (which stands for SCIence to the MARket) I was in marketing at a Fortune 500 pharma company and in charge of scientific communications. I was on the road all the time. I was on a team of only three people and launched a massive product, for hepatitis C. Then, I had my first child. I had this little baby, and I thought, there's no way I can get on a plane four days a week anymore. I asked the company I was working for if I could be home on Wednesdays, and continue to travel on the weekends to talk about medicine and treatment, which is what my main responsibility was.

When I was ready to come back to work, I got a phone call telling me that the incoming CEO – a female – said I had to come back full-time or not come back at all. So I walked away. I consulted from 2003 to 2011, and I had four kids in that time frame too.

How did you transition from a consulting business into a technology business?

By 2011, I had really honed in on what we did well. I had a team of health care practitioners working for me, and we would cull through all of the scientific data manually, essentially going through tons of paperwork. My husband, who was in technology, would look at the giant piles of paper with all their highlights and sticky memos in my office and tell me, "Donna, there's a better way to do this."

After a very stressful year at a corporate technology company, he got laid off, as one of the last ones in his division of 500. When he told me, my immediate response was, "Okay then. Now show me the better way to do this."

We started building these digital solutions for individual pharma companies until 2019. Things were going well, but we started to realize there was a bigger problem to solve. We saw that the industry was losing super valuable knowledge every time a drug failed. This loss created redundant work from not only company to company, but also from function to function within a company. This waste of time could be spent innovating and progressing development of their individual drugs instead. As you can imagine it is also a huge expense to drug development overall.

I told my husband I thought we needed to take a year to regroup and re-envision, that there was something bigger out there. So we took a risk and dropped all our clients to strategize and then build a SaaS platform.

Did you have any fears about starting a SaaS company?

The biggest fear has definitely been putting all our eggs into one SaaS basket. We are a family business and the fear of going broke before we make it hovers in the background. We're essentially walking away from well-paying clients and trying to build something that is going to be more comprehensively used around the globe and better for public health. We're either going to be wildly successful or fail miserably. There's no middle ground. That's exciting, but scary too.

Have there been any challenges in development?

Testing viability in terms of user experience can be challenging, because you need to be surveying people who, in some ways, have the ability to envision a new future and be brazen enough to disrupt the way they currently work. That's a challenge when you think about pharma because you're dealing with risk averse corporations. In the past, they only dealt with very concrete ideas and facts, not with what *could* be.

That being said, I think the market is starting to change. As technology has grown, pharma is understanding and realizing that technology is going to help them develop better drugs, faster and safer. Redundant tasks are being placed into technological solutions that are ultimately freeing up time and space for the scientists, doctors, PhD's, marketers and payer groups to do their best work. And that's changing the game for everybody.

TAKEAWAYS

- If you're in an industry like healthcare, be patient when testing viability in terms of user experience. Your potential customers have to be willing to disrupt the way they work.

Ariel Lipschutz

Title: Co-founder & CEO, Poolpo

Value proposition: Helps car insurance payers save money by applying an algorithm to their insurance policy

Industry: Insurance

Keywords: AI, development, product/market fit

What problem does Poolpo solve?

Insurance companies are not taking care of their customers. They try to get more people in the company, but they don't care about the most important thing – saving people money.

We give people the opportunity to save money with a simple algorithm. We have an artificial intelligence algorithm that can understand the policy of your insurance company, and decide if there are better options with the same coverage condition at lowered prices. This algorithm performs these days before you need to renovate your policy.

How did you get interested in solving this problem with AI?

My cofounder Martin and I started talking two years ago, and decided we wanted to do something together. He had been working in the insurance industry for 10 years, and I had been working in artificial intelligence and building and designing products and services for different companies. But I had never started my own business.

Martin told me that he had a lot of customers calling him and telling him they were paying 50% more than the previous month. In Argentina, we've had around 30% inflation over the last five years. People are looking for ways to save money, and we decided we could automate a process to help them do so.

When you started Poolpo, did you plan to use an algorithm?

I've been working in AI for four years now, and I have a background in software development and innovation. We decided we were going to build an algorithm to help understand customer policies in order to scale our product all over the world. The next step is to create a chat bot that can talk to our users about FAQs or incidents with their cars.

What kind of advice would you give to someone who's wanting to start a company with that AI component?

You're going to need a lot of data. In our case, we have data from my co-founder's company. It can also be expensive. But if you have your own algorithm, that can set you apart from your competitors.

Do not be discouraged! Sometimes it can be frustrating because responses are not always going to be good. You just need to keep training your algorithm!

Is there any other advice you would share with people who are wanting to start a SaaS company?

Know and take care of your customer. If you don't, they're going to leave you behind for a new company.

Nowadays, there's a lot of competition. You should have one eye focused on bringing in new customers and the other one on taking care of your existing customers.

I was a high school teacher for 10 years. A couple months ago, a former student called me and told me his idea for a business. I asked him, "How much time have you spent developing this tool?" He said, "Maybe 100 hours." I said, "But have you talked to somebody who is going to pay for your product?" And he said, "No."

I told him to stop developing. First, you need to understand if there is going to be somebody who will pay for your product/services. Listen to your customers before deciding there is a real problem.

My best advice is this: Always remain in the position of trying to find the problem.

TAKEAWAYS

- Don't forget about your existing customers. If you focus on customer acquisition at the cost of customer retention, you risk losing your customer base to the competition.

Tim Wallis

Title: Founder, Turq.io

Value proposition: Enables everyday people to create signature ready legislation for issues they care about

Industry: Civics, legislation

Keywords: Fundraising, MVP, validation

What is Turq.io?

Turq.io is a platform for funding, enabling, and pipelining signature ready legislation written by everyday people. If you have an issue that you care about, but you can't get the time, energy or attention of elected officials to create legislation for that issue, or if you're intimidated at the prospect of creating legislation yourself, you can use Turq to write signature ready legislation that we pipeline into state and local legislatures. We also enable you to crowdfund with others that also care about that specific issue.

How did you get interested in legislation?

I ran for state Senate down in North Carolina. My goal for running for office was to take the processes that we use in software development and apply them in the classroom to help deliver educational content. I met somebody who was already doing that, and I wanted to take his ideas and his implementation and spread that across the entire state. I didn't win, but my experience on the campaign trail was transformative.

There was a guy who would come to every event and would, for lack of a better term, beg these elected lawmakers to care about his pet issue, which was stray animals. Because this was not a top 10 issue, he could not get the attention of anybody.

I thought to myself, *Why couldn't somebody else just write legislation for him and then hand it off to an elected lawmaker?* The job of the elected lawmaker would be super easy. They wouldn't have to invest anything into research or drafting legislation.

When I looked, I couldn't find anything that made that connection between lawmakers and people who wanted to get involved in the civic space.

How has COVID affected your business plan?

Originally, my concept was to target small businesses with the platform. Small businesses interact with the law all the time and probably see a lot of opportunity for change. Then COVID hit. All of a sudden, small businesses weren't looking to spend money on anything other than the bare necessities. We had to pivot our target audience towards individuals with issues they really care about.

The challenge is that it's much harder to discover those people. I can't say that we've figured that out yet, but we've been getting traction with some experiments. We're going through advocacy groups and seeing who are the types of people that they interact with, like self-identified community organizers. Ironically, it's been easier to find people to write the bills. We've had a lot of software developers willing to help create legislation. They have a lot of experience with documentation. They know how to write crisp, concise language.

What's the best piece of advice you've received?

At first, I assumed that I had to raise money in order to build the product. Y Combinator advises that you build the product and then raise money to scale the product. When you raise money before building the product, you put yourself at a massive negotiation disadvantage with investors. They have all the leverage at that point to dictate how much of their business they want to take and what the valuation is. If you have a product first, you're in a more advantageous position to negotiate with investors.

If you had to do it over again, what would you do differently?

If I were to do it over again, I would have been more willing to not have a full platform upfront. I started out with a Squarespace site, but I could have probably gotten away with something more lightweight, like even just an Air Table or a Google Forum. I wish I had pushed harder on validation without all the technology underpinning. Don't delay validation because of a lack of technology. Go with something basic on the front end and push harder.

TAKEAWAYS

- Build the product, then raise capital. You'll have more leverage with investors.

- Focus on validation first. Go super simple on the MVP.

#30

Christina Layman Holmes

Title: Co-founder, Theta Retail

Value proposition: Empowers teams to make better purchasing, stocking, and assortment decisions; uses advanced analytics to help companies make better decisions

Industry: Horticulture

Keywords: Development

What is Theta Retail?

Theta Retail provides two things—an order flow for companies to stock retail stores and a business intelligence piece that provides advanced analytics to help companies make better decisions.

What's your professional background?

I started Theta Retail with my brother. We grew up in an entrepreneurial household. My parents owned the largest perennial nursery in the Southeast. After my brother and I graduated college, we both worked for the family business and gained a ton of experience. It was a medium-sized business and we wore a bunch of different hats. We were involved in logistics, in marketing, in procurement, and the sales cycle. Basically, we were exposed to everything that you need to know to run a business at a very young age. We did that for about 10 years. Then, as a family we made a decision to sell.

After about five years of working for the company that bought us, we decided that we needed to get back to our entrepreneurial roots. Even though it's hectic and your hair's on fire all the time, it's hard to go back and be an employee for someone. So we decided to break off and start our own consultancy. We knew that the end goal was to develop a product, but we weren't sure exactly what it was.

How did you come up with the idea for Theta Retail?

A couple of years into running our consultancy, we were approached by a connection in the nursery industry who was looking for a replenishment solution. There was only one provider and that provider was not doing a good job servicing the market. So we decided to bring together what we love – technology and horticulture – and create our own product.

Did you create your own MVP, or did you outsource?

We outsourced development. It's been a good experience, but myself and my co-founder (my brother) are both highly technical. I can look over their code and know if it's quality or not. If we were non-technical founders that outsourced development, we would have to have someone internal that could review the code and ensure that it was quality.

What are your plans for the future?

We started within this industry because that's where our Rolodex is. Our entire careers have been spent inside horticulture and we have some very deep connections within the industry. However, it's a relatively small industry.

After getting a certain amount of market saturation within horticulture, we'll look at industries that are very similar to wholesale horticulture, such as cut flowers and packaged food.

What advice would you give to other SaaS founders?

It's going to be cloud-based. No one's developing on-premise solutions. If you're non-technical, bring in a consultant who can walk you through development. Through that process, make sure that you develop your application with cost in mind. Within cloud technology, there are 10 different ways to build a product–and each of those 10 ways has a very different cost structure.

TAKEAWAYS

- If you're going to create a product, make sure it's cloud-based.

#31
Fedor Shkliarau

Title: Co-founder, Alfread

Value proposition: Helps users read and learn from online content more efficiently

Industry: News media and content

Keywords: Customer acquisition, distribution, mindset

What is Alfread?

Alfread is a red letter mobile app that helps you do a better job at reading your saved articles. Sources like Instapaper and Pocket allow you to save articles very easily, but the problem is actually coming back to read those articles.

The goal of Alfread is to create a habit of reading and catching up with what you've saved, so you can learn from content and be a better professional.

How did you identify this as a problem to be solved?

I observed my own habit of not coming to back to Instapaper to read what I saved. I noticed other people complaining about the same problem. I thought, *What if there was a solution for that?*

How are you honing in on the right audience, and how are you reaching that audience and acquiring customers?

We're targeting people who are already frustrated with services like Instapaper and Pocket. We know that we're going to have to explain the concept of saving later to this category of people.

We're targeting customers in a few ways. First, we're observing mentions on Twitter when people are complaining about their service. Next, we're targeting designers, product managers, journalists, and writers by reaching out to them on platforms where they hang out.

We're also writing content ourselves, publishing on Medium where people are already used to reading articles and saving them for later.

What has surprised you about the journey of building an app?

There's a meme that shows that second time founders focus on traction instead of paying too much attention to the product itself. There's a lot of wisdom to that. Now when I'm thinking about a new idea, I never start pursuing it unless I have a clear understanding of how to distribute it. You have to reach people where they hang out versus relying on an "if you build it, they will come" mentality.

Another surprise was how much time it takes to build something worth someone's attention.

Finally, if someone says they want something, it doesn't mean that's true. Sometimes people say that to sound nice.

What does it take to be an entrepreneur?

In order to develop, you have to step up to something you are a bit afraid of and you have to catch up and learn a lot of stuff. Being an entrepreneur uncovers a lot of weaknesses. It can be intimidating, but it's also fun to switch your perspective and learn something new.

TAKEAWAYS

- Think about how you will distribute a product before you build it.
- Starting a business will uncover your weaknesses. It's all part of the process.

#32

Brianna Sturm

Title: Founder, BORN

Value proposition: Birth Support at Your Fingertips

Industry: Pregnancy and birth

Keywords: Chicken or the egg, development, MVP, non-technical founder

What is BORN?

BORN is a platform and a community to support moms in their transition into motherhood and parenthood. It's also a platform for practitioners – including doulas and midwives – so they're able to create a thriving business for themselves.

How did you identify this as a problem to be solved?

I've been a doula and a prenatal yoga instructor. I was very much in the birthing world and realized the struggle that doulas have finding clients and keeping their books full. On the other end, moms were struggling to find the support they desperately needed throughout the parenthood journey.

I knew there was probably a better way of bridging that gap and making sure that the two demographics were able to find each other.

Moms weren't just looking for the doulas. Even after they've hired a doula and they've gone through their birth and now they're mothers, they still need different types of birth workers. Maybe they're having trouble breastfeeding and they can't find a lactation consultant, for example. The way people find these workers now is typically just by word of mouth and Google searching. Bringing everyone onto one platform just made sense.

What have been some of the challenges you've encountered while developing an MVP?

When you set out to create something with a fairly broad idea, you've got to narrow things down. I had a million ideas that I wanted to put into BORN, but they weren't all feasible out the gate. You have to ask, "Okay, what is needed right now? What's really going to motivate people to download your app?" I'm passionate about making sure that this is something that moms are going to want to use and doulas are going to use, and they're both going to benefit. When you're passionate about your product, it can be hard to say, "Business-wise, what are the bare minimums that are going to make this work?"

Another challenge is communicating exactly what I need to my developers. I couldn't have asked for a better partnership, but it's still difficult to translate what I actually want to a developer that's never been in the birth world.

Did you find anything that helped communicate your vision to your technical co-founders?

I finally got a grasp of how their minds work and how their processes work versus how I thought they were doing things. Secondly, I started detailing everything carefully, instead of thinking that we were on the same page. When I conveyed an idea, I stopped assuming they understood where I was coming from. I took the time to make sure there was no room for error.

What's the best piece of advice that you've received as far as starting a Saas?

Getting it done is better than getting it perfect!

TAKEAWAYS

- You may have a million ideas, but you won't be able to implement them all in the beginning. What are the bare minimums that will help your product succeed?

- If you're working with developers, be vigilant about detailing what you're looking for. Don't assume you're on the same page!

#33

Paúl Rivera

Title: Founder, Cognitiva

Value proposition: Makes Industry 4.0 accessible for manufacturing companies

Industry: Manufacturing, Industry 4.0

Keywords: Mindset, work-life balance

What is Cognitiva?

We are committed to making Industry 4.0 accessible for all manufacturing companies. Our SaaS platform allows companies to incorporate data collection on a real time basis to obtain actionable information and deep analytics for decision making.

How did you identify this as a problem to be solved?

I've been working in this industry for 16 years. In 2016, my first daughter was born. It was then that I started to worry because I noticed the consultancy industry was dying. I realized I needed a strong value proposition. As a consultant, you need to offer more than your individual skills. You also have to give them data and something that actually solves some of the problems. My first step was to try to sell European software designed specifically for manufacturers, but I noticed that the existing software was very complex, expensive, and unreachable for local companies.

A specific need was real time information from the shopper, because you have all of these systems, but they are aimed at the executive level. They only deal with big issues. The flows of information are oriented to strategic decisions to this process, and that's fine.

But the manufacturers need specific information on what operators are doing or how the machines are behaving or how the inventory is flowing on a structural basis.

What's the biggest lesson you've learned as an entrepreneur?

I consider myself a persistent person. Maybe I'm not the smartest person in the room. Maybe I'm not the best seller. But I'm able to withstand the heat and keep working. Our company has been through a lot. We've pivoted several times. My wife is my business partner, so problems in the business live at home, too. This company has been a painful process for me. My family and I have had a lot of sleepless nights. But we're persistent. I have also learned to have a very disciplined life, to exercise a lot. I meditate a lot. Here I am, and I'm still learning.

Do you have any advice for Latin American entrepreneurs?

For Latin American entrepreneurs, it's important to look beyond Latin America, especially when talking about investors and business networks and support. In my experience, it was very difficult to believe that somebody not in my country would believe in my company. But when I reached Europe, I realized I was wrong. The entrepreneurial spirit in Europe is very different and more mature than Latin America. So stay open to building new networks and getting support from elsewhere.

TAKEAWAYS

- Be creative when networking–don't assume investors and other partners won't be interested in your business!

Nathan Bakirci

Title: Co-founder, Beacon Dates
Value proposition: Generates local date ideas
Year of company launch: 2019
Location: Washington DC
Industry: Social/Lifestyle/Community
Keywords: Customer discovery, resources

What is Beacon Dates?

Let's say it's Thursday or Friday and you want to plan something for the weekend with your significant other, but you're tired of going and doing the same things. It takes a lot of time to pull together all the information you need to figure out what to do. We took all the information, put it in one place and made it subjective. A lot of websites like Yelp and Google Maps just aggregate data in a very objective way. Beacon is like the friend that knows the city really well and can recommend all the good spots and tell you what to get at a restaurant. We create that by reaching out to locals who are in the know and letting them share their ideas on the website.

Is Beacon Dates community-based?

Yeah, but it didn't start out that way. At first, my co-founder and I wrote all the content ourselves, but that can only take us so far. We needed to get other locals to create content. It naturally evolved into a community as we involved more people into the platform. It was surprising how willing people were to create content. Right now, we are exclusive to D.C., but hope to expand once we prove the idea.

How did this become a problem you wanted to solve?

My co-founder kept hearing the same questions over and over—"I'm going out, what should I do? Where should I go?" D.C. is very transient, so there are tons of transplants who aren't familiar with the city. Instead of explaining the same thing over and over to our friends, we thought, *Why don't we just create a website that has all this information and has opinions built into it?*

What has been surprising to you about building a SaaS?

What people say and what they do are two totally different things. One of the biggest surprises is the difference in how people verbally react to something versus the data. We've tried to be data-driven and remove guesswork from the equation when it comes to our product decisions. You imagine that as you make a change or implement a new feature, it will magically create more traffic or more usage. But that's not the case. You might get a minor bump in your metrics or something. But no matter how excited or enthusiastic people are when you talk about these kinds of things, it rarely translates into hard data.

How have you validated your idea?

It started out as informally talking to friends and family. Once we built the MVP, we would set up video calls with people where we would pull up the site and have them walk through the whole experience. We got a lot of great insight that way. That's how we iterated from our first version of the site.

Are there any other concrete strategies or tools that you've found to help you overcome those challenges?

LogRocket records user sessions. That's a decent replacement for sitting down and talking with someone and having them go through it in person. I've also found bugs that look like they do something that I didn't really anticipate, or the screen looks weird or something. But other than bugs, we can get a sense for how people are using this site. We can make educated guesses and see common trends, just by watching a few sessions. For example, if we see people not clicking on something that we want them to click on, we realize we need to make it more prominent. Seeing people in action adds more context to the data.

As someone who is two years into the process, what would be your first piece of advice to an aspiring founder?

Don't build something great that nobody wants. Take the time to really figure out what people want and solve that problem. It's easy to get carried away with a feature or even a whole product where you do surface level market research and convince yourself that everyone's going to love it and it's going to be a huge success. You might spend a bunch of time building to figure out that no one actually wants this thing. Prove out your idea in the least amount of time and effort as possible.

What do you do to keep yourself motivated and in that entrepreneurial mindset?

I keep learning. The "How I Built This" podcast is a really great podcast about interviewing founders of successful or innovative companies. I feel like every time I listen to an episode, I get a whole bunch of energy. I consume content like that and just generally learn as much as I can all the time.

TAKEAWAYS

- Enthusiasm does not translate into hard data. Adding a feature that people are excited about doesn't mean you'll see a change.
- Make sure you have a tool to help you see users in action.

PART 2

THE GUIDES

Founders who know the ropes...and are willing to share their expertise and wisdom

#35

Melani Gordon

Title: Co-founder & CEO, Evergreen* (fka TapHunter)
Value proposition: Digital signage for restaurants and bars
Industry: Food and beverage
Keywords: Development, fundraising, MVP, sales

*Gordon has stepped down as CEO since the time of this writing, but is still on the board. She is now the Program Director of Techstars Anywhere.

What is Evergreen?

Evergreen is a B2B tool for bars and restaurants. We help them to market and sell more of their food and beverage with digital signage.

How did COVID affect your business?

The amount of small businesses that completely shuttered their doors during the pandemic was pretty alarming for our team. We saw a lot of account suspensions and holds. Their pain was our pain. But we got very lucky because we were super diligent with the Paycheck Protection Program and that helped our business stay afloat. One silver lining of the pandemic was that we saw opportunistic people pick up new locations or business concepts for pennies on the dollar.

Can you tell me about the journey of starting Evergeen?

Our initial concept was launched as a B2C mobile app (TapHunter) where we helped you find your favorite craft beers and beverages through a gamified point system.

We quickly pivoted once we realized that the bigger opportunity was with bars and restaurant owners. They might love creating great beer, wine, and cocktail menus, but a lot of them are not so great at marketing. That's when we built our first tool for digital signage. Most locations don't have to accrue the added expense of hiring an audio-visual company to use our product. We just ship them a tiny device that they can plug into the back of their TV. They're literally up and running in a couple of minutes.

Why did you get into SaaS?

I have a long background in SaaS. I began my career as a sales leader and managing director for B2B SaaS in the real estate industry. That's when I saw the power of subscription-based business models. When I was 28, I left that company and started a marketing agency. The goal with that agency was to find something that we were passionate about, and build out of that. In 2009, the idea for Evergreen was born. We had built software for big clients, but it wasn't really getting me out of bed in the morning. We wanted to start helping small businesses in food and beverage, run by passionate, artistic people that really care about their craft. Being a whiskey and beer connoisseur myself absolutely helped.

We were at the right place at the right time, because that was around the explosion of the craft beer industry – and shortly after, craft cocktails and wine on tap. By now, we've served over 5,000+ bar and restaurant locations around the world to date.

What have been some of the unexpected challenges you've faced?

Initially, we raised a Friends and Family round, and then raised the Seed round—mainly from Angels, but with one institutional investor. It became clear that "growth at all costs" was just not the best way to go for us. I came from a B2B SaaS company that was entirely bootstrapped. They took it to $20 million a year in revenue and sold it a handful of years later for a lot of money to private equity. They didn't raise a penny. That experience taught me that you don't have to raise money to do well.

In 2019, we took a step back. I was carrying the stress of knowing there were 27 investors needing an exit in six to seven years, and I was working 80 hours a week in the concrete jungle to make it happen. That's not what I envisioned when I imagined running my own business. So, we restructured our company and team, got profitable, and bought out our investors through our profits within an eight month time span. Five of them decided to stay on.

Once again, we got very lucky on timing, because we COVID-proofed our business. When the pandemic hit, we had already gotten rid of the $20k per month office space and decided to run the company remotely.

I would encourage founders to think through raising money before taking that leap. Once you raise money, it's very difficult to go back.

My attorneys have confirmed that it's actually harder to untangle and divorce your investors than it is to get a divorce.

Do you have any recommendations for raising money?

There are some pretty big capital companies out there now. SaaS Capital and Lighter Capital lend on your MRR or ARR at 18-20%. That can be very difficult, but we got lucky in that we got referred to a boutique lender and were able to take non-dilutive funding. So no, I don't think raising money is always a bad idea. Once you get your business to flying altitude, there are some really great funding options.

Is there any final advice you'd give to SaaS companies?

I'm mentoring and coaching six companies right now through a fund called Founders First Capital. What I'm recognizing is that some of them have an amazing concept of where they're headed, but they don't understand the technology they need to power the business. Founders sometimes think that by hiring a coder on Upwork, it's going to fix all their problems. And that's just not true. Now they're off spending $10k, $20k, or $100k on a concept that hasn't even been proven yet.

I coached a team yesterday on wireframing their concept. They had never heard of Balsamic, so I went a step down and recommended that they first build out their concept and website on a PowerPoint wireframe, going screen by screen through the user experience. That changed their world. Even so, taking that concept to a coder might cost $50k. They still needed to prove the concept by stitching a couple of other tools together.

Everyone's so excited to have a subscription-based model. Too many of them are jumping right in, blowing cash, and thinking that a coder is going to solve all the problems. A coder is a coder. They're not a CTO. They're not a product manager. They don't understand user experience. Typically they have no front-end user experience design.

Using PowerPoint would be my first piece of advice. The second thing is on sales. If someone thinks that they're going to turn on some Instagram ads and their business is going to be a success, they're in for a long road. If you think that's how you're going to start your company, you better have $50k ready on a credit card to spend on paid ads, because paid ads and cost per click are going up every single day.

I learned how to dial for dollars 20 years ago when I was 23 years old. I have no problem picking up a phone and trying to call someone and demo them. The world has changed drastically through the pandemic. But that doesn't change the fact that in your early days, you have to go out and talk to customers, interview them, and pitch and demo your product.

When we got our business off the ground, I walked around to a 100 different bars in downtown San Diego, and pre-sold them a Twitter tool feature that didn't exist yet for $19 a month. I accepted cash and checks and written down credit card numbers. Then, I walked back to our accelerator and told the CTO, "They like this feature. Now we have to actually go build it."

TAKEAWAYS

- Think through raising money – and what that will require of your business – before taking the leap. From a legal perspective, it's harder to divorce your investors than it is to divorce your spouse.
- Use Powerpoint (or Balsamic) to prove out your concept before building.
- Go out and actively pitch and demo your product to customers.

Craig Zingerline

Title: Founder & CEO of Growth University; Co-founder of Votion; Former Chief Product Officer of Sandboxx

Value proposition: An enterprise grade growth bracket solution for driving audience engagement

Industry: Growth marketing

Keywords: Customer acquisition, chicken or the egg, distribution, iteration, no-code, non-technical founder, side hustle, virality

What is Votion?

Votion is an enterprise grade bracket solution for driving audience engagement. The typical use case is a company that uses our platform to build out a March Madness-style campaign that leverages the more human, competitive side of customers. You've got participants in the bracket sharing it out on social platforms, which creates a series of sequential growth loops that all point back to the product. The brands that run these things generally have a phenomenal ROI. It really is its own flavor of marketing. It's a very, very niche product.

Is anyone else doing anything like this?

We've had competitors come and go over the years, but we've been the one company to kind of survive. It's a challenging product to build because it's a tough UX, so the actual engineering is difficult. It's also a tough business model. You want to position it as an enterprise play, which is great, but there's also consumer demand for it. So how do you figure out pricing? There's an inherent challenge there. It's also an infrequent use case. That third challenge has been really hard for companies that have tried to come in and build a $100 million dollar business with a product like this. It's just never going to get to that point.

Are you a technical founder?

I started my career as what I would call a very bad software engineer. After five or six years, I moved into product management and then into growth marketing. Now I'm doing product and growth. I was the least technical of my two co-founders. Until founding Votion, I was still coding at least part of the time.

I would say I'm smack in between technical and non-technical—just enough to be dangerous. I say "dangerous" because I'm well-versed enough to put out feature requests. But then those requests turn out to take forever, and they turn out to be bad ideas.

You mentioned that this was a difficult product to engineer. How did you tackle that challenge?

I was lucky. When I lived in Encinitas (California), one of my neighbors was Steve Phillips, and it turns out we had a lot of shared interests. When I was spinning this company out, he was in between gigs and we just got to talking. He loved the model for Votion. Turns out, Steve is one of the best enterprise level software engineers out there. I mean, he's absolutely phenomenal. But on the flip side, the earliest iteration didn't really take off. I ended up taking a job in D.C. where I was hiring people to be UX/UI front end engineers, and I hired somebody at the company that became the next co-founder. We pulled him in when we really started to scale the business. His name is Seamus Leahy. It was pure coincidence and luck that I was able to find two highly technical resources like that. Both of them are still with the company.

What are the pros and cons of running a seasonal SaaS business?

I'm doing a bunch of different things outside of Votion. If you don't fully require your niche business to be your primary means of survival, then you can opportunistically generate revenue and have some fun along the way. There's less pressure on you as a founder to get everything right and to build a billion dollar business and scale it exponentially every single month. The con is that you have to take a long view if it's not going to be the primary thing that you're working on. You have to be patient.

For example, there was a while where we built a bunch of additional products and features within Votion as a suite, and it totally failed. We wanted to do that because we wanted it to be a self-sufficient business with venture scale potential. What we realized was that we couldn't get to product market fit with those non-niche products and features. You have to be realistic with where you want it to go, and if you're not, you find yourselves in a situation where you're raising money off of hopes and dreams that you may never reach.

Still, I think building a niche business is especially interesting right now with the no-code movement and changes in the industry that make running a side hustle more viable. A niche business almost makes the perfect side hustle. Find something that you're passionate about and good at. Figure out how to monetize. And you're set. Just don't expect it to be this massive thing that you're going to get rich off of.

What would you say to someone who wants to start a business on the side and isn't technical?

I would do a lot of experimentation. Resist the urge to build a whole bunch of stuff until you start to validate that there is actually demand. How do you do that? For a non-technical founder, your ability now as compared to, say, 10 years ago, is orders of magnitude easier to get something viable in front of an audience. What do you need to build an audience? You need distribution.

There's this chicken or the egg problem. You need to build enough value into the product in an industry that has some potential to meet your financial goals, and you need to get whatever you're building in front of people as early as possible. Go as lean as possible.

I think a lot of founders—technical and non-technical—overbuild and overengineer before they have anybody giving them feedback. You should be embarrassed by your first iteration. When I started my growth courses, I had no audience. The first time I sent an email blast, it was to like, eight people. I'm sitting there working, and wondering, *How do I even justify where I'm spending all this time to my wife?* But over time you talk about it, you pitch it, you get better at it. That actually helps you build a better product because, early on, you're getting it in front of people for feedback.

How did you build your audience for Votion?

Off of distribution from brands that were using the product. We had a couple inherent viral loops into the product. Let's say you're *The Boston Globe*. You put a bracket out there about a topic or about the basketball tournament and you're running it through our platform. We've got a "Powered by Votion" graphic on that destination landing page. In a lot of the social links that go out that people are sharing, there are pointers back to our domain, a kind of product-led growth landing page where we talk about the product and where you can sign up for a trial or a demo and learn about pricing.

Outside of Votion, I'm the Founder & CEO of Growth University. We help founders build their own playbook for growth for their company. Prior to that, I was the chief product officer at Sandboxx, which is a consumer product that allows people in military basic training to receive letters from friends and family during the eight to 12 weeks when they lose their phones. I do a bit of high level growth consulting through my current side-hustle – Growth Minded. Audience development for Growth University initially came via a lot of thought leadership and content production and talking to as many founders as I could and giving away as much content for free as I could. I've done over 150 calls on the Growthmentor.com platform where I've assisted founders with tough growth problems that they've had. I speak at every event and conference that I can, join every podcast. I go into every scenario to be in a book or be referenced somewhere just to build some awareness about the stuff that I'm doing. That's a multipronged content strategy that I've worked on. Everything I do basically feeds off my other brands and platforms.

Any final words for first-time founders?

The process generally takes a lot longer than you think it's going to take. I subscribe to a ton of products and newsletters from thought leaders. Some of these people already have large audiences that they're tapping into. They bypass a lot of the early one-to-one conversations that most of us have to go through to grow our businesses. It took a long time to put significant amounts of people through my growth courses. First, I had hundreds of conversations one-on-one with people just trying to figure out what I was doing, to softly sell, to build my own credibility, and to gain the confidence to be able to sell something.

Launch early and launch quickly. Don't be afraid to be embarrassed by your product. Expect it to take multiple years before you get that compounding effect where you see all the charts that go up into the right.

TAKEAWAYS

- Go lean at the beginning; don't overbuild before getting feedback, even if it's just from a few people.

- Most early-stage founders need to have a lot of one-on-one conversations to softly sell and to get feedback. Be patient.

- Launch early, and don't be afraid to be embarrassed by your product.

#37
Al Bsharah

Title: Co-founder & CEO, Email Copilot; Managing Partner at Interlock Capital

Value proposition: Uses machine learning to identify and resolve problems with email delivery

Industry: Email marketing

Keywords: Co-founder, customer discovery, prioritization, product/market fit

What problem does Email Copilot solve?

Large marketing brands send out millions of emails every month to their user base, which generates revenue. But when Gmail or Yahoo starts blocking those emails, it takes companies three or four days and lots of human effort and digging through log files to figure out why. Meanwhile, their email program is failing and not delivering revenue.

Email Copilot uses machine learning to "watch" the underlying communication. Within two hours, it lets you know if there was a problem with delivery, why there was a problem, and what to do to fix it so you could get your marketing program back to generating revenue.

How did you identify this problem?

We had a very different company at first. We went into a grueling program called Techstars. The first month is validation, where you're meeting with hundreds of people a week, super strong mentors and potential customers, and you're validating that what you're doing is right. Coming out of that, we believed we had a good business, but not a great business. So we literally fired all of our customers and started over, which is not something you want to do in the middle of a high paced accelerator program. We pivoted towards the email space and decided to focus on delivering emails at the right time for each individual user – which we eventually realized was a "down the road kind of need." Ultimately, there was a more pressing problem, and that was actually getting emails delivered. When we sat down and dug in with our customers, they told us, "If my emails aren't being delivered at all, who cares about the timing?"

They had a problem that was right in front of them that we could solve, so we pivoted dramatically again.

If you had to do it over again, would you do anything differently?

Hindsight is 20/20. What I will say is that if I had taken more time to work *on* the business instead of *in* the business, things might have gone more smoothly. As a founder, you have to force yourself to not be in the weeds all the time. That's really hard because there are always like, 70 things that needed to get done yesterday and you're one of the only people that can do them. You almost have to force that time to take a step back and look at the bigger picture and see if you're marching in the right direction. We didn't do that enough.

We did an okay job of setting longer term goals, but I don't think we reevaluated those enough.

One of the things we could have done better is more customer development – talking to your customers, listening to them, hearing their pains, digging in, asking more general questions about their problems. We did that early on, and that's how we got into time optimization. But we stopped doing it once we started building a product for it, and that was a big mistake. Once we built and released the product, we started asking customers questions again and we realized that there was a bigger pain that we had missed. If we had continued that customer development as a part of our day-to-day flow, we might have seen the signal sooner.

How do you find a co-founder?

Don't rush it. It's been said a zillion times, but finding the right co-founder is like dating and getting married. You want to get that relationship right. Work with that person and see if it makes sense. One of the ways that my co-founder and I tested this was going through another incubator, an earlier stage program called the Founder Institute. We were doing separate businesses when we got in, but ultimately decided to work together. And it was because we had time to see each other in action.

Find a way to get to know if it's going to be the right relationship. That could be a side project. That could be working together on a small part of your own business. Or, if you're a business person and you need a technical person, maybe bring them on as an engineer or a developer. If it works really well, then offer them more of a CTO role. But if you commit to that co-founder role right out of the gate and it doesn't work, that's a lot more painful than feeling it out for a while before making a commitment.

Was it always your plan to sell?

We didn't have our minds set on exiting in a specific way. We wanted to build a big company. If we build a big company and we're doing very well, an exit opportunity will present itself. Our approach was, *We're going to run as fast as we can. We're going to build. We're going to grow. And when the time's right, we're going to be in a great position to sell or maybe go public some day.*

If you build a big business and a good business, then all the other opportunities will fall in line.

What would you say about Gail Goodman's phrase, "The Long Slow SaaS Ramp of Death"?

Of course, building a SaaS company takes much longer than you want it to. Every projection you build is likely wrong. There are obviously anomalies to that, but for the most part, it's very difficult. It often boils down to product/market fit. Before you prove that, it's a slog. It's that constant feedback loop, the one that I was talking about earlier, where we got a bunch of feedback en masse, built the product, and then got more feedback and realized we missed some stuff along the way. As you dig into the actual pain that the user has, you'll start to see hotspots. Maybe out of the 50 people you interviewed this week, 20 of them brought up the same issue. Go talk to the others and see if this is a dense pain point. If it is, then get that solved.

It's the whole process of listening to your customers, building a product iteratively that solves important pain points, and not stopping that cycle. Find a way to make that a part of your culture so that it's not a chore to talk to customers. It's just what you do. It's a part of your onboarding process. It's a part of your sales process. Before you even start talking to a prospect, ask them questions. Don't even talk about your business. Just ask them questions for the first 15 minutes of any call.

What's the #1 mistake you see SaaS founders make?

Product/market fit is a term that's used so frequently that people think it's very accessible and that's not true. Product/market fit is probably one of the hardest things to achieve. The worst part about product/market fit is you may think you have it and you don't. A number of times we thought we saw product/market fit and we didn't. We got some good traction but the reality was that people weren't yanking it off the shelves.

Be self-aware. Get excited when you have moments of traction, and don't beat yourself down, but be honest. Is this truly a product/market fit, and if not, what do we need to do to get there?

TAKEAWAYS

- Step back and reevaluate frequently. Make sure you're heading in the right direction.

- Keep talking to customers and digging into their pain points; don't stop after you've built a product. Find a way to make that part of your culture.
- Just ask questions for the first 15 minutes of any phone call with a prospect.
- Be honest when you have moments of traction, and evaluate whether this is truly product/market fit. Product/market fit isn't easy to achieve.

#38

James Davis

Title: SaaS Startup & Product Expert, Founder – Dispersion IQ

Value proposition: Helps SaaS founders and teams grow their businesses at scale

Industry: SaaS consulting

Keywords: Customer discovery, fundraising, validation

What does a "bird's eye view" of starting a SaaS company look like?

There are certain phases that every startup will go through. First, there's the ideation phase. That's where you say, "I have a hunch about something – a hypothesis – and I need more information about it." If you have the discipline to go and do the research, you might save a whole bundle of money later on. But this is the first mistake that I see nine out of 10 startups making. They don't do enough research to validate their own idea. Typically, you're going to create a widget or a digital product with a target audience in mind. But sometimes your hunch might be wrong. There might not be a customer for your product.

At some point you have to take yourself out of the equation. Your product isn't for you. The hunch starts with you, but you need feedback from the people you're targeting. As an entrepreneur, how good of a listener are you? You have to be inquisitive, ask questions, and be willing to get beat up a little. Maybe your hunch was wrong, but be willing to listen to feedback and make changes. That's your MVP phase.

The third phase is when you say, "Okay, I'm ready to make some money. I'm ready to release this thing into the market." This is the phase that everyone wants to get to – but they don't always do the preceding phases well. They read about all these sexy stories and they watch TV and read blogs about startups getting millions of dollars in investment. And they say, "I think my idea is better."

But it doesn't matter how much you believe in your idea – the market is the ultimate judge.

A lot of founders believe that if you "check all the boxes" from a book or a lean startup guide, that all of a sudden, you're going to be somewhere. But it doesn't matter how many boxes you check if you don't have a product that people actually want.

What would you say to someone who's wanting to get started in SaaS, but doesn't know where to begin?

The barrier to entry is incredibly low. Anybody can build a startup. But you've got to identify a problem organically. I've talked to people trying to find a problem to solve, which is an odd way to go about starting a company.

Why do most startups fail?

Nine times out of 10, startups fail because there was no need in the market. Just last week, I spoke to a woman who dropped almost a quarter million dollars of her own savings into an app she wanted to build. She couldn't get investors to get back to her. So I reviewed her material and her product, and I told her "I don't see it."

Sometimes I see founders say, "I've got money, I'm going to create this product, and people are going to like it." But that's not how the system works. Half of all startups fail during the MVP phase, but if you do the ideation-research phase well, that statistic for failure dramatically decreases.

When do founders know they are ready for investment?

Having an effective MVP doesn't mean you're ready for investment. It just means that you kind of have shown that there's a stickiness to what you offer. Give your product a year, and if it hits some metric of success, whether it's downloads or revenue or something else, then you might want to start raising money.

When people approach you as a consultant, what is the core problem they are usually trying to solve?

Nothing lives in a vacuum in SaaS. Everything is intertwined – development, investment, sales. As a founder, you're wearing a million different hats.

The product is central to everything. Then you have marketing and development and all these other things. But if you can't deliver a meaningful experience to users, then nothing else will fall into place.

Most of the issues clients approach me with are fairly minor and can be course corrected easily. The problem, more often than not, is that founders have lost objectivity. They've been in their product for a year or more, and they're sort of living in a vacuum. That being said, I ask two questions of every client: "Should they be here right now?" And, "What should they be focusing on?" The bottom line is that I want everybody that I work with to be as successful as I know they can be.

Any final advice for founders?

Don't underestimate the power of your ability to be creative or to find others that are.

Too often, I see people just trying to create a job for themselves, not build a company. That typically never yields good results. Passion and persistence will win nine times out of 10.

TAKEAWAYS

- Don't go looking for a problem to solve. Let it come to you organically.
- First, make sure people actually want your product.
- Prove your product's stickiness before you look for investment.

#39

Louis Nicholls

Title: Cofounder, SparkLoop

Value proposition: Making newsletters grow faster with referral marketing

Industry: Referral marketing

Keywords: Customer acquisition, pricing, validation

What is SparkLoop?

We help you grow your newsletter 20-200% faster with a referral program that actually works. If you have a newsletter or an email list of any kind, and you want to grow your list, you probably don't want to spend a lot of money or time trying to find new subscribers. SparkLoop helps you do this by incentivizing your existing subscribers to share with their friends and do the marketing for you.

How did you identify this as a problem to be solved?

When I was working as a marketing consultant—mainly focusing on conversion rate optimization—I was working with a client with a newsletter business. They asked if there was any good software out there for generating referrals. I had a friend (now my co-founder) who ran a generic referral tool for e-commerce and SaaS. I knew his tool was good, but when I asked him about using it for newsletters, he basically said, "Look, you can kind of make this work with our tool, but not really. There aren't any other good solutions out there either."

He then told me that I was the fourth person that week who had asked about newsletters. So, we decided to give it a go and build something that would actually work.

What can founders without marketing experience learn about customer acquisition?

I've taken quite a few companies from customer #1 all the way up to well past $10,000 in monthly revenue. I teach founders how to market their product and how to acquire customers. I focus especially on teaching technical founders how to do early stage sales.

One big trap that technical founders can fall into is thinking that if they can just find one customer, there must be hundreds or thousands of potential customers out there. If you're a technical founder and you don't make any sales, that's almost a good thing because in some cases, it's better not to have any hope. The worst thing that can happen is when a technical founder makes one sale and thinks, *I've managed to do it right. I'm onto gold. Let's go and find the next 100.* Then it takes them three years to realize that actually there is no customer #2. With enough time, you can convince one person to buy anything, even if it's absolutely terrible.

How can a technical founder avoid that "three year wait" for customer #2?

The first thing is to get out of the mindset of validating. When you try and validate something, what you're really trying to do is create a false sense of security to tell yourself that you're on the right track. It's never black or white, validated or invalidated. What you need to figure out is, do you need to adjust course slightly?

The absolute worst case is that founders will build a product and try to do sales without knowing if there's a viable audience. The next worst case is to do a pre-launch by collecting email addresses or asking people to pay for the first month, and then to take that as validation. Paying $50 or inputting your email address may be proof that you want to support someone, or that you find the product slightly interesting, but it's not a guarantee that you're building the right thing.

What you want to do is to create a mutual action plan, or a "shared success plan." That's where you sit down with a potential customer and say, "We want you to achieve success with our product. What do we have to build to make that work? What do you have to do on your end? Right now, you are willing to commit to talking to your boss about using this tool. Are you willing to commit to spending two hours with me, setting up the tool, and starting to use it on this date if I build it by then?"

If you can get someone to agree to all of that, there's a good chance that they will actually use it. But unless you go into that kind of detail, you might end up thinking you're building something that people want...and you'll probably end up disappointed.

How can founders learn to correctly price their product?

It comes down to being able to understand the customer's perspective. I think technical founders have a really difficult time getting out of their own heads and into the heads of their customers.

Do you have a basic profit and loss sheet for your customer's business? Do you have an idea of where they spend their time day by day? Then you should be able to guide your customer through the amount of value that your product will add to their life. If you can explain to a customer that they're going to make $1,000 a month with the product, then you can ask for $100 or $200 per month rather than $20 or $30.

What's the most important thing that a SaaS founder should know about starting a business?

Many SaaS founders become SaaS founders because they wanted to start a business. SaaS businesses are the hardest businesses to start. Technical founders can get excited about building the product itself. But there is no such thing as an objectively great product. It's subjectively great for their customers. If you're always focusing on the product, you can get motivated even when you're not quite growing as fast as you want to, or customers aren't as excited about it.

In the beginning, don't focus on the solution or the product. Instead, spend as much time as you can talking to your customers. The thing that you should be really excited about and motivated by is helping your target customers. If you do that, everything becomes easier. Sales become easier. Building the right product becomes easier. You're motivated. You're doing it for a reason. Liking and helping your target customers, rather than building fancy product stuff, makes it much easier to be successful in the long run.

TAKEAWAYS

- Your first customer is not proof of anything.

- The idea of validation can be deceiving. Ask questions that confirm your customers will actually take steps to adopt and successfully use your product.

- Get an understanding of how your customers spend their time, and what their basic profit and loss sheet looks like.

- There is no such thing as an objectively great product; all that matters is how your product serves and engages your customers.

#40

Colleen Johnson

Title: Co-founder & CEO, ScatterSpoke

Value proposition: Provides retrospective insight for agile teams

Industry: Software management

Keywords: Customer feedback, customer acquisition, iteration, pricing

What is ScatterSpoke?

ScatterSpoke is an online retrospective tool for agile teams looking to improve the way they work and deliver value to customers. It creates a way to give anonymous feedback so that everybody on the team can give their feedback before the team gets together to discuss it.

One of the things we found in talking to a lot of our bigger customers is that as soon as we create visibility into patterns and themes across multiple teams, a lot of the leadership says, "If you had just told us sooner this was a problem, we would have fixed it right away" – especially when they can see a compounding impact that it's having across the business.

ScatterSpoke is a way to create visibility into those issues so that you can get them resolved quicker.

How did you identify this as a problem?

I've been working in software for a little over 20 years, on the agile side of things for about half of that time. I've been on the consulting side for four years, and in consulting I facilitate a lot of these retrospectives for teams. The tool was originally born as a simple way to get anonymous feedback from everybody on the team before the retros started.

Typically in these retrospective meetings, you have an hour every two weeks. When you add up the dev salaries of all the people sitting in that room, that's an expensive meeting. What often happens is that you hand out Post-it notes and everybody spends 15-20 minutes making posts of what went well, what didn't go well, and what needs improvement. It tends to be a little mind-numbing. Then you add in the fact that retros are often on Fridays. People are out, or they have deadlines they're trying to hit. It's not really what people want to be spending time doing.

It's also human nature to bookend memories. We remember what happened at the end of our two weeks or what happened at the very beginning. But there might be things in the middle that are important that we don't remember.

I wanted a way to capture ongoing feedback from everybody so that when we got together for an hour, we spent our time talking about how the last two weeks went in an efficient, productive way.

We didn't even have the ability to create an account initially. We checked Google Analytics one day and saw that there had been 30,000 uses of the site at one point. Once we had that ability for people to create an account, we realized we were sitting on really valuable data that allowed us to identify and thread together big picture patterns and analytics on what was happening across multiple development teams.

How did you approach customer acquisition?

We've seen a lot of natural growth. We just started working with a marketing team this year – we had never even used Google AdWords. A lot of our growth was through word of mouth. I do a lot of public speaking and presenting and training, but a lot of people also found us through blog posts or through reviews of the tool. Over this last year, we've spent more time and energy on marketing and really targeted sales around that ability to scale feedback across the organization.

Were people using the tool for free originally?

They were. At that point, the tool allowed you to put your feedback up on a visual board and vote anonymously. We started charging once we added the abilities to link teams and data together.

What has it been like to learn pricing?

It made me really uncomfortable at first. But one of the biggest things we got out of getting funding from Tiny Seed and having mentors who had gone through this whole journey before was getting really comfortable and letting that be a trial-and-error discovery process.

We tried a freemium model with a reduced number of users, where you had to upgrade to add more users. Eventually we axed the free altogether and went with a 14-day trial instead. We added a couple plans in between based on the number of users.

I don't think we're at the endpoint in the pricing journey. I think it will continue to change based on feedback. The ability to scale inside of an enterprise has been our differentiator. It's also where we charge the most, because we can integrate with other products that large-scale enterprises already have in place. If nobody else can do that, that's where we make the most money.

What do you think are some of the most common mistakes that B2B SaaS founders make?

We think, *This is the thing that's going to get people excited* without actually talking to people. I think that gets worse as your company gets more successful, because you feel like you've got all the answers. It's easy to stop doing research upfront like you probably did when your tool was a baby.

We also still struggle with big-batching new features. When we release something new, we tend to get excited and try to stick all this other stuff in it. When we release the feature to the community, it gets diluted. It's hard to figure out what's making the change successful or not, because we deployed a dozen changes instead of two.

Is running a startup company harder than you thought it would be?

Yes. The funny thing is that I coach software teams. More specifically, I coach teams on how to improve the way they work together. I also coach organizations on how to implement lean discovery practices of doing customer-driven research and understanding a problem before you try to solve it and delivering functionality in small batches. It's great to be on the other side of it, but it's hard to put into practice.

Any final advice to other B2B SaaS founders?

Stay connected to your customers, and understand what they're using and what's changing for them. Don't just ask them about tools they're using, though. Ask them about what work is like for them. What are the shifts that are affecting them, and how is that going to affect how they use your tool?

TAKEAWAYS

- Talk to people before deciding they will be excited about a new feature.
- Beware of big-batching new features. That will make it difficult to know what was successful.
- Ask your customers about big-picture shifts at work, not just what kinds of tools they use.

Daniel Goldstein

Title: Co-founder & COO, Trust & Will
Value proposition: Makes estate planning affordable and accessible
Industry: Estate planning
Keywords: Customer discovery, iteration, mindset, MVP, viability

What is Trust & Will?

We're making estate planning affordable and accessible for everybody in this country. That looks like helping families plan for the future. We do that with technology and design. We believe in a future that is online, where everybody's assets and relationships are connected in an online world. That connected online world needs to pass when they die, and they need to plan for that.

How did you identify this as a problem?

In 2017, we started asking the question, *What happens to our bitcoin when we die?* One of my now co-founders was getting married and was starting to ask the question, *What do I have to do to be an adult?* Those two questions became what is now Trust & Will.

We started exploring what happens to your cryptocurrency and your regular assets when you die. We also started talking with estate planning attorneys. Coming from a software background, I realized that the whole thing was insane. It's expensive and inaccessible. People who are setting up estate plans don't know how to do it, where to go, or how much it's going to cost. So we decided to build Trust & Will.

How did you test viability?

The first thing we wanted to do is figure out if it's actually a problem or we just think it's a problem. So we just started talking to everybody we knew. We would ask them, "Do you have a will? What made you set up a will for the first time? Do you have a trust? What made you set up a trust the first time?"

The overwhelming feedback was that people set up a will when they have kids. So I started focusing on my friends with kids. The feedback was split. 30% had a will. 60-70% said, "I know I need one, we just don't have it yet." 10% said, "I've thought about it before, but it's not really on my mind."

We looked at the 60-70% of people who have kids and know that they need a will, but they haven't gotten around to doing it yet. Why don't they have one? We started digging in more and asking questions. We got a lot of feedback. It's expensive. You have to go to an attorney. Nobody likes attorneys, especially Millennials. There are online solutions, like Legal Zoom and Rocket Lawyer, but what we found was that it wasn't really an access problem. It was more of an education problem.

We thought the only way for people to understand where to go is if there's a brand they can reference. That was our original hypothesis. We decided to build a national consumer brand so that people would know where to go. Then we could leverage technology to make it happen.

It took six months to get our MVP to market. It was just a basic online will that you could create in 10 minutes. We sent it out to all of our networks, and started getting paid customers. Then we asked, *What else can we do? How else can we find people?* So we started working with influencers and mom groups. We found that moms were typically the ones who were making this actually happen.

After we launched the will, we launched our trust product, which is much more complex. From there we have a whole suite of products. We just kept learning. We have a hypothesis. We validate it, we invalidate it, and then we learn smart.

How did you learn from customers throughout the process?

From day one, we would use Intercom to talk to anybody who wanted to chat, and ask what problems they were having. We responded in less than 30 seconds at all times.

I would call customers all the time. We used Hotjar so that you could watch people on the website. I used to watch every single user session, which often tells a different story than what people will say. People will tell you, "Oh, it's super easy to use." But when you watch the user story, they stop halfway through. At the end of the day on Friday, I would get the team together and we would drink beers and watch user stories that I had flagged. I would call people all the time and ask them, "What's going on? Why didn't you complete it?" It was less methodical and a lot more obsessive.

What are some of the biggest mistakes you made?

We've made a ton of mistakes. We've been assumptive in product development. We've had a good gut feeling along the way of what our members want because we've been talking to them a lot. That can create arrogance, and caused us to build things that nobody wants.

We're constantly trying to anchor ourselves as a hypothesis-driven organization, not an assumption-driven organization. You can make mistakes because you have tribal knowledge. We've been doing this for four years now, so we have things that we believe now to be true. We have to constantly challenge those beliefs. There's a survivorship bias that happens in startups where you can think because you've made it this far, you must know what you're doing. It's a huge mistake thinking that just because you've got *here*, you will get *there*.

What has it been like to pivot from working for an agency to running your own business?

At an agency you solve a problem that's been defined for you, and hand over the product. SWAT team in, SWAT team out. You don't have to live there. With running your own business, you live with a problem day in and day out. We can go much deeper into the problem and much wider into the solution. There are pros and cons to that.

Where are you in terms of growth?

We're close to 60 employees, we're spread across 10 states now, and we've raised about $23 million in venture capital. We've had 300,000 people start their estate plan with us, and we're growing about 30% every quarter.

If you sat down to coffee with someone who's starting a SaaS company, what's the first thing you'd say?

Defining the problem is more important than defining the solution.

TAKEAWAYS

- Your intended users may not be who you think they are.
- Chat with users. Keep a super fast response rate.
- Watch user sessions. Watch them obsessively.
- Beware of becoming assumptive, especially when you see success. Create hypotheses, then validate or invalidate them, and move forward – no matter how well you think you know your customers.

Jim Lee

Title: Founder, Document Group (Product: Reading Supply), Ecosystem WG Lead, Protocol Labs

Value proposition: Writing is thinking, people deserve the best writing tools.

Industry: Writing, Software

Keywords: Bootstrapping, fundraising, top-down/bottom-up

What is a top-down vs. bottom-up approach in SaaS?

If employees at any given company love the software that they're using, they'll want to suggest it to product management or leadership. You'll see this trend at bottom-up SaaS companies as a way to get a product into the hands of the customers. Whoever controls the budget for resources will decide whether or not to allocate some of their monthly or quarterly budget for any given tool.

At some companies there's a top-down approach – "We're all using Office365. Don't argue; it's just the way it is." This is common because it may be uncomfortable for employees to go against leadership. Or maybe they don't even have an opinion about what productivity products they want to use.

That being said, a lot of people are having a sort of allergy to the more authoritative stance. They're starting to ask questions like, "Why do I have to always trust the lead?" The lead may not be in the deep technical details of the work and may not know how the work is actually being done. This is an opportunity for new software to be adopted at the place you work.

How does Reading Supply fit into this narrative?

Reading Supply is an example of a product that would not normally have an advocate at the Executive Level. It's a simple tool that anyone can use without permission. For example, many academics used Reading Supply because of a recommendation from a peer. All users can use the product with no strings attached. These small groups have led to enough revenue where the business is entirely self-sustaining!

Reading Supply is a result of applying lessons I've learned from working for different SaaS companies to one of my own companies.

I'm not alone when it comes to bootstrapping software services. Stripe acquired a project called Indie Hackers, where people talk about their companies that are making monthly revenue. My project falls into this cohort. I don't ever have to raise money because I'm bootstrapping my limited liability corporation with revenue I'm already making.

Some teams use Reading Supply for company blogging. Some teams use it for other things. I don't care what they use it for, as long as they find value and there's revenue coming my way so I can stay true to my values and my own vision. I don't have the same goals or KPIs as some of the bigger companies, where I would have to grow double digit every year. I'm able to do this because my operating bills are under $100 a month and my revenue is many, many multiples over that.

What's one trend that SaaS founders might want to know about?

There's an interesting thing in the industry today where you assume that the more people work on something, the more secure or stable it is. That might not be true, especially from the perspective of the engineering and what is actually being implemented. We might still say, *They've been around for a while. They have a large company. They must be secure.* But that's not true, right? Look at Equifax or any of the other large firms that have leaked data. They have lots of engineers...but that doesn't mean they implement their systems in a way that protects you.

A few passionate people can give a large company a run for their money. That's not always the case, but it can happen.

How are you taking a bottom-up approach?

My users do all the marketing for me. My users who share articles online and get 200+ likes on Twitter have influence, and when they use Reading Supply, people become curious about it. This is an example of a network effect. There's actually a good article about the 13 network effects from NFX that can help explain the positive impacts of network effects on the growth of your product or platform. I'm in that category of having users who are my biggest advocates, who are sharing my product and getting people to use it. That lets me focus on ensuring it works and it's adhering to its values.

Is there a magic key for referral marketing?

I used to work for Patreon (a membership platform for content creators). There, I learned that the success of our members marketed the platform. We could show and not tell.

It's a quality, not quantity, game for early open source products. If you get a few power users that have a huge audience, their network will follow them into their product. That's a really useful tactic to grow anything. More than brands, we tend to follow people we trust and their choices. An example of this is how valuable referrals are. You would take a referral from your best friend more seriously than you would from some arbitrary advertisement. We have such an abundance of advertisements that it's hard to trust brands. But if you get a text from a friend that says, "Hey, you've got to check out _____," then you're going to be a way better lead for that product.

The same applies for recommendations from family members. The risk is pretty high if you betray your family. You don't want to give your family member a suggestion that would hurt them because that can affect a multi-decade, multi-generational relationship. When you give a referral, you're putting your reputation on the line. Reputation goes a long way.

What are some of the mistakes you see SaaS founders making?

Let's say you raise some money. The moment you have that loan, you're on a clock. You want to grow faster so you can get rid of the clock. If you find yourself in a bad situation, you could start cutting corners around your authenticity, your brand, your voice, and your trustworthiness. You start seeing these opportunities that maybe could help you grow in the short term. You're like, "Let's try it all." Maybe you even feel frantic. I think what people don't realize sometimes is that your customers do pay attention. If you cheat your mission, do the marketing tastelessly, or lose your original value proposition, you could put your business into a bad spot.

I can understand the stress of just trying to survive. But I think founders need to be patient in growing that meaningful cohort – the ones who are, for example, making referrals on your behalf. Don't chase random growth opportunities, like starting a Snapchat campaign if you're selling accounting software. Maybe a better focus would be finding accountants and providing value directly to them.

If you have the right mindset and you have the technical skill, you can scale to 50k paying users on your SaaS product for about $1k a month. The margin is massive–for example, 50k people paying $5 a month. That's phenomenal for $1k a month.

Would you recommend raising funds…or bootstrapping?

I generally trust the people who have an insane amount of enthusiasm and passion for what they are building. If you're passionate about something and you know it's an opportunity you can't miss, then raising money could make sense if you have a plan for how to use it.

But if you don't have a burning need to prove an idea needs to exist and you just want to build a pragmatic business – a meaningful thing that helps people – then you don't have to jump on that fundraising train and put yourself on the clock. You can do it bootstrapped.

Is there a purpose to raising venture capital? If you were to raise from an investor, and they said to you, "I have a couple of hires for you, and I have a plan for how to get you to market faster because I love the direction of this product," then that's one of many valid reasons to raise money. The opportunity to work with people who will accelerate the growth of your business by many multiples is often enough reason to do it.

What's the best advice you've ever received?

In this context, it's to "productionize your work". This tends to be natural for people who build software for a living. Software engineers solve problems and occasionally can identify a way to scale the solution to many people.

In the long-term, you don't make money selling your time for labor. Look at the state of income inequality today. People who are stuck are chasing after metrics that other people are throwing at them. They don't even have control over how they want to break out of the cycle, because they are always selling their time for money. Creating products that make money while you're sleeping – like with SaaS – is the way to go. You can create a new system for yourself to generate revenue while you allocate your time towards other things.

TAKEAWAYS

- Depending on your goals, a bottom-up approach can help you build a self-sustaining business without raising money.

- If you run a small company with big competitors, don't be discouraged. Large companies don't necessarily create better products.

- A few influential power users can go a long way in terms of referral marketing.

- Don't chase random growth opportunities that don't make sense for your space.

#43

Ryan Bennick

Title: Co-founder, MemberSpace

Value proposition: Helps small businesses run membership sites through Squarespace

Industry: Website management

Keywords: Calm company, co-founder, company culture, customer feedback, hiring, pricing, work-life balance

What is MemberSpace?

We help small businesses run membership websites.

How did you identify this as a problem?

I'm a software developer. Over the course of a few years, I helped build 400 Squarespace and ecommerce websites as a part of a five-person consulting company. In the process, my business partner and I decided what we really wanted to do was move into the product territory and start a SaaS.

We decided to keep on focusing on helping small businesses with their sites, and realized that within Squarespace, there was a need for a membership feature. So we prototyped the MVP, got some feedback, and now we're six years in.

What did validation look like for you?

We got the idea from the Squarespace community. We searched the forums and what we found was that a lot of people wanted something for memberships. Then, we let our customer base fuel what was needed in the product. That's helped us identify and build things I might not have thought of, like the ability to run a drip campaign.

Your customer isn't necessarily the best one to tell you how to solve their problems. But if you listen to their problems enough, you can begin to understand that problem landscape and then design a solution. That's your job as a product owner.

You can also build a product by giving customers things they didn't know they needed. For example, people didn't know they needed the iPhone until the iPhone came out.

What kinds of challenges have you faced?

For a while, we struggled to figure out the right pricing. For a long time we didn't do transaction fees because people said that they didn't like them. But it turns out that the market as a whole charges transaction fees. Squarespace really solidified this when they put that into their pricing for their Members Area product.

We've been doing transaction fees over the past two years, and customers are fine with it. Customer feedback can be confusing because oftentimes, all you hear are the vocal ones complaining about certain things. But actually most people don't care.

We also tried a semi-freemium model for six months and our growth went flat. We realized there's something about having a set trial because time sensitivity helps customers make a decision. We're still pretty fluid. If a customer asks for more time on a trial, we usually give it to them. But we also want to encourage customers to dive into the product and make a decision right away.

What have you learned about being an entrepreneur, a business owner or a founder?

To do this for the long term, you have to have a tolerance for risk, financially and emotionally. There are a lot of ups and a lot of downs. But it's really rewarding to create your own business. Some of our employees have kids – it's really cool to be able to support families.

I guess this is pretty classic in entrepreneurship, but our business wasn't healthy in the beginning. I would stay up until 3AM working on projects. Over time we made ourselves take breaks and vacations, and work sane hours. We try to take our cues from the guys at Basecamp and run a calm company.

What does team look like for you?

We have 15 employees total, 10 in the United States, some contractors in Uruguay, one in Canada, and one in Hungary. We're all remote.

If you're going to be a remote company, make sure you're hiring for that. You want to make sure they have the correct skill set, but they also need to work well in a remote setting. They need good written communication skills and the right personality fit.

What does "personality fit" mean to you?

We like to have open and positive debates, because we're trying to figure stuff out as a team. We want to debate about ideas, whether it's a way to code something or the way to develop a better support process. We value a space where people can express their opinions, but not get too emotional about going in a certain direction. We like to say, "strong opinions, loosely held."

How did you meet your co-founder?

My co-founder and I have known each other for a long time. We met in the fall of 2004 at college, have worked together in the consulting company, and have even lived together.

When you start a company with somebody, it's kind of like getting married. So you want to look for a lot of the things that you would look for in a good partner in marriage. You want someone that communicates well, and that doesn't hold grudges against things that you did.

My co-founder and I debate all the time. Ultimately, we go in the direction of whoever wins the logical debate.

What do founders need the most?

You need grit. There were a few years that were really rough, ups and downs with consulting. I would think, *I could make more money if I just got a job*. But you've got to stick it out. Having grit is a core feature of running a business to just keep going. It's just about consistency, showing up every day and putting in a positive effort.

TAKEAWAYS

- Customer feedback isn't always reflective of reality. Sometimes, you're only hearing the opinions of the vocal few.
- Tolerance for ups and downs is critical.
- When hiring remote employees, look for personality fit and communication skills as well as technical skills.
- Find a healthy rhythm of work and rest.
- Be able to debate with your co-founder. And don't hold grudges.

Dina Moskowitz

Title: Founder & CEO, SaaSMAX

Value proposition: Helps SaaS & B2B technology companies go to market through reseller partners

Industry: SaaS and B2B technology sales

Keywords: Fundraising, marketplace, team, validation

What is SaaSMAX and what problem does it solve?

SaaSMAX is a platform that helps B2B SaaS and technology companies go to market through reseller channel partners. Something like 65% ($2.4 trillion) of all B2B tech sales go through resellers. Yet most tech vendors find that 80% of the resellers they sign up fail to drive them revenue. It's an industry-wide pain point that vendors are spending enormous amounts of time, resources and expense to recruit, train, nurture and incentivize the wrong ones. Available reseller discovery, insights and research methods are outdated, manual and take months and hundreds of thousands of dollars, with no guaranteed results.

PartnerOptimizer by SaaSMAX is a game-changing partner discovery and insights SaaS platform that improves efficiency and accelerates reseller channel sales performance. Our proprietary data-driven approach enables channel teams to pinpoint the right partners for their specific products. Finding those companies is not easy. It's almost like fitting a square in a circle, because there are so many different attributes that a partner needs to have in order to really be aligned. It can become a very expensive endeavor when you are investing in building your channel. By speeding up the time to find those right partners, it improves the return on investment. It's basically like having an indirect marketing and sales team.

Our PartnerOptimizer platform is all about data mining to find and profile partners from around the world, and to categorize unstructured data about them into a structured, searchable database that allows us to find these partners much more quickly.

What's one of the #1 mistakes that you see companies making?

One blind spot that I see founders have is not leaving room in their pricing structure to compensate resellers. When you're first building out your business plan and you're trying to project what your pricing is, it's so important to leave room to compensate resellers, not just your direct sales team. Because if you don't, you're really underpricing your product or you're overlooking the fact that if you're a strong SaaS or B2B product, you will need to go to market through indirect channel partners.

How did you identify this as a need in the market?

I started off doing business consulting for dot com companies back in the 90's. Using my experience in investment banking, I was helping companies to build business plans. From there, I created an online data storage product called Critical Digital Data, which I took to market and sold. That's when I learned all about how other data storage companies actually go to market by leveraging channel partners. After I sold my company using a direct sales method, I realized that there was this whole sector called the IT Channel – a middle market that most people have never heard of. That led me to ask, "Is there an avenue to help SaaS vendors get to market through this channel?"

I ended up on this adventure of trying to figure out how to profile and find the right partners for SaaS vendors who were wanting to go to market. Ultimately, we went from a marketplace into a business intelligence data mining platform solution. Today, we make data digestible to channel teams that just want to know, *Are these partners right for me?*

Do you think a startup has to identify a problem that hasn't been solved before?

I think it's really hard to do something truly unique in the SaaS world these days. There is more verticalization and more specific features and functionality that can be developed. But I worry that people are starting their companies in a vacuum. Make sure you are fully aware of what your competitors look like, and what features and functionality they offer. Do a real analysis of how you're going to compete with them and how you would differentiate your product from theirs. Is there really room in the market for you? Because you're either going to be going after new customers or you're going to be stealing customers from other platforms....and you better have something really good besides just better pricing.

We all think we have great ideas, but most of them have been thought of in the SaaS world right now. Do your homework before you get excited and put any money down. We waste a lot of money building prototypes, only to learn that there is a hard road ahead.

What do you know now that you wish you had known starting out?

Just because someone likes your solution doesn't mean they're a qualified sales prospect. A deal is not a deal until the agreements are signed and payment is coming in. That's a really critical lesson, because when you're a founder, you're super excited and you think everyone is just as excited about it. But you really have to understand your sales cycle. Know who the stakeholders are, and who actually has decision-making power.

In terms of raising money, I've also learned that it's not a done deal till it's signed and the money's in the bank. I had one investor who had been planning to invest one million. He lived in Europe and was on his way over to California to meet me when he had a heart attack. He had to slow down, and the entire thing was put on hold. You never know what can happen.

Finally, make sure you have language to articulate the key agreements of your business. When you're first building your team, you're really excited. And the people who are joining your team are excited. And sometimes you get involved with them without having all of your agreements really well-documented. If you hire a developer, for example, you need an agreement that prevents them from retaining the code and claiming it as their own. That could be a critical mistake.

What kind of advice can you give on building relationships and team?

As a SaaS founder, you can't always afford a team. It's really important for you to cultivate relationships with advisory board members, people who will act as sounding boards. That's definitely a good thing to do early on. And success breeds success. So when you do find someone that you enjoy working with, they can refer you to others who will be valuable and helpful. Leverage the networks of people that you want to work with. Finally, don't be afraid to admit what you don't know.

And if you do have a team, remember that as a SaaS founder, it's not just about what you're building. You're going to be asked to wear many hats. No matter what hat you're wearing, you're also a leader. You have to lead by example, especially when you can't lead by compensating people in a big way. You have to lead through cultivating great relationships and making sure that you are letting those people know that they're valued and that you're all in it together.

TAKEAWAYS

- Research the competition before you decide there's room in the market for your product.
- A deal is not a deal until payment is coming in. Same goes for investors.
- Don't forget about key agreements. For example, make sure you have a contract that prevents developers from retaining the code as their own.
- Create relationships with advisory board members, especially if you run a small team.
- Don't be afraid to admit what you don't know.
- Leave room in your pricing structure for resellers, if applicable.

Bruno Bornsztein

Title: Founder, Influence Kit

Value proposition: Influence Kit helps brands and agencies run better campaigns, learn what works, and increase their influencer ROI

Industry: Marketing Analytics

Keywords: Calm company, mindset, work-life balance

What is Influence Kit?

Influence Kit helps brands and content creators work better together. Our mission is to help them build stronger relationships, empower them to have smoother workflows, and to be able to prove the value of their collaborations.

There are two sides to the product. One side helps influencers plan, manage, and measure their content with an editorial calendar. Influence Kit works really well for influencers, content creators, and small publishers because it's a project management tool, plus a reporting tool.

There's another side of the tool that's targeted more at brands and agencies. If you're a brand or you're a small agency and you're trying to get influencers to create content for your client or your brand, you need to be able to measure how that content is performing. Influence Kit allows you to say, *I want to work with these people and I want them to submit these deliverables. And I want to be able to see a report for how that content did on a bunch of different platforms.*

How did you identify this as a problem to be solved?

It's a "scratch your own itch" product. I ran two blogs for over 10 years and we did a lot of sponsored content and worked with a lot of brands and agencies. We couldn't find a tool that enabled us to streamline our workflows, help us become more efficient, and also let us provide reporting. Influence Kit started out as a solution to that problem. It was really an influencer focused tool. As we started rolling out, we found that a lot of brands wanted to use it, too.

What have some of the challenges been pivoting into selling your products and running a SaaS?

The first code for Influence Kit was written in 2011 but we didn't have our first paying customer until 2018. It took a long time to realize that I had a product that I could sell.

The challenge was that I wasn't persistent enough early on in trying to productize it. I had this internal tool that worked great for us. To get from there to the point where people are paying for it is a bit of a gap.

The initial goal wasn't like, *Let's build a business around this.* Approaching it from that point of view, I wasn't ready for how persistent you really have to be in terms of showing it to people – ignoring negative feedback or less than enthusiastic feedback, and continuing to push it out until you find the right audience.

Why face this challenge if you were already running a successful business?

I had been running content businesses for a long time and I was ready for something new. In 2008, my daughter was born, so the content business was really conducive to that kind of lifestyle. It provided me with a lot of flexibility. Around the time I wanted to start focusing on Influence Kit, I had more bandwidth. My kids were getting older and they didn't need me all the time.

Also, the ceiling on a SaaS business is a lot higher. There's just a lot more opportunity there, a lot more control.

What do you see ahead for Influence Kit?

We are growing gradually. With SaaS, it can be hard to know what the right rate of growth is. We're working on a freemium and a new strategy for how we're going to pursue bigger brand accounts that have higher LTV. My hope is that next year, we can see that start to bend upwards.

It's easy to say, "We want to grow faster," until you realize that you don't want everything that comes along with that. We're figuring out how much faster we can grow without sacrificing the lifestyle that we want to have as we're building the business.

Why build a calm company?

The important thing is to understand what your priorities are as a human being. So many people go into entrepreneurship and don't think about what they actually want to prioritize. In my case, I took every Friday off until my kids were three because that was my priority. I just had to restructure everything else around that.

You get good at what you practice. If you practice having a lifestyle that you enjoy or having free time to be with your family, then you will get good at actually doing that. If you want to take Fridays off, you need to start doing that and let everything else adjust around that. It's difficult when there are people pinging me on Intercom and I'm out for a walk with my wife. It's a practice to not answer the call and to continue my walk. Just like anything else, it's a muscle that you have to work at.

I'm an entrepreneur because I want to work less, not more. I see a lot of entrepreneurs who talk about how hard it is and how tired and stressed they are. I'm like, "Wait, I think you're doing something wrong. That's not why you got into it."

If you're starting SpaceX or something like that, then obviously you're going to have to work incredibly hard. But that was never my goal. For me, entrepreneurship is a gradual process of aligning the kind of business you're building with the kind of life you actually want.

What's the most important advice you'd give to a SaaS founder?

When you're starting something, failure and success look a lot alike. It's very easy to mistake something that is actually succeeding for something that is failing. So if you're new and you don't have a lot of experience, then be aware of that. Talk to people who have more experience because you may actually be doing really well.

It's easy to feel like you're late to the game. In 2008, it felt like every cool thing had been built and that it had all been done before. Now look where we are.

You're still early to the game. I think there's a huge wave coming in SaaS. If you find yourself thinking, *Oh, shoot, I just wish I'd been around 10 years ago, then I could have been something great*, stop and realize that it's still really early and there's a lot of opportunity. Start now and keep working. 90% of the people I know who started in 2010 are successful in some large or small way now. The sooner you start and the longer you keep at it, the more likely you are to succeed.

TAKEAWAYS

- It takes persistence to productize a service.

- Be vigilant about your priorities—including the ones that involve work-life balance.

- Sometimes, success looks like failure in the beginning. Get advice from those who are more experienced to help gauge where you're at.

- You're not too late to the game.

#46

Yashar Ahmadpour

Title: Co-founder, AdviceAnalytics
Value proposition: Democratizes access to 401k retirement
Industry: Retirement
Keywords: Fundraising, MVP, prioritization

What is AdviceAnalytics?

We're democratizing access to 401k retirement by making it far more accessible to more people, especially to underrepresented people. We are doing all of this through compliance by helping companies from being hit with massive fines. In fact, around 70% of companies fail compliance every year due to missteps with 401k compliance issues. The end result is that American companies are paying more than $12 billion a year in fines and fees.

How did you identify this as a problem?

My co-founder Jerry worked in the 401k industry as an executive. He noticed that when he solved a few of his clients' problems, they would come back and tell him that he had saved them a ton of money because he had helped put them in compliance. That got him on a mission to find out why companies were paying so much in fines. He and I have been friends for a number of years and one thing led to another and now we're working together. I'm the product co-founder. User experience is my area of expertise.

When did you launch?

The company was founded in June of 2019, but we really got off the ground in May of 2020. That's when we got our first check from a partner with data from 11 million 401k participants. We used that to build our first product–predictive compliance testing. Soon after we were introduced to SAC (Seattle Angel Conference). We would meet with them and ended up entering their pitch fest which we ended up winning, to the tune of roughly $270K. That garnered us some PR in Geekwire and elsewhere, and ended up getting us a lead investor along with angel investors to raise nearly $1M in a few months.

What did it look like for you to develop your MVP?

The mistake that I've seen a lot of startups make, including me in the past, is building your product before finding customers. When we started Advice Analytics, we just had a slide deck with prototypes because we wanted to get buy-in first. So we took that to SAC, and then we built the product and we started selling.

What are some of the mistakes that you see SaaS founders make when it comes to UX?

Too many founders go engineering first, then sales and then finally, user experience. That's why product is usually an afterthought; it's not an early hire. You usually have the CEO and the CTO as the team in early startups.

The problem with that is you are now focusing only on the tech stack, and you're missing a very important element – audience. What are they currently using? How are they going to use your product? Will they have to learn something entirely new?

If you look at the 401k industry, it's very old school. It's primarily pen and paper, fax and spreadsheets. Excel is like, bleeding edge. If user experience was not at the center of how we move forward, then we'd be like any other startup that would say, *We got breakthrough technology. It's the latest and greatest.* But this audience would be like, "Okay, well, how do I use it? Why do I need all this fancy tech?"

It's very important for us to understand the personas that we're building this for, understanding what their organic flow is like, and to translate that into a delightful experience using technology that will not scare off our persona.

What kind of advice can you give on the topic of raising funds?

First, get a customer. Don't build anything until you actually have something that someone is interested in. It's also easier to build for the enterprise market versus consumers or even SME's. With consumers or SME's, you have to have thousands of people that want something, whereas with enterprise, you could have one big customer that's going to drive your entire revenue stream.

We have a hard rule that we try to live by, and that is we commit no code until we have created all the flowcharts and all the user experience. We build based on what the market is telling us. If we have ideas of what we think the next big thing should be, we go through the flow of user experience. But we don't commit code until we hear someone tell us they would love it on our product roadmap.

You mentioned earlier that founders often stack their priorities incorrectly. How would you restack priorities?

Here's how I look at the hierarchy of building a product. Sales finds a customer. Sales comes to the company and says, "I've got a customer." And then the company then says, "Okay, let's start building it." But before they start building, they create the flowchart. I can't stress how important the flowchart is because the flowchart is going to drive not only the user architecture, but it's going to drive the backend architecture of what the database structure ought to be like. That's because of the relationship between the different databases. From there, you start creating the user experience. From user experience you hand it to software engineering, they start building it, and then a UI designer comes in and starts designing based on the UX as well as the user hierarchy.

Is there any other advice you'd give to someone starting a SaaS?

Do as much research as possible. Just because one or multiple people say that you shouldn't do it, you shouldn't let that hinder you from reaching out and doing what you really want to do. Most of the time when you tell people that you're building a startup, they're going to be naysayers. For some people or a lot of people, it's not worth taking that risk. And that's fine. Everybody shouldn't be thinking the same way. But if you're truly passionate about solving a very complex problem, whatever that problem is – then you should do it. As a wise green person once said, "Do, or do not. There is no try".

TAKEAWAYS

- Don't build your product (or try to raise funding) before finding customers.

- Thinking about UX early on will help you build a product that's right for your particular audience.

- Enterprise can be easier; you'll need far fewer customers than required for products for consumers or SME's.

- Do your research before allowing people to discourage you from building your product.

#47

Liam McIvor Martin

Title: Co-founder, Time Doctor
Value proposition: Time analytics tool
Industry: Time analytics
Keywords: Bootstrapping, fundraising, mindset

What is Time Doctor?

We are a time analytics tool. I believe that in the future, you won't be measuring how much time it took you to complete a task. Instead, you'll just look and see how efficiently you actually completed the task. Our tool analyzes a bunch of different variables that you wouldn't usually measure. We have the largest second-by-second work database on the planet. I can tell you how to do your work better and how to make yourself more efficient at what you do day in and day out.

Why was this a problem that you wanted to solve?

I'm a sociologist by training, with a specialty in the sociology of work. There's an interesting dialectic between the amount of hours that you put into a task and the perceived value of it. The amount of time that you put into something does not equal better results. In many cases, it's the opposite.

You need a large dataset to analyze that type of information. I realized that building a tool like Time Doctor would be the only way to get those types of answers.

Did you raise money?

We are a remote first organization. We have team members in 43 different countries right now. We have no physical office. This might not sound weird to people today. 10 years ago, that was nuts. We build products effectively out of the ether. That made it a very long slog to be taken seriously as a company. We got term sheets around year number two to do a Series A, and every single term sheet had the requirement of coming back to the office and bringing everyone to a particular city. They said, "We'll give you the Series A funding, but everyone has to come to Toronto or New York or San Francisco." We said, "We're a remote work company. Our tool literally helps facilitate remote work." They said, "That's great. But we're venture capitalists. Trust us. This is how you build a fast growing business."

We disagreed and continued on being bootstrapped. Hindsight is 20/20. Maybe that was the wrong decision, but based on what happened in 2020, it seems like the right decision. Quite literally, we had a five to six year acceleration in remote work during March 2020.

This last year has been crazy. We personally have been doing a little under 200% year over year growth for an eight figure business. We've hired over 100 people over the last year on top of our current team, so we're close to 200 people right now. We've effectively more than doubled the organization in the last year. In March, April, and May, I was working 12 hours a day every day, seven days a week. We were waiting for eight to nine years for remote work to be taken seriously. COVID literally jumped the curve forward five years.

Have the last 10 years been ups and downs, or a steady uptick of growth?

Steady uptick of growth. SaaS has the best business model for compounding. If you get 1,000 customers that pay you something, and if your product doesn't suck, you're generally going to achieve velocity with that revenue. You don't have to add much more marketing into the top of the pot to see growth. That's the magic of SaaS.

I got in earlier where it was a lot easier to acquire customers. I think the challenge that most new SaaS founders would have is that initial traction of building. The cost of acquisition is going up and up and up. If I had to start Time Doctor over again right now, I'd probably have to raise money to be able to get to the trajectory that I currently have now.

Any final advice for SaaS founders?

Someone gave me this piece of advice recently, and it's been sticking with me all week. If you're going to start something, you better really love it, because you're not going to make that much money at first, particularly in a SaaS model. But every year that you stick with a SaaS business, it becomes that much more valuable. The practice of patience is something that a lot of these business founders don't get.

If I were to start another business today, I would probably just shut up and not do anything and grind for five years before declaring it a success or failure. A lot of SaaS founders don't do that. They look at it after six months and they're just like, "Well, that didn't work."

If you have an initial traction, if you have customers, then you'll grow. If you've got $1 million ARR, you've got the machine in place. It will turn into a $10 million a year business. If it's a $10 million a year business, it's probably going to turn into a $100 million a year business. You just need to sit there and grind. Many people don't have the patience for that.

Put on blinders. If you're good at SEO, then write 10,000 blog posts over the next two years. It doesn't require that much intelligence to do what you're already good at and just keep doing it. I've been a proponent of remote work for 15 years. The pandemic is just one of those things that came out of left field that blew us up. But growth was an inevitability. Just keep going.

TAKEAWAYS

- If you've gotten decent traction and have a good product, you're going to achieve velocity. Stick with it.
- SaaS requires you to sit and grind it out. That requires patience that many founders don't have.

Frank Barry

Title: Co-founder & COO, Tithe.ly
Value proposition: Helps churches grow with affordable technology
Industry: Church management
Keywords: Co-founder, customer acquisition, hiring, mindset

What is Tithe.ly?

We exist to help churches grow with affordable technology. Churches serve a major purpose in the world and yet they're way behind on tech adoption. Most churches are 10-15 years behind the trends. We started off as a simple giving app on your iPhone to make giving easy. We've grown that from a simple app into a whole ecosystem of products that serve churches.

How did you identify this as a problem to be solved?

I went to school for computer science, but I spent the first five years after graduating as a youth pastor. After that, I started working for a tech company that creates software for larger faith-based organizations. On that journey of around 13 years at that company, I crossed paths with three other people and connected the dots to church and technology and payments. All those things converged into Tithe.ly. Our now CEO, Dean, had this idea. He was like, "Hey, you can buy a coffee on a Starbucks app. Why can't you give to your church on your phone?"

Between the four of us, we had the expertise to pull it off. Dean was a pastor for 30 years. Barn was an engineer. Steve had started a couple of companies in previous lives and knows payments. I had experience with product and marketing. So we had this net of experience to lean on throughout navigating the business.

What are some of the things that you experienced in starting Tithe.ly that you didn't see coming?

As I just said, we had a great foundation to lean on. So we've been able to handle and navigate new challenges well.

One interesting thing is that we now have 125 employees all over the world, including Australia, Canada, Chile, and the Bahamas. Those employees get treated differently according to law. Even state law affects how employees are treated. I didn't think through that initially, but we have to write up different contracts in really clear terms.

With every 25 new employees, things change and you have to grow up, have more formality. When we had 10-15 employees, for example, everybody brought their own machines into work. Now, we can't do that. We've had to do employee training around security protocol, sexual harassment, and privacy. I had gone through those kinds of training in my former life at a big corporation. You might hit a stage in your own startup where you actually have to start doing that stuff.

People can be the hardest part of business. I think we have a great culture, and we've got amazing people. But things can still happen. Stuff goes sideways and we've had to grow up fast when it comes to things like employment law and how you handle sensitive situations. That being said, hire for HR early.

What does sales look like at Tithe.ly?

From day one, you could go to our website and create your account in five minutes. In theory, you could be off and running and taking donations for your church digitally without ever talking to anybody at Tithe.ly.

We made sure, however, that from the very beginning we talked to everyone that "came through the door "– our new customers. At first, it was just Dan and I. We called in, made sure they had a great experience, and felt loved. We do that to this day, even as we add hundreds and hundreds of new accounts every month.

We also did tons of content. We did SEO, Google ads, Bing ads, Capterra ads. Almost from day one, we wrote twice a week on our blog. Nobody would read it, but over time it paid off. Two years in of doing it twice a week and sending a newsletter every week, you started to see it grow. Four years later, you really see that labor pay off.

Now, we take an organic inbound approach. People sign up and we don't do outbound sales or cold calling. They just come to us to sign up on our website. If they need a demo or if they need questions answered, our sales team steps in.

How have you handled competitors in this space?

Competition doesn't drive our behavior. We should be smart and aware of who's out there and what's going on. But it doesn't change our mission, which is to be the No.1 tech platform for churches in the world. Five years ago, that was just a dream. But now we have 30,000 churches on the platform, and we're on the path to 50,000. Arguably we've already reached our goal, because we probably operate in more countries than any other church platform on the planet.

What's the best piece of advice you could give to SaaS founders?

Just keep at it. Get really talented, passionate people around you who can help you push through that five year mark. Most companies are going to fail in the first couple of years. But if you can keep pushing, keep paying attention, know your customer, know your market, know the problem you're trying to solve and the value you bring – you'll succeed.

TAKEAWAYS

- If you're building a medium-to-large sized business, hire for HR early.
- Content can pay off. But it will take time.
- Follow up personally with new customers.
- Get talented people around you and keep at it.

Chris Ronzio

Title: Founder & CEO, Trainual

Value proposition: Creates company playbooks for better onboarding/training

Industry: HR, operations

Keywords: Bootstrapping, customer acquisition, customer discovery, hiring

What is Trainual?

Trainual is a business playbook software for small growing companies to document who they are, their culture, their history, their story, their policies, and their processes so that as they grow, their teams do things the "company way."

How did you identify this as a problem to be solved?

Through my own business. I had a video production company that covered youth sporting events all across the United States. Process and quality were really important, and I put a lot of attention into online training and standard operating procedures and trying to really package up how my company did what we did. I ran that for 13 years before I sold it. Part of me getting ready to sell it was transitioning myself out of the business, and that whole journey prepared me to help other companies do that same thing.

I started a consulting firm after that and saw that all small businesses, as they grow, need to delegate responsibilities and train people to do things consistently. But for small companies, a lot of times that just ends up creating a lot of documents and Dropbox folders and it's just chaos. I thought there should be a tool for small businesses that acted as a hub for how you do what you do.

How did you go from a consulting business to a SaaS?

From 2015-2017, Trainual was just a tool on the shelf for my consulting business. During that time we had just 27 customers. Initially, it covered my car payment, and then my house payments, and then I started to think that there was something there. In late 2017, my consulting clients started referring the software to their friends that didn't necessarily want the consulting, just the software tool. So we decided that instead of taking on another client, we'd rebuild the tool. I got so excited about it that I decided to stop doing the consulting and pivot into SaaS. In January of 2018, we spun the software out as its own business.

What were some unexpected challenges of going into SaaS from consulting?

We were selling $10k, $15k, or $20k dollar consulting packages. I thought a $49/month software would be so much easier to sell. But it was actually a lot harder to sell something for $49 a month. People were questioning whether they would use it, wanting to bring other people on the call, etc. I had to do demo after demo. I felt like *this is crazy. I could sell a $10k consulting gig at a coffee shop in half an hour. SaaS is so much harder.* There was a learning curve to that. The consulting business was based on referrals I had. I'd written a little book, and was getting some call traffic, but it was still mostly referrals. With a SaaS business, I exhausted my referrals in my inner circle. I spammed everyone on LinkedIn and then we had to figure out where to go from there. So we had to learn digital marketing pretty quickly.

How did you overcome the challenge of sales?

In the beginning, I was learning through demos. I was trying to understand my customer. But after I did 30 or 40 of them, I was hearing the same things over and over. What I was hearing became the bullet points for our website and our ads. After that, it was all about exposure. How do we get thousands of people to the website and start to figure out a funnel? How many people do we need to get to the website, to get to this many trials? How many trials do we need to get to this many conversions? We started with some pretty simple Facebook ads to drive traffic. We did Instagram as well.

Another helpful thing that we did early on was go to a couple of industry conferences to see what other people were doing. Overwhelmingly, it felt like B2B software was so polished and corporate, especially in the HR/operations space. We wanted to be really different, raw and authentic, no stock photos and no silly cartoons. So we hired a photographer and a videographer to tell our story. We started putting out a lot of blogs and content about our own growing pains. A lot of those ads were just shot on the iPhone, while walking down the street.

That started to work. We were getting hundreds of people, then thousands of people, to the website. In the first month I think we got six conversions. Then it was 25 conversions. It kept going from there.

What did it look like to fund the business before it took off?

I initially funded the business through the profits that were sitting in the consulting bank account. When we stopped consulting, the income stopped coming in. We went from having a multimillion dollar consulting firm to a $2k per month recurring revenue app. We bled through cash pretty quickly in the first six months. But at that time, I was starting to see these early signs of the ads working. I knew that if we were putting $5k into Facebook and we were getting 15 or 20 customers out of that, we could make our cash back in three months based on the monthly subscription revenue from those customers. After that, it felt like free money. Why wouldn't I tap into every ounce of debt that I have to pump customers into this business? It was a measured decision, but it was still painful to have all my credit cards maxing out, taking Kabbage loans, and writing myself 0% interest checks from the credit card companies. It got to where I was selling stuff out of my garage to my neighbors. My wife was at the supermarket calling me because none of the credit cards were working, so she had to put back all the groceries. It finally got uncomfortable enough. But at the same time, we had built this business that had close to a thousand companies on it. There was some real value to it.

I financed it through the customers first. I accelerated it with debt. The cautionary thing there is that I wasn't experimenting with debt. I was fueling the business with it.

What does the team look like at Trainual?

At the time of creating Trainual at the beginning of my consulting firm, I was a solo founder. When we decided to launch the company as its own business, there was a team of five of us. By the end of this year, we'll have about 90 people.

How do you find the right people for your team?

I think the best advice is to have people that love being generalists and that can do a lot of different things. My chief of staff was employee #1 and she has done almost every job in the business other than coding. She's talked to customers and done research. She ran our customer support. She's done sales demos. She's done the operations and office management.

My brother, who is the CMO, has been the perfect complement to me right out of the gate. I was the operations/business guy and he took on the creative side, the marketing. Early on, he was able to come up with cool ideas that I could execute on or I came up with cool ideas that he could execute on. That magic was so important at the beginning.

What's the #1 mistake you see SaaS founders make?

They immediately start with features. They add a bunch of stuff and make sure it's really polished. Then they have something great that no one ever finds out about and the opportunity missed them. It's more important to come up with something that is good enough for a specific use case and then figure out marketing and sales. If you figure out marketing and sales and you've got that engine, then you can start investing more in product. A lot of people do that backwards.

TAKEAWAYS

- Hire people who are happy to wear many hats—especially in the beginning.
- Don't focus too much on polished features in the beginning. Figure out what your sales funnel is, and then let that fuel more product development.

#50

Dean Hantzis

Title: CTO, Tapple

Value proposition: Tapple establishes an interactive pathway for brands to gather first-party data in the physical world

Industry: Marketing

Keywords: Company culture, mindset, team

What is Tapple?

Tapple is a SaaS platform that facilitates the connection between brands and consumers in the physical world. We capitalize on the rich data that is uniquely available at a specific location to provide a new type of targeting. It's point-in-time physical world marketing.

We then marry an abundance of real time environmental data points with in-the-moment consumer engagement data. From that, a new type of data payload emerges, which Tapple uses to generate business intelligence for its clients.

Let's say you're targeting a group of people at TD Bank Garden for a Celtics game. Tapple gives you the ability to create content that targets people in that environment in real time. So, you catch people's attention at a point in time when they're immersed in a specific environment, and optimize content based on their mindset, which takes conversion rates to places the digital web can't touch.

How did you identify this as a problem to be solved?

Every successful business is trying to do one of two things. You're either trying to solve a problem, or you're trying to address a desire. We first got excited about the potential opportunity of physical to digital pathways when Google and Apple enabled QR scanning directly from smartphone cameras—essentially opening up the gateway to drive instant, digital engagement in the physical world. After about a year of testing the product in industries like hospitality, the arts, and restaurants, we identified a market that was already heavily invested in physical world engagement, but had very few tools to measure their impact.

By enabling a data-centric value exchange between brands and consumers outside of the web, we give marketers the ability to collect first-party data from anywhere in the world in a meaningful way.

How did COVID impact your business?

When COVID hit, it was very difficult for me to put this passion on hold. There were no Celtics games. Every in-person event on the planet was canceled. We had many opportunities cued up that evaporated overnight.

We came together as a team and asked, "What can we do right now to help people to solve a problem?" Businesses needed to open back up, but they also needed to put some kind of attestation protocol in place to ensure employee safety. They would have to adjust agreements based on government requirements and contact tracing. We knew this would be an administrative nightmare.

So we decided to solve that problem. We refocused completely on giving businesses like construction and live TV production the ability to securely screen everyone who arrives on site, whether it's a contractor or an employee. This effectively gave them a way to offload liability and perform contract tracing quickly and easily at every work site.

That was a very difficult decision given all the unknowns around COVID-19. But I'm glad we did it. Initially, I really didn't want to do it. But my team convinced me, and we made the decision together. We then launched a pillar from the platform that we productized as the Touchless Health Screener. We have done really well with the screener, and are generating recurring revenue because of this difficult decision to refocus on solving a "less exciting" problem. It's part of the reason why we're looking to raise our seed round now.

What would you say to someone who had a passion for something that hadn't necessarily identified a place in the marketplace for that passion to generate revenue?

It's a risk, potentially a large risk if you're in the position of supporting family or something similar.

When you start with a passion instead of a problem, you're going to spend a lot more time before you really get to the point of solving a problem. Say you do push forward and you're a dreamer—which I think I am. If you're not disciplined, you run the risk of failing persistently. If you're too immersed in the dreaming aspect of it, you're not going to succeed. I think startups that are more successful are the ones that have a healthy mix of both, maybe 75% discipline and 25% dreaming. It's part of my personality to constantly reevaluate and be disciplined about what I'm doing day to day. One of the biggest challenges in any startup is that you can get so immersed in the details of your day to day, that you can't see the forest from the trees.

How has "team" played an important role in your company?

Everyone brings something to the table. They keep me balanced. "Organizational culture" is a term that's thrown around a lot, but it's so important. In the culture at Tapple, I'm bringing in a group of people that have the mindset of teamwork and are less about structure and hierarchy and more about creativity. Structure and hierarchy need to exist, but when it comes to the hierarchy of personalities, I think it really benefits the organization to have that as flat as possible.

Everyone should be excited about coming to work. Generally, there should be more positive vibes than negative vibes. Culturally, we hire more based on outlook and attitude than proficiencies.

Is there any other advice you'd want to give to SaaS founders?

Creativity can often be overlooked when you're building a technical product with technical people. I used to be extremely concrete in the way I thought. My eighth grade science teacher said to me when I graduated, "Dean, you're a real smart kid. But you got a B- in my class. You need to think less concretely, let your mind wander a little bit more." I'll never forget that. Doing computer science, I started to observe how differently I was thinking about things compared to my peers. I'm not thinking about how to programmatically get something done by moving from step one to step two. Instead, I'm tying what we're building to the value of the business and thinking of creative ways to get things done efficiently.

One of the best pieces of advice that I can give to building a SaaS – or really, any startup founder – is to be disciplined enough to step out of your world and reflect. I catch things I'm doing wrong every day, but that number would be much larger if I didn't reflect. You have to want to understand the mistakes you're making. We have a very open environment where constructive criticism is a real pillar to us making progress. But you've got to do that with yourself as well, independently of others. I think that's the best way to succeed.

TAKEAWAYS

- Stop and re-evaluate every so often. Are you too caught up in the details to catch larger mistakes you might be making?
- A strong company culture values positivity, passion, and constructive criticism.

#51

Rahul Pandey

Title: Founder & CEO, Bonzai

Value proposition: Build personalized and scalable content for digital advertising

Industry: Marketing

Keywords: Hiring, mindset, product/market fit, team

What is Bonzai?

Bonzai is a content creation platform to help you build content for your digital advertising space.

What's your professional background and how did you decide to create a product like this?

I started my career with AT&T in the telecom space. After about a decade, I moved on to the media content business, where I worked with CNBC and CNN in India on the digital content side.

Being a brand manager, I realized that the biggest challenge for marketers was the content gap, which would continue to grow because of new channels, new devices, and new screens and screen sizes. How do you scale your creative content across devices with different sizes and orientations? At the same time, how do you personalize content to different customer segments? That was the genesis of this company.

What does the team look like at Bonzai?

I'm the founder of the company, and I have a team of 25 people in India. We operate largely in Asia, Australia, and New Zealand. In fact, we were the first platform from Asia which got integrated with Google, Apple News, and Adobe.

What has been the biggest challenge to building a team?

Getting the right sort of people, with the right mindset. You can get a lot of people with the right skill set. But the mindset is what will make the difference. Look for people with grit.

What did you learn during COVID-19?

The pandemic put everything to a full stop with meeting potential customers in person. We were forced to ask, *How do you keep those relationships? How do you still service them effectively and make them happy and stay with you for a long time?*

As a result, we've learned to spend more time with customers, to keep talking to them, and to keep asking about pain points. Serving your customers is the most important thing. Go the extra mile to empathize with them. We spend a lot of time trying to understand customers so that we can build our product better.

What's the most important thing someone needs to know about starting a SaaS company?

Product/market fit is the most important thing. But it rarely happens the first time. I've seen a lot of people invest too much in functionality at the very beginning, because sometimes access to capital is easier. Keep fine-tuning product/market fit before you scale your operations.

What kinds of traits do founders need to succeed?

An openness to "unlearn." Like me, many of us might have a lot of professional experience before coming into the space. But you need to keep an attitude of being open and continuing to learn. A lot of people wrongly think, *This is the way it will work because that's how it worked before.*

The second thing is that you need to listen to what your customers are telling you, rather than what technical capability you can bring. Spend a lot of time consistently revisiting your UX and UI and figure out how to keep tweaking it.

You need to figure out how to make yourself the dumbest person in the room. That's what's going to make your business a success – a team that's better than you are.

TAKEAWAYS

- Hire people with grit.
- Hire people who are smarter than you.
- Product/market fit rarely happens the first time around.
- Keep fine-tuning product/market fit before you scale.

Daniel Huss

Title: Co-founder, Gravity AI

Value proposition: Dual-sided marketplace for AI, increasing speed of data science adoption

Industry: AI and data science

Keywords: AI, co-founder, mindset, resources, work-life balance

What is Gravity AI?

The boom in data science infrastructure and available data means there are now thousands of out of the box AI solutions available to companies today via small third party vendors. But large enterprise has trouble accessing these solutions because of slow procurement and strict compliance requirements. In fact, the only time in my career as a product manager I was ever frustrated enough to throw a chair (gently) was when my own procurement department told me that it was going to take 18 months to buy the super simple algorithm that I needed for my product I was building at that time.

So we build gravity AI to save future chairs. We do that through our platform – a dual-sided marketplace for engineers and enterprise product teams connecting them to thousands of high-quality AI Models from various third party vendors. These teams can browse third party tech that we've vetted for security and compliance, standardized in our own custom docker container and API endpoints, for a very simple low code implementation of that AI. The goal is to increase speed to market for engineers and product teams, and reduce the need to waste resources on solved, non-proprietary problems.

Are you a technical founder?

I'm just technical enough to be dangerous. I'm not an engineer, but I grew up in a household of engineers. My brother Jon is a very accomplished creative technologist that I suckered into being my CTO. So we've got a double brother team here.

My adult life has been focused on product management as a discipline – validating product concepts and then building and regularly shipping something that, hopefully, people want. I've really tried to live the product management mantra of "outcomes over outputs." Jon is incredibly complementary to me. His whole life has been around solving meaty technical problems. He started his career in bioinformatics for pharma, working on incredible AI based drug discovery, protein folding, and more. He was then a lead solution architect at an antivirus company in San Diego, where he architected the whole backend. We're a very well-positioned team to tackle the data science problem that we're trying to solve.

How did you identify this problem in the marketplace?

My last full time role was head of product management for a product at State Street, one of the largest asset management companies in the world. While there, I quickly realized that building AI at such a large regulated company was going to be difficult. Namely, I started facing the challenge of not being able to access third party data science models that would have accelerated my product development process, but was forced instead to waste resources solving solved problems. The story about the chair is true. I mockingly knocked over a chair one day when my procurement department told me it was going to take 18 months to buy this model.

There's a major interest in data science across all organizations, big and small. This frustration with procurement is compounded by the fact that right now, data science is becoming even more accessible. There's sufficient enough infrastructure that's available for small data science companies to start building lots of different models. For the first time ever, there are widely available public free data sets that can be used to build interesting models.

We're seeing a massive increase in high performing third party data science solutions, but as mentioned, the companies that need them either don't know they exist or can't get them quickly through security and procurement.

What did it look like for you to shift from a full-time, well-paying job into the life of a startup founder?

I'm not a first time founder. I've had a couple of ventures in the past, including running an analytics company for four years and building it up to just shy of $1M in annual revenue. That was very different from what I'm trying to do now, however. That was a services company, with low upfront investment needs, but a business model that was difficult to scale. What I'm trying to do now, however, is build that scalable model and solve some big, hairy problems for companies. This is much more capital intensive, and this is my first time raising substantial amounts of venture capital, so there are all sorts of learnings.

There's a fantastic book called *Just Start* that outlines the steps that you mentally go through as a founder. Namely, you take small steps of action to learn whether or not you want to invest more into the venture, learning at each step and deciding whether to push forward. It's basically a variation on *The Lean Startup*. The first small steps of action for me were to conduct tons of user interviews validating that the problem is real, huge, and painful. After that, I spent some money getting low fidelity wireframes built and trying to reach other people through platforms like Respondent, where you can pay to do interviews.

Step by step, people got more and more excited about what I was doing and validated that the concept was on the right path. When I finally made the decision to leave my job, I had already spent a good deal of energy validating the problem and business concept. I'd already done enough legwork to say I'm on to something.

The jump back into startup life was jarring, but it was needed. At my previous job, I was showing up to work around 10:30 AM and leaving at 4 PM. I loved my team and what we were building there, but the slow pace was killing me. Now jumping back into start up life, I was returning to 12 or 13 hour days.

Fortunately, I have a deep comfortability with uncertainty and reminded myself that the worst case scenario is that I fail, and I get a job again. Maybe I go try something else again in the future. I have the luxury now of knowing I'm not going to starve to death.

Was the journey lonely?

It was very lonely until I brought on my co-founder full time. I wanted one of the best engineers I knew to join me, and that just happened to be my brother. But he had a very well-paying job and unlike me, he has a kid and a mortgage. Leading up to working on the start up full-time, I had structured my life in a way that I was able to give up stuff very quickly. For example, it was easy to give up my expensive Soho apartment in Manhattan. I started digital nomading, going to hostels or hotels around the world, working on the business. But Jon doesn't have that luxury. He has fixed bills that he continues to have to pay. So one of the major milestones for us was raising our first friends and family round and figuring out how we could get him on full time and still be able to take care of those bills.

Can you talk about what it takes to be "wired for entrepreneurship"?

I've always imagined that I have this iron ball of optimism that sits in my chest, which can be shaped and molded but not shattered. A lot of founders have this intense optimism. It should be noted that's different than comfortability with uncertainty, which is also super important. But with this optimism comes the belief that we're in control of our future. In psychology, they would call that a "high locus of control." I have a high locus of control. I believe that when I do certain things and I work hard, certain outcomes will happen.

I romanticized the idea of entrepreneurship before it was cool. When you actually get into it, you realize how much BS it is. There's no romanticism about it. But because of that draw I had towards the entrepreneur lifestyle, I started fostering a set of values in myself very early that I believed were important to succeed in building a sustainable company.

One of those values I mentioned already is to embrace uncertainty. Sometimes that level of uncertainty when I'm working on a new feature or product or approach reaches peak levels, and even *I* get a little uncomfortable. Then, I remind myself that when we are faced with uncertainty, we're simply looking at an incorrectly scaled time horizon.

For example, right now there's some uncertainty about if we should continue targeting large enterprise businesses, or go more towards targeting venture-backed startups. It's really difficult to predict what will happen in three months, but what I can do is say, *You know what's not uncertain? What I can learn right now.* I can set up a meeting tomorrow with some venture-backed startups and learn more about whether that's the path that we should be spending time and money and energy on and make a better decision by shrinking that time horizon. As some of my advisors would say, I have to figure out what decisions I can put off for "future Dan" versus what things I can do right now.

The dumbest question we were ever asked as kids was, "What do you want to be when you grow up?" Because you're like, "I'm five! I just finished watching Rugrats. I don't even know what professions exist." When I was five, I wanted to be a chemist and an ice cream man. I was operating with imperfect knowledge and being forced to think on the wrong time scale. I needed more information to make such sweeping life decisions!

Another way I work with uncertainty is to approach this whole thing as an adventure. We're on our own hero's journey, with ups and downs. If you were to watch an adventure movie that didn't have any moments of danger, challenge, or difficulty, that movie would suck, right? We need to recognize that as founders, we're on an adventure and it's those challenging moments that make a good story.

TAKEAWAYS

- Small steps of action can help you determine whether to keep pushing through with your idea.

- When you're facing uncertainty, you might simply be looking at the wrong time horizon. What can you do tomorrow to make a difference?

- Believe that you are in control of your future.

Zachariah Moreno

Title: Co-founder & CEO, of SquadCast

Value proposition: Allows remote content creators to create studio quality recordings

Industry: Podcasting, content creation

Keywords: Bootstrapping, co-founder, mindset

What is SquadCast?

SquadCast is a platform that empowers remote content creators to collaborate with their guests, co-hosts, and co-creators in a private Cloud Recording studio. We have an emphasis on being a recording platform first, and a conversation platform second.

That's the biggest differentiator with Zoom, which I would say is our closest competitor. They're a conversation platform first with a feature that has recording. Our hypothesis is that content creators need and want high-quality recordings because research has shown that quality preserves credibility.

How did you identify this as a problem?

In 2016, we started working on a remote podcast – a science fiction audio drama – and found this challenge regarding quality when we set out to collaborate remotely across a team in California. I was a software engineer, my brother is a sound designer, and my best friend is a decorated playwright. We had the skills to get the job done, but quality was the bottleneck.

We took a step back and looked at podcasting and what "state of the art" technology really was. What we found was that nobody was happy with what was out there.

How did you test your initial hypothesis?

When I was teaching at Cal Berkeley in 2018, one of my students suggested that we take our MVP and not just attend, but sponsor, one of the largest conferences in the podcast community. Thankfully, it was within driving distance and we did everything on the cheap except for the sponsorship. We put ourselves out there and took that step into the abyss, but we were prepared to fall flat on our faces. Within the first five minutes of the event, people started coming up to us and saying, "I was hoping to find the answer to this problem at this event." We got our first customer and our founding adviser that day.

Where are you now in terms of growth?

We have over 14,000 active customers, including podcasters, content creators, and producers at studios and enterprises. ESPN, VOX, Marvel, and Spotify are really amazing teams collaborating on the

SquadCast platform. I would say an inflection point in the COVID-19 pandemic propelled us to where we are today.

What's your professional background?

I had an amateur art career, and then went to college to learn web development. From there, I did an open source internship on the Google Chrome team in 2012, where I got exposed to how Google engineered software. I then did some writing for a software engineering magazine, and eventually wrote a book called *AngularJS Deployment Essentials*. That's what led me to teaching at Cal Berkeley in their extension program. All the while, I was a full time software engineer for the government here in California.

I wanted to do a creative side project that was out of my comfort zone. I was a big fan of podcasting, and science fiction is near and dear to my heart. That ultimately led to the idea for SquadCast.

My co-founder, Rock, and I are long time friends. We went to high school together and stayed connected through college and went on different career paths. He became a financial auditor and CPA, where he was auditing large companies in tech. Both of us thought about founding something on our own, having an impact beyond fulfilling somebody else's mission. Rock also introduced me to podcasting as a listener. He was the first person that I approached with this idea because I knew our skills were symbiotic. He had business and finance skills, and I had design and engineering skills.

What have been some unexpected challenges of running a business?

We've had technical challenges. We've had PR challenges. But I would say the biggest kind of category of challenges was that we chose to bootstrap. We did that as an experiment – and that experiment hasn't ended.

We're essentially our own angel investors, so we wear a lot of hats and that has its challenges. The biggest one is not being able to grow the team as fast as we would like to because we aren't spending other people's money. We essentially have to get our product and our business model to a place where we can sustain new hires from revenue. That's a tall order, but that's also where I'm super proud of overcoming those challenges and being able to grow the team the way that we have.

How have you handled the rollercoaster of running a business, from a mental health perspective?

We look at challenges from a design thinking perspective. We do experiments. We come up with hypotheses. We test the hypotheses. And we've gotten a lot better at measuring the results so we can have a clear outcome.

As for being persistent, it's hard to ignore the reality of the right timing – that's such a big factor in success, and it's completely outside of anybody's control. I've learned not to take outcomes of experiments too personally and just to trust the process.

Mental health is paramount to success in a startup and being a founder can be a lonely role. We practice, and encourage our team to practice, mindfulness meditation to help develop what we call, "microscopes and telescopes." This is the ability to dial your perspective from between zoomed-out to the vision of the future and zoomed-in to the small details of today.

Any advice for new founders?

The narrative you might hear is that you're not a real startup unless you raise money. I don't believe that. You always have the optionality to go out and raise capital. Sure, it might be tough to get at certain times, but it will always be there. Once you opt in to venture capital, you're on that track. You can't put the genie back in the bottle. Our mentor and investor, Rob Walling, says that fundraising is a one-way door. If you choose to bootstrap, you always have optionality.

Try to bootstrap before raising money. You will increase your valuation, reduce risk for investors, and you will likely end up owning more equity over the long run.

TAKEAWAYS

- Learn how to dial your own perspective between the big picture/future and the details/present.
- Bootstrapping can be challenging, but it's a wise choice for founders who want to keep their options open. Plus, you'll likely end up owning more equity in the long run.

#54

Segun Temitope Omisakin

Title: Founder, Trackboard by Kinetic

Value proposition: Helps develop, map and create strategy implementation and a transparent, flexible OKR for organizations

Industry: B2B technology

Keywords: Customer acquisition, development, distribution

What is Trackboard?

Trackboard is a strategy design and implementation platform that's uniquely designed to drive objective key results (OKRs) and key performance indicators (KPIs) for organizations. It helps align strategy implementation from top executives to downlines in real time with clarity, focus, and transparency.

Everybody is used to project management tools. But the majority of the time, project management tools are not transparent enough to key stakeholders. In Trackboard, if any variables change in real time, they can be implemented quickly and transparently by cascading down to different lines of management. When you come into your dashboard, you can see exactly what everybody's working on and where alignment falls.

We're focused on developing markets like Africa and we'll hopefully extend to Asia soon. All of our current customers are in Africa.

How are you reaching new customers?

Every one of our customers so far has been referred. I've never personally reached out to any CEOs. Instead, we're using high-level networking partnerships with key consulting organizations. We're still in beta; we're keeping it low-key. We've never taken any venture capital. All the co-founders invested in the product. That's been good because the cost of acquisition of customers has been practically zero so far.

People don't just adopt your product because it's good. There are many competing products out there that could do close to whatever you're doing. People will actually use your product if it is very good *or* they know someone that uses it and refers it to you. If you look at one of our main competitors, they're actually a lot less expensive than we are. But we've made it easy for consulting partners to introduce our products to the consulting organizations. We don't intend to just stick to that route, however. By the time we leave private beta, we'll introduce our product to the public and take a more traditional approach.

We're still fixing bugs and building new features. We can't do that when we have thousands or millions of customers. Our approach right now is to continue to be profitable because it's far better that we don't spend money on marketing when we're not ready for it.

Would you say that Africa is an underserved market overall in SaaS?

Very underserved. Digital transformation is happening, because companies are realizing they need transformation to be competitive. Things are gradually changing, but there are still far more businesses competing for these markets in the developed world. People often hold the perspective that there's always poverty in Africa. There is, but there's also a lot of wealth. A lot of organizations need tools that will help them do better or perform better.

What would you say to another SaaS founder who is wanting to break into an underserved market?

The most important thing in the developing world is your relationship with others. The majority of the time, people buy things because they trust the seller. In the developed world, you don't need to know anybody before you buy Slack or Zoom, because those are the de facto tools.

You need to network as much as possible with the key market or the key people that will use your products. In fact, we have actually brought in key users and stakeholders into product development. They have a voice in the product that we are building, so they are very enthusiastic about using it. Finally, in Africa, companies won't buy a product they don't need. They have to need it, not just want it.

Any other final advice you'd want to give to SaaS founders?

The important thing about SaaS is developing an architecture that is scalable. If a person is not technical, they need a very technical person to start with and must have a long term vision in terms of the functional use. Because you don't want to create a new product while people already know your product. When you're designing the architecture of the product, you have to make it scalable, balanced, and stable.

TAKEAWAYS

- Don't underestimate the power of referral marketing; people will use your product if it's been personally referred to them (even if your product is more expensive).
- A soft launch can help give you much-needed time to fix bugs and add features.
- Focus on developing a scalable architecture from the start.

Ryan Shank

Title: Founder, PhoneWagon

Value proposition: Helps small businesses ensure they are getting high quality phone leads from ad spend

Industry: Telephony

Keywords: Customer acquisition, development, enterprise sales, mindset

What is PhoneWagon?

PhoneWagon is a call tracking and call analytics software. There are a lot of industries where you need a first phone call as a lead, like a dentist, a remodeling company, or a personal injury lawyer. Those businesses want inbound phone calls from qualified high intent buyers. Phone Wagon helps prove to those businesses that the marketing agency that they're paying to manage their ad spend actually drove them high quality leads.

How did you identify this as a problem?

I was COO of a company called mHelpDesk, which was a field service software company. We ended up getting acquired by Home Advisor, a marketplace for homeowners to find local service professionals. During that time, I learned more about the needs of small businesses who were out in the field all day. What I realized was that phone calls are the lifeblood of their business. They need to be able to track and see if calls were high quality leads, but there weren't a lot of great solutions for small businesses. There were some options, but they were cumbersome, often required annual contracts, and were very difficult to use. There wasn't a beautiful off-the-shelf solution that enabled them to actually track calls.

When I left mHelpDesk, I knew I wanted to do something with small businesses, and I knew that not a lot of people were tackling telephony. I didn't know anything about e-commerce or B2C. I'd pretty much only been in like B2B SaaS and B2B SMB. I wanted to stay in my lane for my next gig. I think founder/market fit is really important.

Are you a technical founder?

I'm not technical at all. But I've learned to manage engineers. When I started Phone Wagon, I had no technical co-founders. I hired offshore contractors to build the first prototype. That took us to $50k in MRR. We raised over a million dollars before we brought in our co-founder and CTO.

How have you learned to communicate effectively with engineers?

I wrote an interesting blog post for Neil Patel's blog called, "How I Built and Launched a SaaS Company for Less than 40k." If you Google "Build SaaS Company," it's one of the first organic results. In that post, I outline a lot of the documents I created when I first started Phone Wagon that I passed over to the engineers.

It's important to write down everything about the product at a very high level. Don't even try to get technical. Instead, just describe all these different use cases. Literally type out, "Nick owns a painting company and spends this much money on advertising." Your goal is to highlight the problem you're going to solve. That's one document. Then you'll want to create wire frames, and maybe another document that lists features and why they're important.

When you hand all that over to the developers, they understand what needs to happen from a functionality standpoint and what the actual vision is. Then let them put together a plan for you. They'll scope it out and tell you what kind of infrastructure you need to get a first version live. I tried to not get too technical with them because I'm not technical. Passing over a high level overview was what we needed to bring it life.

Ultimately, that helped us get off the ground quickly. But we eventually needed to rewrite the code. So there are pro's and con's to this approach.

What's the #1 mistake that founders make when it comes to sales?

They try to pass the baton too early and outsource sales. Founders can do sales for way longer than they think. Everyone's obsessed with making things scalable, but they often try to scale before they get the repetitions in themselves. Honestly, people appreciate when the founders reach out to them.

But there are also other learnings. In the beginning of Phone Wagon, I was making all of the sales calls, and what I found is that we shouldn't even have been calling businesses directly. If I tried to bring in someone for sales, they would have just said, "We didn't make many sales today." But what we realized is a lot of these businesses work with agencies to manage their ad spend. We needed to go to the agencies instead of the businesses.

What's one of the biggest challenges you've faced while building Phone Wagon?

Like I said before, I worked with offshore engineers at first who built the product and got us to $50k MRR. That was great for getting it off the ground, but I let it go too long before realizing that we needed to do things right. Rewriting it was time-consuming and expensive.

Second, I tried to scale too early. We had a working product with hundreds of paying customers. However, we were short on a lot of features and integrations that were key requirements for bigger customers. I added sales reps, but when we would try to sell to bigger customers, we would realize that we needed, for example, a Salesforce integration, and we would get rejected. We were spending all this money and not converting because there was a feature gap or an integration gap. The tricky thing was that we had just raised over a million bucks and we needed to get the growth rate up. But the product wasn't ready to scale. We should have just had cash in the bank and focused on product, product, product.

Any final advice for SaaS founders?

There are so many tools you can use nowadays—like no-code tools, even Canva—it's not that difficult to get something up and running. If you can figure out a problem to solve, I think you're going to be able to build a product without too much difficulty. People like to chase shiny objects. But to succeed, you need to stay heads down and grind for years. It's not fun, but that's what we did. If you just add 10, 20, 30 customers every month for four years, you will sell for mid-seven figures. You can make millions of dollars, but you have to grind it out and be consistent.

TAKEAWAYS

- If you outsource development, write down a high level overview of your product for your engineers. This includes use cases and different features.

- In the beginning, make your own sales calls. Customers will appreciate it – and you'll learn who your customers really are.

- Don't be too quick to scale. Make sure your product is ready, especially for larger customers.

- Keep your head down and grind it out. Don't give in to shiny object syndrome.

#56

Will Stackable

Title: Founder, Arbor XR

Value proposition: Makes it easy for companies to deploy XR at scale and manage the in-headset experience

Industry: AR & VR

Keywords: Enterprise sales, mindset, prioritization, resources

What is ArborXR?

Arbor XR is a software that makes it easy for companies to scale XR, or augmented reality (AR) and virtual reality (VR).

COVID-19 forced companies around the world to look at remote tools for work training. The problem is that companies today are using consumer hardware without business software that lets them scale. They go from these small private projects to large deployments, and they get stuck. In some cases, they're even mailing flash drives and headsets back and forth for updating and plugging in cables every time they need to update anything. Arbor XR is a SaaS platform that makes it easy for companies to manage thousands of devices, build a content library, deploy apps remotely, and completely control the in-headset experience.

How did you identify this as a problem?

When VR had just kind of taken off and the first tethered headset device came out, we launched a VR arcade in the middle of the country in Oklahoma City. It was one of the first five in the world. We bought consumer headsets and put them into a mall where people could come and rent them. There was no software for any kind of retail solution for VR headsets, so we built our own software for that location. Very quickly, we realized it was going to be needed for anybody that was wanting to use headsets in a commercial setting. We started selling it and quickly pivoted away from retail to software. Within 18 months we had customers in 40+ countries. We were the market leader for licensing commercial entertainment and gaming content, and ended up having the largest commercial marketplace outside of Asia.

One thing we didn't expect is how much we would spend just on legal fees for things like GDPR compliance, or tax compliance. Scaling up global support, but also building a product to work in multiple languages and navigating all the data protection. In the U.S., it was already a challenge, but once we bumped over into other time zones and particularly getting into Europe, it became more of a hurdle.

How did you overcome those challenges?

By making a lot of mistakes. We always try to stay close to the fact that we don't know what we're doing. There's not a school we could go to figure it out. VR is in an emerging sector where everybody is on an even playing field. We built an informal advisory council, a mixture of experienced people. We were quick to ask questions. Any time we got stuck, we went to find somebody who had been down that path before. It was often a "just in time" thing where when we faced some new challenge, the right advisor would get parachuted in at that moment.

What advice would you give to somebody who is building a SaaS product that deals with an emerging technology?

One thing comes to mind is the importance of just being in the market. Any chance we could go to a conference, whether it was in Amsterdam or in Las Vegas, we would go, attend workshops, try to get a speaking slot. We were just trying to be present and have conversations. We started getting the sense that enterprise training would be big. It seemed like there were similar problems to scaling. You have companies that are doing small pilots and then going to larger deployments and they get stuck. IT departments are stressed out of their minds because they don't know where the headsets are and they don't have control. They're giving consumer headsets to employees that can literally start playing games or jump on the Internet and get lost in settings and menus. So we started to investigate that problem space.

Early on we went to an XR enterprise conference in San Francisco. We bought the smallest booth we could get and put up signs for a product that we were still building. But we had a prototype, and over the course of the week, we had hundreds of conversations with companies large and small. We asked a lot of questions.

When you're in an emerging market, you need to be having conversations, particularly with the people that you want to work with. They're learning and things are emerging and rapidly changing as people adopt the technology in surprising ways. Because of our conversations on the frontlines, our product identity shifted multiple times.

Most founding myths are constructed "after the fact." Mark Zuckerberg had no idea when he started some Hot or Not copy that it was going to turn into Facebook. My only thought at the very beginning was that when I put on a headset, my mind was blown. My co-founder Brad did the same, and we both had the sense that VR was going to be massively impactful. We had no idea where we would land, but we wanted to get our foot in the door. It wasn't strategic. We were just present. We listened. We shifted – sometimes later than we should have. But we tried to be agile as the market changed.

Any advice you'd want to say to someone who was interested in starting a SaaS company, specifically in the enterprise space?

Everybody knows that enterprise sales can be a huge mess and a massive time suck. It can also be easier than you think, because enterprise companies are more and more familiar with SaaS platforms and SaaS business pricing and models. It's not as difficult as it used to be to sign contracts, even with Fortune 100 companies. But on the flip side it's also a massive investment. The imbalance in resources and power becomes apparent on the legal and sometimes on the business side. As a SaaS company, you really have to know yourself. Sure, there are times when you need to be willing to offer custom pricing or add new features for a unique client. But if you do that for every enterprise deal, you may end up just becoming a custom software development company, without a true product. You need to ask yourself, "Are we a dev shop or are we a product company?"

It's so much easier if you have good hardware partners or channel partners. We joke sometimes that we're like the little suckerfish on the side of the whale. We've been surprised at how easy it is to have conversations with big players. They actually like working with small companies. But you need to be proactive and talk to them early.

There's also good reasons why even big companies do rollouts regionally. There is always the temptation with SaaS to go to market globally. It doesn't seem that difficult to add another language. In reality it starts getting complicated very quickly. Pricing, language support, time zone support, legal considerations, et cetera. Start with whatever region you're in and then work your way out. We let customers pull us into growth instead of feeling like if we build in another time zone or another region, that they'll come.

What are three qualities or three words that a founder needs to know?

Focus, focus, focus.

All of our biggest mistakes involved us doing too many things at once and not having clarity on what was truly important. Time and time again we'd overextend and end up paying for it.

Greg Mckeown, who wrote one of my favorite books – *Essentialism* – said "Sometimes what you **don't** do is just as important as what you **do**."

Even big companies with thousands of employees have trouble doing many things with excellence. If you are a SaaS company, chances are you've got less than 50 employees. You should really be doing one thing. Do it and do it really well.

Focus always wins. Sharpen that axe!

TAKEAWAYS

- Acquiring enterprise customers might be more realistic than you think – but you'll have to stay true to who you are (not a custom software developer!)
- Resist the urge to quickly expand your product to other regions. Let customers pull you into this kind of growth, not the other way around.
- Be vigilant about staying focused, and make sure you have clarity on your priorities.

#57

Neal Bloom

Title: Co-founder, Portfolium; CEO, Rising Tide Partners, Managing Partner, Interlock Capital

Value proposition: Student portfolios for showcasing skills and accomplishments to potential employers

Industry: EdTech

Keywords: Chicken or the egg, customer acquisition, fundraising, metrics

What was Portfolium?

Originally, Portfolium was like LinkedIn for college students. Employers would pay to access talent. Eventually, we had to pivot the buyer to universities. For example, UC San Diego might display student profiles and show all the things that students were working on. We were going to be a consumer-facing social network, but it turned into more of a tech company where we were selling a product to universities.

Why did this become a problem you wanted to solve?

I graduated in 2008, right when the financial crisis was hitting hard. As an engineer, I was lucky enough to get a job in the last year or two of new grads to be recruited to our company for the next three years. I was working in aerospace, specifically on the space side. Then in 2011, the space shuttle was retired and 60% of our workforce was let go. I immediately saw 20,000 engineers released into the workforce who had only really worked on putting people in space. So I started thinking about new career tools we could use to help engineers showcase their skill sets beyond the bullet point resumé.

Portfolium was a way to showcase your body of work in a visual format. What if you could walk into an interview with an iPad and show people things, as opposed to them looking down at your resumé and barely looking at your face? It became a tool for people to connect with you during the interview process. That's when we realized maybe there was also a social networking component to it.

Can you tell me a bit more about that pivot from social networking platform into a tool for universities?

It was a classic chicken or the egg problem. Do you first get a whole bunch of students who are looking for jobs on the platform, or do you first get employers?

It was a real struggle. What we found is that to get students to actually fill out their profile, they kind of had to be forced to do it. They really didn't care about getting jobs until they graduated from college. We thought students would be building profiles throughout their entire university journey. But we found that 95% of students didn't really have career aspirations until graduation week.

We had to find a way to get students on board, and that was getting universities to mandate this. They would run classes and curriculum so that you turn in your homework through Portfolium. Once it's graded, you could hit save and *boom*—Now you're starting to build up your portfolio of work.

How difficult was it to find universities to use your product?

If we thought it was hard to reach 40,000 students and get them to individually join, it was almost harder to find the buyers at universities. It took around 40 interviews at UC San Diego, our pilot, to figure out the buyer–alumni services. It turns out career services don't really care if you get a job or not. Once you leave campus, you're not their customer anymore. But alumni services measure who is going to donate back to school over a specific time period.

Was it always your goal to get acquired?

Yeah. Originally, LinkedIn was a very natural place for us to get tucked in. But once we realized we were more of an education technology software being used in the classroom, we started to look into the big edtech platforms and specifically, the learning management systems being used for universities. Ultimately, Portfolium was bought out by Instructure.

What kind of advice would you give to somebody who wants to enter the edtech space?

People who want to enter edtech often feel like they have to have a background as a teacher. That's not true at all. It turns out that because it's such an insular environment, they really do respect innovation coming from outside. You just have to learn how to speak their language.

Because it's not a huge universe, there aren't a lot of players. You're going to butt up against your competitors kind of quickly. I find that founders are shy about reaching out and getting to know their competitors. Don't be. Go and get to know them. You never know what could happen. You might be able to get acquired by them, or you can acquire them. You've been hustling in the same industry as them. Usually people respect that.

After Portfolium, you shifted to Hired.com. What did you learn in that process that you didn't learn with Portfolium?

Originally we built a marketplace for Portfolium. I don't think we really knew a lot of the KPIs that you need to understand to balance supply and demand. At Hired.com, we had those down. A big learning for me is understanding funnel optimization and marketplace KPIs and lingo.

Another learning was around a sales regimen. We really didn't beat the drum hard on hitting sales goals at Portfolium. But at Hired.com, we'd taken on a lot more venture funding by the time I was there. We had goals we had to hit. We had to understand how to run sales sprints and pre-launch. Launch playbooks were huge.

One thing that I started thinking about and discovered during sales calls is the importance of KPIs. A lot of founders don't focus on the right metrics. It's easier to go for vanity metrics, especially when you're pitching to unsophisticated investors who may not know how to ask the right questions. These metrics may get you a check, but you may be tracking the wrong thing.

Any insights on the "right" metrics to track?

The actual KPI is going to vary from business to business. Where are you in your life cycle–pre- or post-revenue? There are specific KPIs for each part of the cycle.

Is there any advice you'd give on raising money?

You should be talking to the smartest money you can find as quickly as possible. You want to surround yourself with people who've done the things you've done before and made money at it, so that they're not just going to write you a check, but they're going to help you afterwards. Even the people you dream of getting acquired by–go try to see the highest level people. Get sophisticated capital as early as possible, reach out to your dream VCs who have funded companies similar to yours. Even before you raise funding or see any revenue, start to find out what KPIs they look for so that you can know when you're ready to be on their radar.

TAKEAWAYS

- If you're in a small space, get to know the competition. That can open up valuable new opportunities that you haven't thought of.

- Beware of focusing only on vanity metrics. They may get you funding, but they don't always indicate potential.

- Talk to smart money–to people who have done what you're doing successfully, and who can help support you beyond writing a check.

PART 3

OVERACHIEVERS
Founders who keep starting SaaS companies

#58

Brian Casel

Title: Founder, ProcessKit; Founder, ZipMessage

Value proposition: Makes your client onboarding process repeatable & predictable

Industry: Project management

Keywords: Customer acquisition, development, MVP, work-life balance

What is ProcessKit?

ProcessKit is based on specialty processes that run repeatedly with a team.

The idea came from an online content agency I started (Audience Ops) where we had these documented standard operating procedures in Google Docs, but they were siloed from where the tasks actually happened. ProcessKit functions like a project management tool that offers the convenience of having everything in one place, but also automates processes. If we know that this client purchased Plan A and this other client purchased Plan B, then we can show or hide certain tasks for our team to follow, depending on what that client needs. You can't do that sort of level of automation on something like Trello.

How did you get involved in the SaaS space?

One thing I've noticed in SaaS is that everyone's journey is very different.

For me, the productized service model was huge. I was a freelance web designer for a couple years, spending literally all of my hours making websites for clients. What broke me out of that was building a productized service. First, I built a business called Restaurant Engine, which was part software, part service. I sold that business in 2015 and then started Audience Ops, an online content agency that ran itself through the productized service model. That gave me the time and the self-funding to spend years working on software. A lot of other people I know either do consulting or they're in a full-time job, and they build a SaaS product on nights and weekends.

The productized service model is much faster to launch and grow than a conventional SaaS. There's this phrase from a talk by Gail Goodman – "the long, slow SaaS ramp of death." It takes a long time to build a software product, and then if you're charging $50 a month or $100 a month, it takes a long time before it becomes a sustainable business. With a productized service, each individual client might pay about a thousand dollars a month. So you don't need that many clients.

How did you build ProcessKit?

This is another area where I took a bit of a different path than most founders take.

I come from a background as a web designer, but I didn't have the skills for application software development. With previous businesses, I would hire developers to build the backend and I would design the frontend. From 2016-2017, I used this approach to build a SaaS product, but it ran into technical hurdles. I felt frustrated because I probably could have designed a better product if only I knew how to architect the backend.

I essentially spent all of 2018 learning backend development. I had the benefit of having all this free time on my hands from building AudienceOps, which ran itself in many ways. I took courses, worked with coaches, and did some practice projects. By the end of the year, I was able to build a very simple product. In January 2019, I started building ProcessKit. I spent six months building the first version and then later, I hired a developer.

What kind of advice would you give to aspiring entrepreneurs?

There are a lot of different paths that can work for people. One path that a lot of people suggest is the stair-stepping approach. Start with something very small. If you're already a developer, instead of building a whole SaaS, you can just build a WordPress plugin.

There's also value in the opposite direction. I started with consulting first. Charging more for fewer clients can give you more space and bandwidth to explore other products.

Learning to code and building something yourself is not for everyone. It can help to either partner with a technical co-founder or if you have the funding, to hire someone. That's not cheap, but it doesn't have to be outrageously expensive either. I'm working with a developer now in India. It still costs money to pay for full time work for over a year. But it's not the same as hiring someone in the U.S.

What would you recommend for customer acquisition?

Everyone tackles this a little differently. My recommendation is to go with the inroads you already have. The hardest part is getting customers and getting traffic. Whatever you can do to shortcut that, use it. For several years, I've been talking and teaching about productized services. I have a course about productized services, and I built an audience on my email list who tune into my podcast and read my stuff. Most of those people are freelancers, agencies, and consultants. It just made sense to try to build a product aimed at them. That was my go-to group of people to get the very first users. The harder part after that is growing traffic beyond my audience. That's been primarily through content, which we're doing now.

What's the biggest challenge about building a SaaS product?

I've done productized services, I've done WordPress plugins and I've done WordPress themes, and I've done freelancing and services. SaaS is definitely the hardest out of all of those by far.

The length of time it takes to build and then roll something out, and then just having to deal with that length of time is very difficult. The challenging thing is that you could spend a whole year or more on a product and if you haven't quite nailed product market fit, it's not that it'll be completely wasted, but it will be a lot more difficult and it will grow a lot slower. If you're solving the right problem for a market that is growing and that is actively searching for that problem, things click and move a lot faster.

Any final advice for SaaS-preneurs?

Everything is harder when you're building something alone and not getting feedback and constructive criticism from other people doing the same thing.

I'm active in online communities, and I'm in a couple of small mastermind groups. Before COVID, we used to meet up twice a year and go skiing and talk about our businesses. That kind of thing can be really important.

If you're brand new to startups, it's very easy to be attracted to the VC path. That's one way to go if you want to try to build the next Airbnb. But know that there is a whole world of other startups that are bootstrapping their businesses. Companies raise millions of dollars in VC, but then they feel pressure to work 100 hour weeks and make it work. I prefer having a family, having fun, and taking on interesting work.

TAKEAWAYS

- When it comes to customer acquisition, go with the inroads you already have. Where do you have influence and a voice?
- Nailing product-market ASAP is critical.
- A productized service model of SaaS means you can have fewer, higher-paying customers.
- Community is key. Make sure you have people who can give you feedback and constructive criticism.

Doss Church

Title: Founder & Chief Development Officer, Galaxy Digital

Value proposition: Helps organizations manage and engage their volunteer bases

Industry: Volunteer management

Keywords: Customer acquisition, metrics, mindset

What is Galaxy Digital?

We build simple technology that's designed to connect people, organizations, and resources specifically for the purpose of bettering communities through volunteerism. The technology itself is volunteer management and engagement software for any organization that has a volunteer base they need to manage.

How did you identify this as a problem?

I started the company in 2009. I had developed a social networking platform in a previous company, and wanted to use it as a platform for product development. I began looking for a product that we could develop and put the whole company behind. That product didn't become clear until about a year later when we met United Way, a network of non-profit fundraising affiliates. The global organization that manages United Way had just announced that they all needed to do a better job of managing and engaging their volunteers because those volunteers were their future donors. After a volunteer would come into their office, United Way would connect them to one of their agencies and then they would have no idea what happened to that volunteer after they left the building.

Oftentimes, volunteer management software was an afterthought in a much larger system. United Way might be happy with the functionality of donor management, but they were never happy with the volunteer management side of the software.

Is this your first SaaS?

No. My prior startup was called Livekite, which was a social network that allowed church groups (small groups, service groups, music groups, etc.) to connect, share, and meet online for free. I raised a little over $100k from Friends and Family (and myself) and another $160k from a high net worth investor. I built and launched the social network in 2007. The 2008 financial crisis plus the explosion of Facebook killed the dream but, thankfully, the idea for Galaxy came to me from the ashes of Livekite. So it wasn't a true loss, just a stepping stone – as most of these things are.

What's been the biggest surprise about starting SaaS companies?

I tend to dream things up, and I am either driven enough or naive enough to believe that I can pull them off. I've had ideas for businesses, and it has never occurred to me that I couldn't do it. I would raise the money that needed to be raised. I would make all the connections that needed to be made. I would recruit the people that needed to be recruited. I loved building the team. When I got to about 10 people, I realized I was overwhelmed. I really like creating things, but I don't like to manage people. I am very much a people person, but I don't love the operation side. That was a surprise to me. I thought I wanted to oversee this large company and be the CEO and be the one in the middle kind of directing everything.

Fortunately, I was able to pass the CEO title to a mentor of mine who was active in the company from early on. He now runs the day to day. I get to build my own little empire within an empire, as I develop new alliances and partnerships for Galaxy that allow me to stay involved in product development. The real joy for me in my new role is that I get to stay involved in product development, marketing, branding, and sales. Being able to have my hands in all of these areas of the business without having to manage 30 people is what I love the most.

What is the #1 mistake you see SaaS founders make?

The "if you build it, they will come" mentality. A lot of founders that I encounter tend to come from a marketing or creative background. On the marketing side, it's easy to think, *We're going to come up with this incredible branding and we're going to put it out there on all the channels, and it's just going to take off.*

We went heavy into direct sales, which tends to get lost on other founders. That has enabled us to grow consistently every year at a predictable pace. That's kept us from exploding, but also given us numbers that we can give to our board that are actually realistic. We can always say, "We did this many phone calls, we do this much outreach, and we get this much back."

It's much more complicated than creating beautiful branding or doing great SEO. As a result, entrepreneurs who get into SaaS for the first time can come out with really unrealistic projections.

What metrics do you focus on?

Obviously there are new sales. You can break that into a couple of categories. There could be new direct sales – outbound – and then new online sales – inbound. You want to grow 20-25% year over year with your new sales. Your recurring sales should continue to build at a good pace, and you should track cancellations. This year, we want to lose less than 8%.

Then you want to look at traffic to your website and conversions on your website. What kind of conversions are you getting? What's your highest conversion percentage on your website for requesting demos? What's the percentage of folks who request demos that are then converting and choosing to purchase?

In summary, watch new and recurring sales, customer attrition, customer satisfaction (via net promoter score), and inbound traffic to your website. Determine the quality of your web traffic by monitoring your conversion rate to demos and then to actual sales closes.

What are three qualities it takes for an entrepreneur to succeed?

　I use the word naivete, because it can be really helpful to be naive. It can be helpful to not know what you're getting yourself into. At the same time, it wasn't too long after we got the company going that I realized, *This is a lot harder than I thought it was*. It takes a tremendous amount of courage. I've worked harder than I've ever worked before. I want to say creativity is super important, but it's not necessarily required. It may be more just commitment to the vision. That's what keeps you going when you're crossing the chasm.

TAKEAWAYS

- "If you build it, they will come" does not typically apply to SaaS. Consider going heavy into direct sales.

- Metrics to focus on: new and recurring sales, customer attrition, customer satisfaction (via net promoter score), and inbound traffic to your website.

- It can be helpful not to know what you're getting yourself into.

Taylor Cavanah

Title: Founder & CEO, PetDesk

Value proposition: Helps pet owners better engage with their pet health through a deeper relationship with veterinarians/pet care providers

Industry: Pet care

Keywords: Chicken or the egg, co-founder, mindset, work-life balance

What is PetDesk?

　PetDesk is an app to help pet parents better engage with their pets' health through their relationship with their veterinarian or pet care providers. What that looks like is a platform for managing communications, including appointment and health service reminders. Veterinarians pay us for the reminder services to get people back in.

Is this your first SaaS app?

No. A number of years ago, we were trying to build a better Foursquare. But we failed at launch. We launched a 10-by-10 booth next to Foursquare when they had a Pepsi-sponsored pavilion and $40 million in funding. After nine months, we realized we were failing. My wife's uncle, who is a retired veterinarian, told us that we needed to build a pet service app and bring it to veterinarians. I remember looking at my dog Molly Sue, who was missing a paw and her eyebrows. She was keeping me sane through this crazy roller coaster ride and I wasn't even taking care of her. We realized that we could solve this problem, and that there was no existing technology in this space. It was a no-brainer.

We didn't want to build an app for consumers and then monetize it. Instead we decided to build software for local businesses that worked with the consumers. The local businesses would pay us for the tool that we provide, and later, we'd be able to monetize the relationship with consumers.

With our original app that we built – the tool similar to Foursquare – we would go into restaurants with our app, but no one was about to pay us for a tool when we only had around 2,000 users.

I heard somebody once say that as an entrepreneur you should never complain about having a "chicken or the egg" problem. That's why you're an entrepreneur. You have to find a chicken or the egg problem and you have to be the one to solve it.

On a mental and emotional level, what was it like to pivot to an entirely new product?

It was insane. My two other co-founders – Ken Tsui and Aaron Bannister – and I talk about how we got emotionally dead inside. The highs were so high and the lows were so low that the only way for us to cope was to not have any emotions. You can talk to our wives, and they would say the same thing. The worst possible thing you can do in your 30's is to work all the time, completely stop doing exercise, and not pay attention to your emotions because they will eat you from the inside out.

What I would say to early founders is to make sure you take care of yourself. But almost nobody will actually listen to that, because when you're in it, it doesn't matter.

What advice can you give to founders?

Listen to your friends. I had a friend who knew the founders and the people over at Foursquare and he knew that what we were initially doing was not going to work. He said it in very nice ways, but I did not listen to him or anyone else who told me it was a bad idea. You shouldn't listen to just one person, but if enough people are telling you something, then pay attention. Make sure that you're super self-aware and you're not letting your ego blind you to doing what's right.

Don't compare yourself to success stories. I think this fallacy is finally disappearing, but the "overnight success story" just isn't true. It takes seven to 10 years to go and do something. You're not a failure if you've failed. You're only a failure when you just stop trying something new. There's a direct correlation between failure and learning. I'm a trained physicist and that's how science works. You just fail a whole bunch of times until you succeed, and you learn from all those failures. Besides, failing fast means that you still have the energy and the money to go and find other opportunities, if necessary.

Take everything with a grain of salt. Remember that there's selection bias in any piece of advice given from personal experience. Someone might think they know why they were successful, but there's also luck involved.

What was it like to start a company with your friends?

This is always the hardest part. I mentor a lot of early founders and they always want to know how to find a CTO. I'm like, "I can't tell you, because my two best friends just happen to be tech guys." That being said, I think the best possible way you can meet a tech co-founder is by working in a tech company. If you're still in school, hang out with all the engineers. Surround yourself with the type of people that you want to meet.

Of course, we've all heard the stories where friends are no longer friends because they started a business together and it didn't work out. But that obviously hasn't been the case for me.

Ken and I had already worked together for six or seven years at a nanotech startup.

We knew how to work with each other. It also helped that we played no limit hold 'em together. We're very competitive, able to really talk to each other and get in each other's faces and argue. But we always come up with a solution. Having lived with Aaron, we knew each other very well. You can't be a roommate with somebody without being a little annoyed about what they do or don't. But it was an easy roommate relationship, so I thought we might work together well as founders. I was right.

I'm amazed at solo founders who become successful and get through all of this without somebody else. I couldn't have done it without them, not just from the technical side of it, but from being able to talk to someone about what was really going on. There are certain things that only other CEO founders will understand. You won't be able to bring certain things to friends, or family, or your spouse.

I'm actually a part of a CEO group here in San Diego, where we get together every two to three months and talk about not only strategy and tactical stuff, but about the tough side of it.

You launched in 2014. Where do you find yourself now?

We've now raised about $16 million through our Series B. We've got about 90 employees, over $10 million ARR and 2,500 locations across the US and Canada.

TAKEAWAYS

- Never complain about a "chicken or the egg" problem. Your job is to find a chicken or the egg problem and solve it.
- Take care of yourself.
- If enough people you trust are telling you something is a bad idea, pay attention. Is your ego blinding you?
- Failure is just another part of learning.

Jane Portman

Title: Co-founder, Userlist
Value proposition: Email marketing automation for SaaS companies
Industry: Email marketing automation
Keywords: Co-founder, female founder, mindset, prioritization

What is Userlist?

Userlist is an email automation tool for SaaS companies. It helps you onboard and engage your users based on what they do and what they don't do, as well as nurture your marketing leads. Our secret sauce is SaaS-specific features, like in-app notifications and full support for company accounts.

How did you identify this as a need in the market?

Four years ago, I was running another SaaS product called Tiny Reminder. At the time, I couldn't find a tool to help me manage my users and send them behavior-based stuff. Once I sold Tiny Reminder, the new idea was immediately on the table. We got together as a team of co-founders and started in the fall of 2017.

What was Tiny Reminder?

It was a small productivity tool. My big mistake with that product was that it was useful, but it didn't have a clear target audience or use case.

With Userlist, we have settled on serving SaaS founders like ourselves from day one. That's part of our company ethos – to be helping people who are starting out and chasing their SaaS dream.

You've been both a solo founder and a co-founder. What would you say about the pros/cons of each approach?

Of course, there are drawbacks and benefits for each approach. If you're a solo founder, you can call the shots, and be your own boss to a certain extent. But it's much more exciting and enjoyable on a daily basis to have someone else who cares about the business as much as you do, and to share the ups and the downs of running a business.

The whole thing is about the journey, anyway. It's not like you can launch something and reap the benefits and then retire in two months. You've got to enjoy yourself in the process. That means setting up a comfortable working environment for yourself and your team, and making sure you share goals, values, and a vision.

Why is running a business rewarding for you?

One of my joys in life as a product person is crafting a tool that's genuinely useful to other people, but also matches my design standards and the ideas of what a good tool should look like. Bringing that to life is highly rewarding, even when we have limited resources and have to strictly prioritize where those resources have to be spent. As a consultant, you never get that experience. You rarely get to follow along with implementation, let alone gain creative control over the projects.

Owning something useful and then watching it grow and bring value to people is rewarding for me. That's at the top of my Maslow pyramid.

How can SaaS founders learn to prioritize allocation of resources?

If you eat less, you're going to lose weight. But it's really hard to follow through on that. It's the same with priorities in a startup. As a founder, you're bombarded daily with new information, new opportunities, new feature requests. You also get partnership ideas, different marketing ideas. Ideas are jumping out from every corner. Deciding what's important and sticking to it is challenging. But if you do that, it will bring you more success than if you try everything and "die by a thousand paper cuts."

You're a mom of three. How do you balance life as a mom with being a founder?

I don't have a silver bullet solution to that, except for getting as much help as you can. I couldn't have gotten to where I am today without the help of babysitters and parents helping to drive the kids around.

For me, being a business person and a mom is easier than just being a mom alone. Running a business helps me keep my mind active. With my first child, I went on a proper maternity leave and spent three months not working. It was fun, but I didn't last long. With the other two kids, I didn't take that much time off. I still kept working, just at a comfortable pace. It was enjoyable to watch my kids grow, and also watch the business grow.

Any final advice you'd give to founders?

Don't get stuck in a certain mindset. For example, there is this bootstrapper mindset where you decide that you do things small, stay small, and never hire help. And then there is the VC route, where you get millions of funding and burn it off quickly. But there's balance to be found. You shouldn't be stuck in one way or the other. Don't burn everything off for the fancy offices, but don't try to do everything alone either – especially over a long period of time – because you'll be outpaced and outnumbered by your competitors.

What do you see in the future for Userlist?

This year, we are scaling up our marketing team. We are also excited to extend our usual feature set into a couple of new directions, including the marketing feature set. So it will become an all-in-one solution for SaaS companies.

We've got some of the hardest work behind us. We've grown authority to the place where we're at the table when the big conversations are happening. We're on top of the mind when people talk about behavior-based email. That's an exciting place to be. We want to escalate that, grow, and improve.

TAKEAWAYS

- Be cautious about trying every new idea that comes your way.
- You can strike a balance between different approaches to SaaS– for example, between bootstrapping and raising VC funding.
- Learn to enjoy the journey. That means creating a comfortable working environment and creating a healthy team culture.

Helena Ronis

Title: Co-founder & CEO, AllFactors

Value proposition: Reimagining web marketing analytics to be insight driven instead of vanity.

Industry: Marketing Analytics

Keywords: Customer acquisition, female founder, prioritization, mindset, MVP

What is AllFactors?

AllFactors is a web marketing analytics software that solves the frustrations that founders and marketers experience when they use Google Analytics. We built a software tool that automatically configures itself on a website to display actions and user engagement.

We also focus on insight-driven reports instead of vanity metrics. We show granular attribution, conversion paths, and funnels, as well as activation of data through integration with the entire marketing, sales and revenue stack – including Salesforce, Hubspot, Marketo, Stripe, and everything in between.

How did you identify this as a problem?

I've been working on tech products since 2012. I've always had that problem with marketing where I did not have the full view of what actions my users were taking on my website. That made it hard to make data-driven decisions.

This problem came to a head last year when I was experiencing this specific frustration with another business I had built, a product that converted blog posts into podcasts. You could see how many people listened to your embedded audio player, but if only 10-20% ended up converting to listeners and 80-90% read, you didn't know how much they read or if they read at all. When we tried to figure out how to solve that with existing tools like Google Analytics, configuration took too much time.

When you have a pain point that's also a pain point for similar customers, that's a pattern. You then have a great opportunity on your hands.

What are the other lessons that you carried over from your previous businesses into AllFactors?

When you start working on a new product, the first step is to do research before you begin building anything. Learn to understand your ideal customer profile, or ICP. Have conversations and take notes. Be relentless about learning the space and the pains, and you'll start connecting the dots in understanding how to build the best solution.

Do not build for the sake of building. Build for the sake of solving problems.

How are you finding customers?

I join every possible online community for people in my target market. I explore the communities and jump in with a few questions. In this case, I ask, "What are your frustrations with Google Analytics? What do you use right now to get insights out of your marketing so you can improve your business?" This way, I collect feedback *and* leads. LinkedIn has also been a great place to find customers.

What's it been like to be a female founder?

Many women experience frustration around being underestimated when you fundraise and when you pitch to investors. Another thing women often experience is frustration in finding a co-founder. Both of those things can definitely be overcome with hustle, work, and perseverance.

Planning is the number one key for any founder. In fundraising, the more you can execute, the higher your chances are that the investor is going to move faster and invest because it's really about the speed of getting the money. Sometimes they need to see your progress for a few months and then make a decision, That's fine because we should be building a solid product and company regardless of fundraising.

When a female founder experiences fundraising challenges, it's usually because she's underestimated. She didn't come from an Ivy League school. She didn't work at a company like Facebook or Google. She didn't have a previous exit or some big win. Of course, this applies to all founders. But for female founders, it's extra challenging because there's still a "Boys Club" mentality.

Female founders can overcome this with solid and relentless startup execution, as well as creating a relevant conversation with investors when fundraising.

What would you say about building a product?

To create your MVP, you don't need sophisticated architecture. You just need good planning. You can validate wireframes before anything is built. In the beginning, the founder and CEO is a glorified product manager. You need to talk to your Ideal Customer Profile and ask them questions around the pain and problem.

Having a lot of empathy for your prospects and customers is key. I really like the framework of Jobs to Be Done where you basically think about what job your product does for your customer.

Any final advice?

If you don't prioritize, you waste time. You can also lose motivation and energy. That's the last thing you want as a founder. When looking at your daily tasks, ask yourself, *What's really critical for this* phase of my startup? Which tasks will really move the needle and take us to the next step?

TAKEAWAYS

- Join online communities where your ideal customers hang out. Ask questions.
- Remember that in the beginning, a founder is really a glorified product manager.
- A lack of prioritization can sap your energy and motivation.

#63

Michael Anderson

Title: CTO, Blueprint Title

Value proposition: Increases speed, transparency, and cost-savings for title insurance

Industry: Real estate

Keywords: Company culture, iteration, mindset

What is Blueprint Title?

We are trying to bring modern technology access and a modern approach to title insurance. We work with real estate investors, loan officers doing refinance, flippers, and folks that are thinking about residential real estate as assets.

The market for title insurance and escrow and the closing process are still very paper-based and obviously very regulated...and different from state to state and even county to county. There are a lot of challenges there, including a pretty slow pace.

At Blueprint Title, we're bringing a startup mentality to the industry. We're able to bring a lot of transparency, more speed, and cost savings to the process.

How did you come on to Blueprint?

I came on as the CTO in February of 2020. It was a heck of a time to change careers. Previous to Blueprint, I founded a couple of companies associated with SaaS.

What was your previous experience in SaaS?

I had founded a company called Game West, a SaaS business for gaming influencers on YouTube to monetize their fan bases through fan clubs and subscription programs. The founder of Blueprint Title, Steve, also had a gaming company. The two of us were on our gaming island here in town, and none of the other folks in the ecosystem knew what the heck we were. There are a lot of healthcare-related companies with all of the universities and hospitals here in Nashville, but not a lot of gaming companies.

We got to know each other really well through that and built trust and rapport, and supported each other. When the opportunity came to work with Blueprint, I was able to bring those credentials in technology and team-building, and pick up the real estate side.

What were some of the most important lessons you brought from your previous experience in SaaS?

It's really easy for me to want to engineer my way out of a problem and throw in a bunch of features, but maybe it's not a product problem. Maybe it's a marketing problem, a sales problem, an efficiency problem, or a product market fit problem. Having done that the wrong way multiple times, I now build hypotheses and validate them or invalidate them by gathering information. It sounds pretty simple, but that product process is critical.

With Blueprint, I'm able to step back and go, "This isn't my baby." I'm passionate about it, but there's a distance that allows me to apply that process in a very direct way without feeling good or bad about it.

It's been challenging but rewarding to build the DNA of building iterative SaaS software in this company. The folks that work at Blueprint are amazing at getting a real estate transaction to go from contract to close, but they had no idea what QA meant or a staging server was. We've seen a significant cultural transformation, going from a services company that has software to a tech-enabled services business with a heavy SaaS component. But it's really rewarding, for example, to see escrow officers testing software and giving feedback on product enhancements.

How do you talk about software in a way that makes sense to people outside your industry?

It takes a lot of setting your own ego aside. Maybe you're an expert at building software, building sites, or running a JIRA process or building a team. But they're an expert at something else; in this case, closing real estate and dealing with all the random, crazy things that can come with that.

There's a lot of empathy required. Take the time to understand people's businesses and the nuances of what you're building and the difficulties of your customers.

The other part goes back to cultural transformation. As people start picking up iterative software, they think it's cool to be part of the process. But before they think that, you've got to win them over and help them understand why it's going to be valuable to them.

What's one of the #1 mistakes you see SaaS founders make?

You can get so passionate about what it is you came up with initially, but one thing I talk about a lot is "strong opinions held loosely."

I don't want to waste time building something that nobody wants. At the same time, you might have a great idea that nobody believes in yet. That story exists, but I think it's the anomaly.

Talking to people gives you so much insight. Be willing to adjust your idea based on feedback. That will transform your ability to make an impact on people's lives with software. Instead of jumping into making something, ask questions and be willing to adjust based on the data you're getting. You'll come up with something even better than you thought you had in the first place.

TAKEAWAYS

- If you've got a problem, don't assume it's a product problem. It could be a problem with your sales, marketing, product/market fit, or something else. Build a hypothesis, gather information, and test.

- Empathy is key–whether you're talking to people on your team, your customers, or contractors.

- Ask questions, gather data, and be willing to adjust your original ideas...before building.

#64

Omri Dekalo

Title: Co-founder & CEO, Ubeya

Value proposition: Workforce management for the gig economy

Industry: Human resources

Keywords: Development, hiring, mindset, prioritization, QA

What is the elevator pitch for Ubeya?

In 2017 we started Ubeya, the place for on-demand employees to work and find jobs.

Today, we're serving hundreds of businesses all over the world, helping them manage their employees. We've recently added the option to find employees through the platform, and to extend your existing database of employees by joint venturing with local agencies in your region. We've raised $5 million from a couple of VC's here in Israel and from Cornerstone OnDemand, a publicly traded company in the States in the HR tech space.

What is your professional background, Omri?

I spent five years at the Intelligence Corps in Israel, the IDF. When you turn 18 in Israel, you go to the Army for three years. I stayed for two more years as an officer. In the IDF, you learn that there is nothing that you cannot achieve. You leave there with the idea that anything is possible; you just need a way to do it.

After the military, I studied computer science and accounting at Tel Aviv university. I worked as a consultant at Deloitte and Ernst and Young and later moved to New York to work for Palantir. I then started my first startup, Proonto, a marketplace for online salespeople. After a few successful years I started Ubeya.

What's one of the most important lessons you've learned about running a SaaS?

All of your developers should be full stack developers. In the beginning, we thought that dividing front-end and back-end developers would be the right kind of approach. Very quickly, we understood that when you're a small startup, you cannot afford to separate the two, because then you need another person to manage the two operations. You need one full spec developer that takes on ownership of the whole thing.

The second important thing is that QA should be done by the full stack developer that is taking ownership of the product, so that they can make sure that everything was solved on his or her shift. The third thing is that DevOps should be done internally.

Up until recently, I was doing the big client sales myself. This was the only way for me to crystallize our clients' pain points, and to see those pain points reflected in the product.

What kinds of lessons did you take from your first SaaS company, Proonto, into Ubeya?

Focus. You'll have new opportunities all the time, options to grow, new partnerships, people you can hire, and new products that you can build. But if you don't focus on the right thing, you won't be able to succeed.

What's one of the most common mistakes you see SaaS founders make?

The first mistake is low-budget hiring or hiring people that are not very good. The next mistake is spending money on things that don't really make a difference, like swag and games. You might make this mistake in the beginning, but it's recoverable.

Finally, you've got to have product/market fit, a solution that fits the market and that's good for the clients. When you're there, then you can invest in marketing and bring in more leads.

What's the biggest challenge you've faced in starting a SaaS?

The biggest challenge is yourself. There are so many situations when you suddenly don't believe in yourself. Even people with a lot of self-confidence experience this. There are times that you're doing something that no one else is doing and you totally believe that this is going to be a game-changer in your life and your employees' lives. But at the end of the day, you go home and ask yourself, *what the f**k am I doing now?*

I think the biggest challenge is that you need to pump yourself up and find ways to know that you're doing the right thing. You need a supportive family. You need supportive friends and supportive employees.

Any other advice or insights you'd want to give to potential founders?

Prototype a lot of things. Throw things out there. Even if they're not working behind the scenes, it helps to see the traction. You don't need to build everything in order to test it out.

TAKEAWAYS

- You need at least one full-stack developer that takes ownership of the product and does QA.
- Take charge of relationships with large accounts. That will help you, as the founder, effectively crystallize and solve client pain points.
- Low-budget hiring will only hurt you in the long run.
- You need to know how to encourage yourself and continue to believe that you're doing the right thing by starting the business.
- Prototyping new ideas – without building – can be a useful learning exercise.

#65

Srikrishnan Ganesan

Title: Founder, Rocketlane

Value proposition: Accelerates customer onboarding & implementation projects

Industry: Customer success, Professional services

Keywords: Customer acquisition, MVP

What is Rocketlane?

Today, you have tools for CRM, for salespeople, support tools, and customer success. But when it comes to your customer onboarding, companies usually use a hodgepodge of generic tools. There's no specialized product that helps you collaborate with your customer in that journey.

That leads to a lot of pain and a suboptimal experience for the customer. It's not a customer-centric experience and ends up causing delays in projects or abandoned projects, and bad implementations. That's what we are trying to solve with Rocketlane. Rocketlane streamlines the customer journey and unifies communication, collaboration, and project management into one experience.

Are you a first-time founder?

Rocketlane is my second startup. The previous one was called Konotor, which I ran from 2012-2015. Konotor was acquired by a company called Freshworks in 2015, but we continued building the product. With all that we learned from 2012-2019, we wanted to use our learnings to build a new startup. In April 2020, we started Rocketlane.

How are you building your MVP?

We're taking a slightly different approach to our MVP. Because we're building a unified experience, we need to go to market with something more complete. We're taking time to build the product and validate it along the way, showing it to customers at every stage. We decided that we're going to go with a beautiful, full-featured product at launch.

We launched on June 23, 2021, and we've been growing super fast since then.

How do you plan to approach customer acquisition?

We've started a community for customer onboarding and customer success leaders to discuss problems and learnings. So we already have a community of people who know about us and can give us a shot. We have over 750 people all over the world, with local chapters in different cities.

Once we launch, we will also do ads to acquire customers from different places, as well as cold outreach. We have an outbound motion with SDRs and AEs, and an inbound motion fueled by ads and popular software listing sites.

What would you tell a founder who wants to build a community?

In my previous venture, we realized that we were focused more on our product than how relevant the problem was. So this time, we focused the community on the problem.

That strategy isn't going to work for everyone. If you are entering a market where there are already communities for the specific problem you're solving, then adding one more community is not going to help anyone. In those cases, you may want to go and participate in the most active community by serving your customer persona, being present, trying to be helpful, and making connections.

What are some of the other lessons you learned from your previous startup?

Konotor provided a messaging experience inside other people's mobile apps. For example, the 1-800 Flowers mobile app could use us, and when a user would try to reach out to support, there would be a chat feature. Most of the big startups in India were using our product, and we were seeing some success outside of India in Southeast Asia. But Europe and the US were still very nascent.

What we later figured is that mobile apps weren't necessarily as dominant a medium for as many brands in the U.S. as they were in India. The reality was that in 2014-2015, most people were still figuring out how to build a successful app. They were at a stage where they weren't bothered about great customer engagement and great support experiences inside that app. We were sort of ahead of the market.

The biggest lesson is to chase momentum. In 2017, we pivoted after the acquisition and relaunched our product called Freshchat, for web and mobile. This time we had seen that the players who were building a modern messaging experience for the web had faster growth than those who were focused only on mobile.

Once we did that, we saw that there was latent demand for a credible, modern, and mature web chat product. The product was beating our internal records of reaching various new revenue milestones in the company.

We knew that if we were going to do another venture, it was going to be something where we understood how much momentum there was.

Any advice on how to sell a product in a B2B context?

If you are selling outbound or top-down, understanding ROI is key. If you can't sell executives on business outcomes, then it's not going to be a super appealing product.

What's the best advice anyone has given you?

Make sure you're climbing the right peak before you start climbing. Is the problem high priority? Is there a big enough market? Are there other competitors doing well? If so, that's actually a good thing. So these are some of the signals to look at….and then start building!

TAKEAWAYS

- Customer acquisition strategy: Build a community that focuses on the problem you're solving.

- Chase momentum! Make sure the problem you're solving is high priority, and that there's a large enough market.

Moritz Dausinger

Title: Founder & CEO, Refiner

Value proposition: Provide actionable customer feedback to SaaS companies through inb-app microsurveys

Industry: Customer experience

Keywords: Bootstrapping, customer acquisition, customer feedback, fundraising, MVP

What is Refiner?

We help our customers – SaaS startups with traction and scale-ups – to better understand who their users are, what they think, and how they can help them to succeed with their product. We do this with microsurveys, which can be embedded into their product.

If you look at the customer surveys market, you have either very generic tools like Typeform or very specialized solutions which focus on one single use case – tracking customer satisfaction, for example.

Refiner is unique in that our solution was built from the ground up with the needs of modern SaaS companies in mind. We support different use cases that are all highly relevant for revenue and product teams alike. You can, for example, have an NPS survey running, asking your users how likely they are to recommend your product. But you can also do surveys that are targeted to product management or feature research.

How did you identify this as a problem?

I've built a couple of SaaS companies before. Refiner is my fourth startup. With the three before, I went through an acquihire and two acquisitions.

For the last venture, Docparser.com, we needed a tool like Refiner. What we wanted to do is ask some simple questions to all our new sign-ups while they were using the product. We wanted to use those questions to better qualify new signups. But there wasn't a tool that did exactly what I wanted it to do. I had the choice to either go with a very generic service software, or go with a tool built for NPS surveys for example. But I would need to tweak this tool in a way that it was not supposed to be used.

This is when Refiner was born. Refiner is a very flexible and powerful Microsurvey tool built for different use cases, but really specifically built for SaaS. By that I mean your user base is always synchronized with our tool. You can target specific users at a certain point in their journey. And we make sure that survey responses are synchronized in real time with your other tools.

Our sweet spots are data-driven SaaS companies who are scaling up and want to better understand their customer experience.

How have you learned to acquire customers in the SaaS space?

Our ultimate goal is always to rank organically in search engines through content. But whenever we can't do that because it's too competitive, we target potential customers with Google ads for specific search terms.

Another channel would be comparison platforms like Capterra, where people go to compare different software solutions. This strategy works especially well if you're in a very crowded category, like we are. I had the opposite sort of situation with my previous startups, which were more niche. With those startups, we faced the problem of creating awareness around the problem.

Our biggest challenge right now is to increase the top of the funnel and get more trial users. Once users are testing our product they usually love it and our conversion rates look good.

What lessons did you learn from running your previous companies that you have carried into Refiner?

The biggest mantra for us is iteration. We always try to break down big ideas and start small. Once we validate an idea, we use our learnings to build on top of that.

How do you build a great MVP?

There are different definitions of an MVP. Some people say, for example, just keep it scrappy, build something with a no code tool, and it doesn't matter if it's not that beautiful. My approach is a little bit different.

We always want to provide a great user experience, even if it's an early MVP. We prefer developing less features than our competitors, but we make sure that the features we develop provide a lot of value and are well executed. There are people who don't care if a product is ugly and a little bit buggy, as long as it does the job. But that's not how we operate at Refiner. I think most people out there value quality products over scrappy hacks.

Where do many SaaS products go wrong, in terms of user experience?

A lot of companies seem to want to cater to a large market right from the beginning. Basically, they want to do everything and in the end, they don't do anything really well. With Refiner, we have a specific target market – data-driven SaaS companies – and we want to become the best tool in this specific target market first.

What are some of the personality traits or qualities you think are needed for a SaaS founder?

I think my competitive advantage has always been that I can wear different hats. Depending on the stage of your company, different skills are needed. I'm definitely not the best developer in the world, but I was able to develop the first version of Refiner. Now that the company is scaling up, hiring and management has become a much more important skill. The bottom line is that you need to be good at many different things and adapt along the way.

Is there any advice you'd give about funding?

I admire people who can build a billion dollar company by raising funds from VCs and scaling up the team really fast. But the traditional Silicon Valley way of building a startup is not the only option available these days. Bootstrapping a SaaS company to profitability or getting funded by alternative funds are other viable options. At Refiner, we raised money from Earnest Capital, which gives us a lot of optionality further along the way.

TAKEAWAYS

- If you're in a crowded space, consider marketing your product on a comparison platform like Capterra.
- Niching down means you can offer a better user experience.
- Founders need to be able to adapt and shift roles.

Preetam Nath

Title: Co-founder & CEO, DelightChat
Value proposition: Customer support tailor-made for E-commerce
Industry: Customer support
Keywords: Customer discovery, distribution, validation

What is DelightChat?

DelightChat is customer support software for e-commerce brands.

Customer support used to be only over email, but there's a new move towards brands talking to their customers over chat mediums like Instagram DM's, WhatsApp, and Facebook Messenger. We are building a chat-first tool, which is much simpler to use than a traditional help desk tool.

Secondly, a lot of the larger help desk tools (like Zendesk) have gone upmarket. They have a lot of features, but they are very expensive for smaller brands. We're keeping the simplicity of the Instagram or Facebook Messenger interface while offering the same powerful functionality of industry leaders at a price point that medium-sized brands can afford.

How did you identify this as a problem?

Support is one of the oldest problems in any industry. Communication between a customer and seller is based around the question, *Can I trust you?* In other words, *Does the product do what I want it to do?*

If it doesn't, then the customer must return to the seller – even in the offline world. The problem hasn't changed, but the interaction has.

That's what we are capitalizing on. There are a lot of ideas that are based on new problems which may or may not exist. We wanted to pick an idea that will 100% work. The question is, will the brand choose our software versus someone else's?

Tell me about your journey from student to founder.

I graduated from university in 2015 with a degree in engineering. I studied electronics and communication, which turned out to be useless. Even then, I knew I didn't want to wear uncomfortable pantsuits and go into an office at 10 AM, take a biscuit break at 11 AM, and then barely work after lunch. I started looking at startups while writing for online magazines. I eventually joined a marketing team, but when I was told that I needed an MBA to get a product management role, I said, "Screw this."

So I moved to Bangalore and helped a friend from college start a business by applying everything I learned in marketing. A few months later, I found my first job as a Product Management Associate at a very early-stage startup. I was isolating problems and figuring out if they were real and if they needed solving immediately. If they were high priority, then I would think through the smartest solution. I loved the process of asking the right questions and trying to determine what the right problem is. After working there for nine months, my learning curve started to plateau.

I was already working with restaurants, so I decided to build a product for the restaurant industry. One year of hustling and trying to push the market to buy my software, and it failed. I realized the market doesn't care what I sell to them. Instead, they need to tell me what they need. But it was a fun journey. I met some people who became co-founders and employees. When we realized there was no course correction, we decided to drink for a month and reminisce on our mistakes.

I came home to my parent's place in Hyderabad and spent the next three months studying everything I could find that was interesting. I knew that every business exists to make money, so I looked at the boom and bust cycles, and looked at why people invest and how some of them get rich. I was trying to understand more deeply where the previous ventures I had worked for went wrong.

Eventually, I joined Unacademy – a tech startup – as the first PM hire. I built their mobile app, their website, the first version of the revenue arm Unacademy Plus, internal dashboards for the support and sales teams...basically anything I could lay my hands on. We had this insane, unlimited roadmap of things we needed to do, because the company was growing 10X every six to eight months.

When I joined in 2017, there was already a unicorn from India called BYJU, which was bringing in $100 million in revenue. Turns out that we had something that these guys don't have, which was mind blowing distribution, mainly through YouTube.

I started asking, *What if I treated distribution as the product?* Once you have the audience, you just keep building things for them.

We know that DelightChat could fail. But if we do our marketing right and we build distribution channels correctly, then even if by some chance this product idea doesn't work, then we will still have an audience for which we can build more solutions.

What have you learned about getting validation from your audience?

We always ask, "What is it that we can create for e-commerce merchants that will make their life better? What are they asking questions about?"

In my first company, I learned that customers will often tell you, "Of course I want that solution." But what they really mean is, *I want what you're building because I want to support you, I'm a good person, and I don't want to make you feel bad.* That doesn't help me at all. That just makes my life harder.

So I went back to the same people and asked stronger, more confrontational questions like, "Here's an alternative solution that already exists in the market. Why aren't you using it?" They would respond, "That existing solution would work perfectly fine for me."

What I learned is that validation works on three levels. The highest level is when somebody is already doing something to solve a problem, such as using a tool. That's the highest level of validation. You don't need to ask them if this is a real problem.

The second level is if people are spending a lot of time manually to solve a problem, like maybe six to eight hours a week on a spreadsheet or even paying someone to do the grunt work every week.

The third level of validation is complaining about the problem. That's not really sufficient validation because if the problem is painful enough, you act on it.

What would you say is the biggest lesson you've learned throughout this journey?

I was always chasing this notion that I had to build something that turns into a unicorn, but that's just BS that VCs push. They want $500 million/year revenue, and that stopped me from building a real business for a long time. 99.9% of businesses solve everyday problems.

The reason for building a start-up evolved into wanting to build a business that helps others and wanting to live life on my own terms. I also want to share my learnings and failures in the hopes that others can build successful businesses. I built a business that made $30k per month and I found that the real cash was way better than trying to build a unicorn.

TAKEAWAYS

- Make sure you have proper validation. Would your customers be willing to pay for a solution, or do they just like complaining about a problem?
- Consider building a product for an "everyday problem" that's already been validated.

#68

Karen Frame

Title: Founder & CEO, Makeena

Value proposition: Rewards consumers for buying better while providing brands the data and insights they need to grow

Industry: Natural products

Keywords: Fundraising, pricing

What is Makeena?

We incentivize consumers to buy better through cash and rewards. We also provide healthy and eco-friendly brands the data they need to become more effective and efficient with their marketing dollars.

We don't care whether the user shops on Thrive Market, a brand's own website, Walmart, Piggly Wiggly, or Whole Foods. We just want the consumer to get rewarded for buying better.

How did you get started in this space?

I'm a lawyer and a CPA by trade, but this is my third startup in the natural products space. I was a vegan for 12 years, and my former husband was an organic farmer. My dad was a science professor at the University of Illinois, so I've been involved with technology since I was a little girl.

The other piece of my story is that my parents built a house on a lake across the street from a cornfield that was sprayed with pesticides every year. As a result, most everybody in my family is either sick or dead. I'm actually recovering from cancer surgery. So I'm super passionate about what we put in and on our bodies. And I'm not alone. 98% of consumers in the U.S. want transparency. They want to know what they're buying and also need those products to be affordable.

How do you balance having a social mission with making a profit?

We're not just building a hub with consumers and brands. We're a social impact, a triple bottom-line kind of company.

How do you describe that to an investor?

What I've learned is that you have to find the right kind of investor. Is it somebody who's interested in data, but doesn't give a hoot about social impact? Or is it the conscious capitalism crowd, who are maybe more interested in taking all of the plastic products out of the ocean?

The bottom line is that the investor needs to fall in love with the team and believe that you can execute on the vision.

The most important thing for SaaS founders to know is that you need to figure out your go-to market strategy – not just your paying customer, but also your investor.

What have you learned about pricing?

We've tried all sorts of things. We tried a single upfront payment, where brands are on the platform forever. That didn't feel good to us because we're continuing to work on the product without getting additional revenue from existing customers. Then we changed it to a monthly fee and that didn't feel good either. We gave some people some special concessions and then they didn't pay.

Then we had to change it to a launch fee plus a monthly fee so that we can recoup most of our costs upfront. If they decide six months in that they don't want to use the platform anymore, then I don't have tremendous heartburn if they want to come off.

As far as specific pricing goes, we look at the competition–such as Nielsen and Spins–and what they're charging for access to data. We know, for example, that the lowest level of data that you can buy from Spins in the natural product space is about $30k a year. So we're always going to be more effective and efficient than they are. Plus, we give consumer access to brands.

There's a science that goes into pricing, but it's also about talking to your customer.

In three words, describe what it takes to be a founder.

Knowing your space.

I was going to say the typical founder thing – "grit, tenacity, problem solving." No, you just got to know your space.

TAKEAWAYS

- Focus on investors that will be excited about what you're building, especially if you've got a social mission with your product.

- You may need to experiment with your pricing. Consider what the competition is doing and what works for you – and most importantly, talk to your customers.

Blaine Killen

Title: Co-founder & CEO, FitLift

Value proposition: The most accurate technology for strength training that maximizes performance while decreasing injury

Industry: Fitness

Keywords: Customer acquisition

What is FitLift?

Poor technique while training leads to 12 million sports injuries per year due to incorrect training technique, leaving a huge opportunity for a technology that corrects form. FitLift is a mobile application plus motion tracking wearable that gives real-time feedback and post training analysis to trainers, which allows them to be more effective than ever before. Now the trainer can maintain a safe distance from the athlete as they now have the ability to remotely confirm that their athletes are performing their routines correctly.

How did this become a problem that interested you?

In high school, I played golf and had aspirations to take it to a professional level but was also an engineer at heart. To understand how to get better, I would film my swing and draw lines on the video to better understand my hip rotation, velocities, and impact. These are things that the pros get tracked, but that aren't typically accessible to an amateur, or even college players.

Then I got into weight training after college and I couldn't get past certain plateaus in the gym. I thought, "I just need the same information. I need to know if I'm doing it correctly." I thought that a wearable might be a good solution, but there were no wearables that gave this data on the market.

I did some research and saw a $233 million opportunity in the college space for a very focused market just in the United States alone. I thought, *What if we help college trainers become super trainers through something that never existed?*

What are some pro's and con's of SaaS?

Things move very fast in SaaS, but they can also move very fast in the wrong direction. If you're in SaaS, you are expected to launch faster and meet customer needs faster than a traditional CD and box company.

In the old days, I could ship you a CD once a year, and then I have a whole year left before I have to respond to your worries as a customer. The advantage is that I have a lot more time to test things and develop new features. The disadvantage is that revenue is all cycled around when that CD comes out. So you get all of your revenue the first three months after launching, and then you have to use that three months' revenue for the full year.

In SaaS, I get revenue every month. Even if the customer only uses the product for a month, I still get paid. If they pay me next month and they don't use it at all, even better. The flip side is that in the SaaS world, because you can deploy and launch features every two weeks, your customers expect a lot more from you. And they are a lot more willing to go to other solutions.

If SaaS has these downsides, then why go SaaS?

My margin in SaaS is 85%. It costs me way less to acquire a customer. I can use web tools. I don't have to go to a supplier. I don't have to get a box, or write code on CD's. Comparatively, when Microsoft used to ship Office on CDs, their margins were only 45% after shipping.

Tell me about your first SaaS company, and what you learned from that experience.

As a freshman in college, I founded a company called Meeting Sprout. It basically did what Calendly does today. We got admitted into an incubator and got funded and learned a lot of lessons. The first lesson learned is to build a product, not a feature. First time founders often make this mistake as they try to build Facebook, because everyone likes to dream big. Instead, start with building something small at first that offers unique value.

What the market was really pushing us to do was build a platform that would allow any shop or facility to build an embedded calendar. But we didn't listen and that led to our eventual failure.

That was a big lesson—listen to your customers. If the market's pushing you in a direction, listen, because that's what keeps your business afloat, not your idea.

The second one is that you really have to have the talent. I programmed a lot in high school and it was something I'd done as a youth for fun. But I had never seen what a professional code base looks like. I never knew the business side of it. I never knew all the things you needed to make a software product succeed that were more than just writing code, which are all needed when starting a business.

Where did you gain that experience?

I worked for Microsoft OneDrive after college. I was fortunate enough to work with very talented people and still look up to my first boss I had while employed there. They taught me the processes and separate skill sets needed to successfully run a company and how to scale it, how to think on the business side, how to not just write features, but write malleable and changeable code.

How have you made sure that FitLift is something people really want?

When we first started, I put a website up with a mocked-up UI. I talked to my customers, and asked them, "If this was real, would you buy it?" That gave me great feedback and allowed us to co-develop it with our customers.

One of those big customers is Team DSM, which we've been partnered with for three years. They're one of the top three elite cycling clubs in the world and have over 160 combined wins a year. So they're very good. Every week we talk to their head strength training staff, we get feedback, and we iteratively build it with them. By mid-April (2021), our product will be on 58 of their athletes' wrists for use with weight training.

Our partnership with Team DSM was very fortunate, but it was honestly lucky and kind of a fluke. The more realistic story was with the University of Iowa. We've just had two devices arrive at their strength training department, and that was more of a "warm lead." We reached out to them and basically said, "We'll send you two free devices and set up two free accounts. It will take 15 minutes of your time, that's it." So they agreed. At the end of the day, customer acquisition is often about being bold. We even went and stood in front gyms looking for customers. I was asked to leave some of the time, but that's what you have to do. That's how you get customers at the beginning when you're nobody and you've got to operate lean.

What's the #1 advice you'd give to somebody who wants to start a SaaS?

I'll share two things: one practical, one inspirational.

First, if you can avoid it, don't try to do cloud at the beginning. There are a lot of costs that will run you under the table, unless you have a big investment right now. The cloud will eat into your margins a lot more than you think it will.

Second, running a startup will be the hardest thing you ever do in your life. Every founder has what I like to call a porch moment. A porch moment is when you're sitting on your porch and you think the business is going to fail and it's time to move on. We've had three of those at FitLift and we kept going.

There are going to be moments like that, where you're facing a technical barrier or a business barrier. Keep going, because at the end of the day, passion and hard work will always win. We're a group of four people that pulled something off in less than a year that most companies take three years to do. That's because we've worked hard and we're passionate. Keep going. Take your porch moments, never give up, and you'll be surprised what that leads to.

TAKEAWAYS

- If your customers are pushing you in a different direction, listen to them.
- Cloud can be expensive in the beginning.

#70

Jenn Bonine

Title: Co-founder, Valhalla and PinkLion.AI

Value proposition: Builds digital twins in industry verticals to create meaningful connection

Industry: Technology

Keywords: AI, co-founder, top-up/bottom-down

What is Valhalla?

We build internal digital footprints. Valhalla builds digital footprints for connection and collaboration where you can seamlessly move between home, school, work, and your social life without physically having to be in those buildings or spaces.

How did you identify this as a problem?

Our first startup aimed to create ease of use for new technologies to solve problems for businesses. We focused particularly on using machine learning and AI to get data and insights more quickly. We realized that while people are getting more accepting of new technologies like machine learning and AI, it can still be a bit overwhelming.

We wanted to create digital spaces to connect in more meaningful ways than through the traditional mechanisms of conference calls or video calls. We wanted to create an ad hoc connection like you used to have, where people could hang out and pop by someone's office spontaneously.

What's it like to have four co-founders?

We believe in the "beauty of four." Being a single founder can be lonely. You don't have someone you trust to bounce ideas off of, or someone that's been there from the beginning that shares your passion and vision. Venture capitalists are also reluctant to take on a solo founder. We've been fortunate to have four of us. We've also known each other now for over a decade, working on some big challenges with very different perspectives.

I come from a background that was more around consumer engagement, leadership, marketing, sales strategy, and thought leadership. I worked as a consultant across many different companies, providing unbiased feedback about what worked and didn't work. My other co-founder is your traditional CTO. I come up with these wild ideas of how to solve problems in the world, and he can actually architect these solutions. Our third co-founder is a traditional COO. She creates the financial projections, and understands the terminology of the customer acquisition cost, and the total addressable market. The final founder is the money person. He understands private equity and capital and can raise the most founder-efficient capital.

We talked about our ideas for two years before we committed 100% to our startup. Once we did that, we went from zero to almost $7 million in revenue in under six months because we were fully committed.

What's one of the most significant lessons you brought from your first company into Valhalla?

I think one of the things that often can trip up founders is whether you want to go top-down or bottom-up.

Clubhouse, for example, has taken a bottom-up approach. Slack is another great example, which was used by individual developers or employees first. Or, you can take a top-down approach, where you sell it to the top first, and then it's widely distributed through those organizations.

That's a big decision point early on. I've seen people try to do both and really struggle, because a top-down takes a very different sales and marketing approach than a bottom-up approach.

If you take that bottom-up approach and you're not ready, then you're not going to see massive growth. But if you take a top-down approach and you get purchased in different verticals within enterprises, you can really refine that product before you take it to bottom-up consumers.

We tested Valhalla in B2B markets in a couple of key verticals to see if we were too far ahead of where people's thinking was, or if it would work. We wanted to make sure it was easy to use, and could be adopted quickly. So we tested with schools – with very young people – and we tested with senior living facilities, with older populations. We wanted to see how easy the UX actually was, so we tested it on both the very young and the elderly.

Any final advice?

If you really want to commit to something and see the dramatic results, give it your full attention instead of trying to do it as a side deal. We literally planned two years before we were able to do that, but we did get there.

TAKEAWAYS

- A top-down approach can help you refine your product before taking it to consumers or bottom-up users.
- If you want to see dramatic results, go full-time on your product.

#71

Michele Hansen

Title: Co-Founder, Geocodio

Value proposition: Saves customers time and money in their location data processing

Industry: SaaS

Keywords: Customer feedback

What is Geocodio?

Geocodio is a geocoding and data matching service that helps people convert addresses to coordinates. It also helps computers convert coordinates to addresses and adds other data that is only available when you have the coordinates (such as Census data).

How did you identify this as a problem you wanted to solve?

In 2012, my husband and I launched an app that helped people find grocery stores, convenience stores, and coffee shops near them with open hours. The idea was if you needed milk at midnight or a coffee at 3 AM, you could just pull up the app and it would show you what was open.

That app was moderately successful. In Denmark (where we live now), it was really successful. 10% of the Danish population downloaded it. It's only a population of 5.5 million, but that's something.

At the time, however, we lived in Washington, DC. We ran into this problem with Google where you were limited to getting 2,500 address lookups per day and you weren't allowed to store the data. The only alternative was to pay tens of thousands of dollars a year to get 100,000 lookups a day. But we just needed 5,000 per day. So we ended up having to build a solution ourselves. It was rough, but it worked.

We talked to our friends who were also developers, and we realized they had the same problem. One of our friends suggested that we just slap a paywall in front of what we had built, so that instead of having to go pay Google tens of thousands of dollars a year, we could have other people pay for the servers for it and then keep our app running. We spent about six months preparing it for launch and ran it as a side project. Within the first couple of months, it quickly surpassed the ad revenue from the original app.

Did the success take you off guard?

Yes. The first day of launch, we were on the front page of *Hacker News* all day. That was a huge shock.

I remember making this spreadsheet of what would constitute success for us. An acceptable success was that we would launch this product and that we would be able to keep our apps running. A moderate success would be that we would launch it and other people would pay for it enough to cover its servers. A wild success would be that it more than pays for its servers. Our expectations were very low.

We were so surprised that we had actually forgotten to write the billing code. When the day came to charge everyone, we had to scramble.

Has your vision stayed the same, or have you pivoted?

The vision for who we're serving has always been consistent, which is GIS (Geographic Information Systems) for non-GIS people.

A lot of the tools for geographic data are built for people who are very experienced in that area. It's important to us to make GIS accessible for those with a non-geography background – developers, marketers, researchers, people who are not steeped in the tools of the trade.

What does it look like for you to get feedback and listen to customers?

In the beginning, we received a ton of emails. Being on the front page of *Hacker News* for a day gets you some visibility. Of course, our traffic dropped off significantly and never went back to those levels. It really wasn't important for the long term growth of the company. But in the very beginning, we just emailed everybody that signed up and said, "Thank you for signing up. We'd love to hear more about the projects you're working on and if you have any ideas or suggestions."

That led us to some really critical early decisions, such as adding reverse geocoding, which is turning the coordinates into addresses–which had not been part of our own personal use case. We also added functionality for uploading spreadsheets. At the time, the only option to be able to decode a spreadsheet was that you could send it to this guy and he would get it back to you in a couple of days. So we created a tool for that. Since then, our revenue has been pretty evenly split between people who are uploading spreadsheets and using the API.

I have an ongoing "listening bucket." The first week of every month, I send out an email to everyone who had their first charge in the past month. In this email, I try to understand the building context of their use case, or what they're trying to do overall. Sometimes I even make a phone call, depending on what the person wants to do.

We also use NPS surveys as a temperature check for how we're doing. Until recently, that question was "Any suggestions?" Most of the time, people just said, "Everything is great." That made us feel good, but it wasn't helping us improve. I recently changed that question to, "What did you use before you used Geocodio?" The range of answers has been fascinating and super helpful.

I also do regular check-ins on certain sets of customers – particularly high value customers – at least once or twice a year. Finally, I will do discreet research projects, depending on if there's a particular topic that I'm interested in or if we're considering changing some functionality and we need to do usability testing.

If you had to do it all over again, would you still start a SaaS business?

Absolutely. It's the best kind of business to run. I started out working for an agency, so I came from working with clients. After a couple of years, I decided that I wanted to be in a product business and did not want to work with clients anymore. I switched to working at a B2C company, and eventually to working on Geocodio full-time. Running your own SaaS business combines all of the great things about working for a product business, but it's calmer, there's more flexibility, and there's more decision making autonomy. It combines the great parts of being in a product business with the freedom that comes with running your own company.

That's not to say it's easy. There's always a new hill to climb. Every business owner has challenges. But in my experience, the difficulty does not outweigh the benefits by any means.

TAKEAWAYS

- Check in with new customers shortly after their first charge. What's their particular use case?
- Check in with high value customers regularly.
- There may be a problem to solve within your existing product. Be creative about identifying new challenges and ideas for new products.

#72

Sam Schrup

Title: Founder, TextRetailer

Value proposition: Provides a way to make purchases with "zero clicks" using text messages

Industry: E-commerce

Keywords: Side hustle

What is TextRetailer?

TextRetailer is a text marketing platform designed for small business and e-commerce businesses. What sets us apart is that we've taken the Amazon "one click" buying concept and put it into text messages. The idea is that you can send out a campaign featuring a product and all your subscribers have to do is reply "Yes" in order to buy. We've already captured their shipping information, and we have their credit card stored securely. As soon as they reply "Yes," we process that order, charge their card, and then ship the order. It's a completely frictionless way to sell to your existing subscriber list.

Is there anything else like this on the market?

There's a ton of people that are in the text marketing space that might send a promotion with a link to their Shopify website or their e-commerce website. You click on the link, put the item in the cart, and check out. It's relatively easy, but there are many steps there for the customer. TextRetailer eliminates all of those extra steps. It's a seamless process, all done through text message.

How did you get into text message marketing?

I have a background in retail, but I also learned software engineering in college. One of the things that I did when I was running a retail store is that I built a rewards program. Word got out about this program, and a few other shops came on. That was kind of my first taste of building software for businesses. That didn't work out – there are a lot of challenges selling directly to small businesses. But this experience led me to want to make a rewards program work for restaurants.

Ultimately, that didn't work out either. It was too difficult to get businesses to sign up. But that experience led me to start a business called Textiful, where you capture email addresses via text. It started off as a side hustle, but ultimately did so well that I was able to quit my job and do that full time. We had public speakers, musicians, and podcasters capturing emails through text message, using our platform.

TextRetailer is inspired by one of Gary Vaynerchuk's products, called WineText, where they sell wine through texts. They built their software in-house. I wanted to take that idea and turn it into a platform that any business can use to start running their own shop-by-text program.

As a three-time founder, would you say that entrepreneurship can be an isolating journey?

Yeah, it definitely can. I have some contractors that I rely on, but for the most part, it's me, myself and I, day in and day out. So yeah, I think that's one of the challenges.

I'm a part of a Mastermind group, and that's been really helpful. It's with a group of five other entrepreneurs that are building software companies. Just being able to have that connection and bounce ideas off of each other has been really helpful.

Do you have any other advice for people who are wanting to start a SaaS?

I've always said that if you have that luxury of being able to build stuff on your own, just do it. You don't have to hire a developer. It's not costing you anything financially. Take a weekend or two or five or six or 10, and spend the time, especially if you have it to give. If nothing else, you build your skills from an engineering and a developer standpoint. You become a better developer. And if it turns into something bigger over time, that's a bonus.

TAKEAWAYS

- If you're a solo founder, find people that you can connect with and bounce ideas off of.
- If you're a developer, building something just for the sake of building can be helpful for improving your skills.

#73
Alex Delivet

Title: Founder, Collect
Value proposition: Creates custom client portals for professionals
Industry: Client management
Keywords: Chicken or the egg, MVP, validation

What is Collect?

Collect creates individualized portals to help professionals automate the process of collecting documents and information from their clients.

How did you identify this as a problem to be solved?

In the past, I was an event organizer, and every time I was organizing my event, I struggled to collect all the data I needed from different speakers and partners. I did it manually for a while. Then I tried to use form builders like Typeform. But this didn't give me any way to send the information back to the speakers and ask them to modify it if necessary. And it didn't give me a clear view of who had filled out the forms, and who hadn't.

That's when I realized that lots of professionals—in real estate, law, or accounting, for example—probably had the same problem. I decided to build a customizable client portal that could work across industries.

How did you validate and launch your product?

I built the MVP in 2017. At the time, I was working at it part-time and it wasn't moving that fast. Still, I was offering it for free to some users, and getting feedback. I didn't feel comfortable about launching, but my wife told me, "You've been working on this project for a long time. It's time to move on. You need to launch." So we did a soft launch in December 2019.

Initially, we used Ship (under Product Hunt) to launch, and though we got the interest of 600-700 people, that ultimately didn't amount to anything. The problem was that there was too long of a ramp up until launch, and I think people lost interest.

What was your first business like?

In 2012, we launched a company called Trip XP. It was a marketplace for activities, similar to what Airbnb does now with "Experiences."

Our main mistake at this time was that this kind of business doesn't work as a standalone from a financial perspective. It works for Airbnb because it's an additional sale. They already have all the community and they don't need to pay anything to access people.

But in our case, we needed to do some client acquisition on both sides of the marketplace. There are typically very few repeat customers with this kind of platform, and the conversion rate is very low.

Lesson number one from this experience was that you need to be able to improve your product technically on a daily basis.

The second lesson was about the business model. Even before starting this business, I was not a huge fan of marketplaces. I prefer SaaS because you can start with only one client, but with a marketplace you need to grow very quickly to please everyone.

The third lesson is to focus on the customer experience and the product. A lot of startups perform well because the marketing and the sales process are well done, but the end product is not that good. Salesforce is not that great of a product, for example. Sometimes it's quite slow or quite complicated. But their funnel marketing and sales are very good.

What's the most important thing that a SaaS founder needs to know?

Sometimes you have to take a counterintuitive approach. A lot of people will tell you that you should start niche with your product, and then you can broaden your ideal customer profile. I did the opposite, and started by targeting many different industries. If I had niched down from the start, on real estate for example, it would have been challenging to change my positioning later. I'm happy with this choice. It was complicated at the beginning, but now it's paying off because I see lots of use cases.

TAKEAWAYS

- Make sure your business model is solid. If you're creating a marketplace, for example, will you have repeat customers? Can you gain growth quickly enough to please both sides of the marketplace?

- Sometimes, you have to take a counterintuitive approach to SaaS. Niching down, for example, might not be the best option for your particular product.

PART 4

THE LONE RANGERS
Founders who are going it alone

#74

Bridget Jones

Title: Founder, Chisel

Value proposition: Builds SaaS products for small to medium sized companies

Industry: Software development

Keywords: Female founder, pricing, resources

What is Chisel?

Chisel is an American business and financial software company that develops and sells software and human capital services to small to mid-sized businesses, local governments, and individuals.

Why did you start Chisel?

I was working in the legal field for about 10 years. A few years back, I decided to go to law school. One day, I was sitting in class as a freshman in law school when I realized, I can make an impact here, but it's going to take entirely too long. I wanted to make an impact in people's lives, but without the barriers of bureaucracy and red tape that can sometimes come with law. But in tech, I saw how quickly groups were able to move large sums of people to do something. Tech was wide open, and I didn't have to ask anybody for permission.

I started off by going to two boot camps where a) I learned about entrepreneurship, marketing, and sales; and b) I learned object-oriented programming. I then worked for a couple of months for a company that built webinars for local colleges and universities. I've been doing freelance work ever since.

I've always had this desire to impact people's lives. Now I'm creating software that moves things, makes people's lives easier, and makes a difference.

What have been some of your "dream come true" projects?

We've done a lot of really cool things in healthcare and education. Some of the engineers on our team built internship portals, webinars, and virtual maker spaces for a few colleges and universities. We've served as mentors in residence for a few accelerators. Our strategists have provided consulting for the Fortune Global 100. We've done some cool work with Black Lives Matter out of their Boston chapter and a few other notables.

Last year, we made the decision to move into SaaS. One of the things that struck us over the last couple of years of being in business is that while we were able to do some really cool work for the bigger companies, we weren't really able to do so many projects that impacted small businesses or startups, and we were serious about trying to figure out why. We noticed, of course, that one of the biggest challenges was money. Smaller companies really struggled to understand their numbers, their balance sheets, their profit loss statements. Even the ones that were really good at sales didn't have a good understanding of where they were in terms of numbers. So we created a fintech platform, a SaaS product, where we teach financial models to founders, specifically in accelerators, small banks, credit unions – anybody with a portfolio company. One of our core values is financial literacy.

What's been one of the biggest challenges so far?

When I first got into SaaS, one of the biggest challenges was information overload. Knowing where to start was a challenge. But I also had mentors and coaches to help me along the way.

What kind of advice would you give to someone who is just starting out in tech?

I think it's irresponsible to offer advice to someone without some sort of background on who they are. The very first question I'd ask them is, "Are you more analytical or creative?" If a person presents as more analytical, I'd talk to them about data science, workflow automation, and coding. If they're more creative, I'd talk to them about UX/UI development and branding and the many different things that you can do in those areas. While there are folks that fit in the middle, most people lean in one direction.

What's one of the most important pieces of advice that you would give to new SaaS founders?

Do research on this business model, read a ton of books on the subject, and learn from those who know how to run a successful company.

One of my favorite books is called *The Automatic Customer*, by John Warrillow. Start there. Get an idea of how this works so that you can think about how you want to get paid. SaaS models are attractive hooks that reel investors in because of the predictability of future earnings.

Finally, think about aligning your pricing structure to your customer acquisition costs. Think about your gross margins. Right now, average gross margins for SaaS founders is about 20%. If you can get above that, you're in the money.

What has your experience been like as a Black female founder?

The numbers are abysmal. Black women don't even make up 1% of people in tech. But what I like about tech is that it's open-entry. In corporate America, you have to "show your papers" or show a measurable validation process to prove that you're worthy to work for these companies. In tech, you can work for yourself. While there are still bouts of "showing your papers" in regards to raising capital, not everyone goes that route. You can jump right in as long as you use a good business model, focus on getting a return on your investment, and learn how to make a profit. You don't need to ask anybody for permission. You can set your own prices and live the way you want to live.

TAKEAWAYS

- Learn from founders who have gone before you. Read – a lot.
- Make sure your pricing structure aligns with your customer acquisition costs.

#75

Michael Greenberg

Title: Founder, Call For Content & PodcastScore
Value proposition: Building Tools For The Business Of Podcasting
Industry: Podcasting
Keywords: Fundraising, no-code

Why did you leave your previous company?

I left because the CEO wanted to go with his gut instead of the customer research. That ended up killing the company. I was leading product, and I knew what the customers were saying and I knew what we needed to build to get people to buy it. I knew it was nothing that was going to be sexy.

The game of building a SaaS business is totally separate from the game of building a venture-backed business. I was interested in game #1, not game #2.

Is it always a bad idea to raise capital?

If you want to attract good venture capital, don't raise money till your Series A. Because if your business can't be profitable from the start, what are you doing? There are too many micro-SaaS options to say you can't build your product without a million dollars – or even a quarter million – in capital. Now, the vast majority of SaaS ideas are cheap to build, especially if you have a working knowledge of no-code tools.

What are investors looking for?

Once you hit $10k MRR, people will throw money at your business. If you look around on Twitter, you'll find venture capitalists who put out tweets that say "DM me if you hit this," because that's their sole requirement. They want to see that you can become a million dollar business. And if they're making an angel investment, a $1M/year SaaS will pay itself off. If they're looking for an exit, then they need the 100X scale. They might be looking for 20k or 30k or 50k before they throw money in. Once there's one or two going in your space, then they're just backing that space of assets. As soon as your team shows that you can develop traction, they don't care about anything else.

What's the #1 mistake that you see SaaS founders making?

Building a SaaS company. The vast majority of founders are not qualified to start their company. They need time in the industry, whatever they're trying to build for.

I'm from the Midwest. My brother went to a very, very good school on the East Coast. I dropped out of school, went to a coding boot camp, and moved to the Bay Area. My general opinion of SaaS founders from the coasts is that they are younger, less qualified, and more entitled. The SaaS founders from the Midwest are beasts and you never hear about them until they sell their company for $200-$300 million.

The flashy stuff comes from the coasts. That's where you get entertainment, marketing, adtech, and social. But I see way more money in industrial companies that are coming out of the Midwest and the inner corridors.

A lot of SaaS companies should be selling services alongside the product. You do a ton of work in the early days of SaaS to brand your company as reliable. In doing so, you open yourself up to the opportunity to take on some very lucrative consulting engagements, or custom enterprise work. While doing that might seem counterintuitive, it can give you a massive head start in market research and provide much needed revenue.

What's a practical way to start a SaaS company?

Building a $5k/month SaaS company – or a micro-SaaS company – is a lot easier. It's not too hard. It's highly salable. It's got everything you want in an asset. People build micro-SaaS companies, and somebody else buys them and grows them after. You're making maybe 50, 60, maybe 100k on the actual revenue, but then you're selling the asset and picking up $100k or $200k.

At the end of the day, you've got to know the market gaps, and how to validate your idea.

TAKEAWAYS

- Explore your options for building a micro-SaaS or a SaaS with no-code tools before you raise funding upfront.
- As soon as you're making $10k MRR, you're in a great position to raise capital.
- Make sure you're qualified to build a SaaS company in your particular space.
- Consider selling a service alongside your product. Consulting gigs, for example, can help provide revenue and provide market research.

#76

Debbie Schwartz

Title: Founder, Road2College

Value proposition: Guides families on the process of college admission and tuition

Industry: EdTech

Keywords: Female founder, fundraising, MVP, non-technical founder, validation

What is Road2College?

Road2College is a platform to help educate families and guide them on the process of college admissions and paying for college. It gives them the tools, the resources, and a community to help them make smart decisions when it comes to thinking about where their kids are going to go for college and how much it's going to cost them.

How did you identify this as a problem?

I worked in the financial services world for many years. When my oldest daughter was about to go to college, I was doing consulting work for a student lender. It was the first time I had seen the student loan business, even though I had been in other parts of financial services. It was a very confusing world for parents and for students. The information in this space is scattered all over the place. There's some government information, there's some private information, there are a lot of good websites, but nobody was pulling it all together.

Going to college is a major financial decision that potentially impacts two generations. But no one was taking on this challenge to make sure that parents and families were navigating this properly.

How did you decide to develop a product, rather than a service, to address this challenge?

I'm a non-technical founder. So I started to address the problem with the skills that I had, which were marketing and education – taking complex information and systems and explaining them to people as easily as possible. I started off with the newsletter. I wrote articles and shared information with people. That gave me time to be in this space. I like to use the word "marinate" for that process. I could marinate and see what was happening and what people really needed. I saw the problem, but I didn't have a solution yet.

If I had jumped in then with what I thought the solution was, it wouldn't have been useful, and not even close to what we ultimately started with.

What was the first step you took to create a product?

We started simply by trying to prove that this was a solution that somebody would pay for. So we created an Excel spreadsheet with collected information about the college admissions and tuition process. The spreadsheet was just to see if people were interested in having all of this data at their fingertips. We did that for six months. Turns out, people were willing to pay for it because it cut down on their research.

We took that spreadsheet and converted that to the first MVP. The MVP was similar to the spreadsheet, but it gave people more tools to filter and sort and compare the data.

I couldn't move as fast in building the actual product, so I spent a lot of time building the audience. By now, we've got a tremendous audience that has already fed us information on how to build the MVP. We don't have to spend as much time and effort on the marketing because we already have people who want this. Now, we're focusing on building out a second iteration of our original MVP.

What have been some of the biggest challenges of this journey?

The biggest challenge from an entrepreneurial standpoint – especially as a non-technical founder – is translating what I see in my head to developers. They might take me really literally or they might not ask me a lot of questions. All of a sudden they've gone down a path I didn't want, and now they've got to redo the code. That type of back and forth can be frustrating. It's been a huge learning process.

What kinds of advice would you give to other female founders?

I don't know if this should be on the record or not, but I think it's really difficult. I've gone into different conversations with a lot of men. If I had gone into the same conversation as a male, it would be a very different conversation and very different outcome. That is just the reality.

It's a frustrating position to be in for a lot of different reasons. My audience is primarily female, because it's often the mothers that drive the decision-making. It's ironic that 95-97% of the people in the industry are men. An executive pointed this out to me – that I was one of the only females in this space trying to solve the challenge of financial decision making for college education. I think that's why the right product has never been created.

Any final advice for SaaS founders?

You can't get caught up in trying to make it perfect. You can't satisfy everybody. There are always going to be people who don't love what you're doing or have suggestions to improve it. You have to have a thick skin and say, "I hear you, I understand, but this is where we're at." Women especially might feel the pressure to satisfy everybody. But you have to step back and say, "I can't satisfy everybody, and 80% of the people are happy. We'll get to the other 20% soon."

The other thing is, you can have a great idea. But an idea goes nowhere unless it's executed well. You can even have the right financial backing, but you need the right people to help put the idea into action and work together.

TAKEAWAYS

- Use a super simple MVP (e.g. a spreadsheet, if applicable) to prove people will pay for your idea.
- A great idea will go nowhere unless it's executed well.

#77
Arsalan Bashir

Title: Founder & CEO, LiveDocs

Value proposition: Modern day office suite that helps you build documents that update themselves

Industry: B2B SaaS

Keywords: Customer acquisition, distribution, hiring, metrics, prioritization, virality

What is LiveDocs?

LiveDocs enables teams to bring live data from their existing tools into their reports and other data-rich documents without losing time updating these documents manually or building data pipelines.

How did you identify this as a problem to be solved?

Before LiveDocs, I worked at companies of all sizes, from two-person startups to Fortune 500's. I noticed that in all of these teams, there was always somebody tasked with manually updating documents and pasting numbers and screenshots into reports. Even documents like PRDs ("product specs") and OKRs, required constant back and forth between the overarching business process and the document itself. These are documents that are *live* by default, and must be constantly updated based on activity and feedback from multiple stakeholders.

The bottom line is that teams run on documents, but there is still a lot of arduous labor that goes into having a document and aligning your team around it.

It was also clear that API-driven apps and rapid adoption of SaaS tools in modern teams meant this was a solvable problem for most teams. All the documents built by these teams and their other tools were already online, unlike 20 years ago. If you could somehow make them talk to each other and enable operators at modern teams to build "live" documents, we could save these teams a lot of time and money that they would spend on updating documents. And so, we set out to build the first truly programmable document editor for modern teams, aptly named "LiveDocs.com."

What's been the biggest challenge so far of running your business?

Hands down, it's been hiring. Hiring has multiple effects. The most underrated effect of good hiring is that if you have a team of players who are committed to the vision and are on the same page as you, it gives you a greater driving force behind what you're trying to achieve. It's not just about hiring the right people, though. It's about retaining them.

That's definitely been the hardest part because it's easy to hire an engineer or a designer, but it's hard to find people who are a combination of these three factors that are on the same page as you, who are available, and who want to join you. The last requirement of course is that they have the technical chops to execute.

How have you learned to hire well?

There's an engineering adage that goes something along the lines of "two hours of planning can save you two weeks of coding." The same applies to hiring. I had to pay a little bit of a tuition fee, metaphorically speaking, to learn this lesson.

You've got to set a standard for the software or service or the product to deliver. You need to measure everyone you hire against that standard, be very clear in setting expectations and aligning on where we're going together as a team.

Balancing immediate output with investment in the professional growth of every hire is vital. Hire them for what they can do today while having a concrete idea of how you can help them advance their career to where they see themself in five or 10 years.

How have you approached customer acquisition?

We rely on a product-led model with a deep obsession with in-product viral loops. We designed LiveDocs knowing that one of its key differentiators was inherent virality. That's been an emphasis since day one. It's something we measure and try to improve upon. So every time you build a report, a deck or a document, you're bound to share it with somebody, whether that's somebody internal or external.

We started off manually onboarding customers, and we optimized everything in the customer experience around increasing the virality of the product. How do we incentivize people sharing this document outside the company or inside the company? That has been something that has high reward in terms of customer acquisition, and that continues to be a key part of how we get customers.

Besides that, we launched a template gallery for LiveDocs, meaning if you want to come up with a sales report, we don't really want you to start off with a blank screen and a blinking cursor. We've worked with industry experts to come up with templates that are ready to go. Simply connect your tools, say your Salesforce or HubSpot account, and your sales report is ready to go. This feature was designed to reduce the barrier to entry or friction to adoption.

The overarching principle is to keep experimenting. We run at least one new growth experiment every other week, experimenting with a new channel and measuring what works and what does not.

What metrics do you focus on? What have you learned in that journey?

When I started out, I was looking for literature around metrics. What metrics make sense for a SaaS company? I quickly realized that with metrics it's not just the "what" that matters, but the "when." Before deep diving into what you should measure viz a viz retention and compound funnels inside the product, it makes sense to do the basics right, particularly early on.

When you're onboarding very few users, especially early on, qualitative metrics make more sense to evaluate how well you're solving the users' problem. Gradually, you might consider adding qualitative metrics in other performance indicators, such as drilling deeper and refining how you define an "active" user (eg: Facebook's infamous "seven friends in 10 days" metric to evaluate if a user has "activated" and whether they would stick around for the long run).

I was really fascinated by what Slack does with their definition of an active user. They define an active user as somebody who sends a certain number of messages per week or exhibits some level of activity on the platform. This clear distinction between an engaged user and someone who just wanted to check out this tool and entered their email address is very valuable, particularly to SaaS startups.

Any final advice for SaaS founders?

If your core product is software, then software needs to be a first class citizen in your team. For as long as possible, the team must be aligned around "What problem are we solving for our customers?" and evaluate every product decision in light of the answers. The software must fundamentally serve that purpose.

It's surprising how many teams fail to get this right, by either front-loading monetization-related jargon too early, leaving the user confused and not solving the core problem for them or by attempting to solve a problem that doesn't exist yet or never existed in the first place.

A counter-example is something like Uber. Uber's mobile app is not the product; you're not paying to use the app, you're paying to get from point A to point B and the software is simply a means to an end. In that context, it might make sense to think about other business objectives and prioritize them over the actual software. But if your product is SaaS, then software needs to be a first class citizen that is designed around the problem. No dark patterns, no jargon, just delivering value to customers. Everything else will follow.

TAKEAWAYS

- Don't focus only on hiring great employees; you also need to learn to retain them.
- Have a clear idea of how you want to help your team members advance in their careers.
- Be creative about building virality into your product. How will users be able to share your product with others?
- Make sure to have a clear definition of what an engaged user is.

#78

Henry Moore

Title: Founder & CEO, REsimplifi, Inc.

Value proposition: Discover, maintain, and distribute web-based commercial real estate data for property site selection

Industry: Commercial Real Estate

Keywords: Development, fundraising, mindset, non-technical founder, team

What is REsimplifi?

We discover, maintain, and distribute web-based commercial real estate data for economic development site selection tools. All over the United States, there are economic development offices that promote industry within their local markets. We collect and maintain relevant property data and syndicate it to our clients so that they can effectively recruit business to their target markets.

It's expensive and time-consuming for our clients to collect the data. Our IP enables us to do it at scale. Think about market sites like Zillow and then apply that to commercial real estate. If a commercial real estate broker has a property listed that's available for sale and it was removed from the website, we have the ability to track that. Was there a transaction, or was it simply taken offline? We then communicate that back to our clients so they have an idea of what's happening within their market to help others make informed real estate decisions.

How did you identify this as a problem to be solved?

I started out in technology sales. In the mid-90's, I was exposed to CRM technology. Ultimately, I went to work for an early-stage company that went public in 2006. I was very fortunate to be one of the earlier hires. I enjoyed being a part of a team that was building something that was largely not yet defined.

Ultimately, I left that company to spend more time with my family. I was covering the Mid-Atlantic region at the time, covering nine states and living on an airplane, with three kids under the age of two. I interviewed with a commercial real estate company in 2008, and quickly realized that the industry lagged in technology adoption. They didn't have the tools to which I had grown accustomed. The ones that did exist were not very good. CRM specifically was not built for commercial real estate.

I decided to *initially* build a CRM specific to the commercial real estate industry. I thought I could do it passively, and just contract out the work. I quickly discovered that in order to make this work, I had to go full time. In February of 2015, I went all in.

What has your journey been like as a non-technical founder?

As I said, I initially thought I could contract all the work out. Ultimately, that was very expensive for us. If I had been fortunate enough to know someone in the space, having a technical co-founder would have been the best way to go. But having a traditional business background, I didn't have those connections.

So we partnered with different people along the way for equity, and that enabled us to bridge the gap in an efficient way. We didn't have to raise too much money. We worked with a great company out of Seattle and they built the beginnings of our current application for equity. That's a great way for people to kind of bridge the gap until they find the right person.

I'm very fortunate that our current CTO and lead developer has made all the difference in the world. We started to take off when I got a technical partner. In the long run, if you're a SaaS company, you need someone on your team that has a technical background.

What do you know now that you wish you had known before?

I wish I had realistically understood how much it would take to get the company to a stable position. You hear people say, "It will cost twice as much and take twice as long as you think." In my experience, it takes much more than that. I am sure that the multiplier for each successful company is different but for us the number was certainly greater than x2. Ultimately, if people aren't willing to pay for it, your idea is likely not there yet. Pivoting is normal and defining "aftermarket fit" may take more than one iteration for your company. It takes a lot of time and resources to really define what it is that people want.

What has it looked like for you to start a SaaS company in the South – a region not as known for tech?

Venture capital at early stage companies looks different here than perhaps West Coast VC does. That's not to say that you can't raise money here; you can, but it might be a lesser amount, or you might have to approach it differently.

The investors here take more of a conservative approach. We were fortunate enough to raise money through Friends and Family, and then partner with the South Carolina Research Authority – a quasi government entity that is tasked with promoting the knowledge based economy in the state of South Carolina. Most of the jobs in this state are in manufacturing, and they are interested in recruiting and growing home-grown technology companies like ours.

Especially in this region of the country, you need to start small and raise enough money to prove your concept out. Keep your operating expenses low so that you can generate enough revenue to show your investors that this can be sustainable. But the speculative dollars are not what they're really looking for.

How do you approach recruiting in the region you're in?

Honestly, most of our current team came from networking. Over time we have been fortunate to connect with like-minded people who are skilled at what they do and interested in being part of our company. Some of our best hires started out as consultants or contract employees.

Any final advice you'd give to SaaS founders?

I wished I had known about the emotional wear and tear of starting a business. To make a company like ours successful – especially starting from ground zero – you're going to come to a time where you don't have capacity to do the things that you used to do, or connect with the people that you used to have things in common with. That only compounds the stress and worry that you have because perhaps you borrowed money from your friends and family. Plus, your own personal investment will be at risk. It may feel like you have everything on the line and that it isn't working yet. This can be a really difficult place to be.

The perseverance required to get out of that is something that I wish I had better understood. Ultimately, it was worth having the freedom and satisfaction of running my own company. But I wish that I would have prepared my friends and family for this aspect a little bit differently. I feel very fortunate to be where I am, but it was a much larger effort than I would have ever imagined.

The bottom line is this: It's going to take more than you realize on every level. It's going to take more of your time. It will take more than your talent. It's going to take you away from your family, hobbies... you have to be all in.

TAKEAWAYS

- Starting a business is going to take more time and resources than you can imagine. Are you all in?
- Be prepared for the emotional wear and tear of starting a business. That includes preparing for a shift in personal relationships.

#79

Peter Solimine

Title: Founder & CEO, Beulr

Value proposition: Attends Zoom meetings and online classes in your place

Industry: Future of Work
Keywords: Customer acquisition, distribution, virality

What is Beulr?

Beulr is a cloud-based bot service that attends, records, and transcribes online meetings and classes on your behalf. Users just need to tell the bot which meeting to join, what time to arrive, and how long to stay for. Then our servers automatically send a bot into the meeting or class. Users can even upload a video of themselves pretending to pay attention, which loops through the duration of the meeting. If you're in college, Beulr guarantees your perfect attendance and you can come back to watch your lecture recordings on your own time. And yes, the name is derived from *Ferris Beuller's Day Off*.

How did you come up with this idea?

In March of 2020, I was a student at Tulane University when classes went online overnight. In hindsight, it's crazy to think back on how unusual and exciting that was.

It was also driving me nuts that I had to get up so early every day. I had been reading the book *Why We Sleep* by Dr. Matthew Walker, and I knew that early mornings were killing my sleep and my education. I thought, *Great, I'll just write a little script that'll show up to my class for me*. As soon as I said that out loud to my friends, they started asking me, "How much do you want for it?"

I built an early version that ran on my computer, showed up to class for me, and recorded it. Then I started going around campus and installing it for friends for a small fee. I knew there was a scalable business opportunity at hand but had never built a scalable web application. I would need a team of computer scientists if we were going to achieve scale. So I called up a buddy of mine who I had met in China at a hackathon while I was studying abroad. He is an absolute tank of a software engineer. Together, we hunkered down and worked on it like a hackathon for two or three weeks and launched in April of 2020. We've seen incredible traction ever since. Right now, we've got 52,000 users in over 175 different countries. The growth has been explosive. But there's been a lot of ups and downs along the way, too.

How did you gain so many users so quickly?

We knew Beulr had viral potential. We just wanted to make as many little sparks as we could and try to get a flame going.

TikTok was our preferred route. We knew that's where our audience is. I just wish I had jumped on it earlier. I should have spent more time in the early days focusing on creating our own internal content. But instead, we went out to try to find the right person to make videos to get the word out. I found this girl who was doing a series on her TikTok page about "quarantine websites you need." But her name wasn't on her page, and you can't DM people on TikTok. I ended up going through all her videos and on one of them, she mentioned her Venmo handle. I found her on Venmo and sent her a penny and said, "Hey, I have a sponsorship opportunity. If you're interested, DM me on Instagram."

I ended up paying her around $75 and the video got 3 million views. We ended up getting 3,000 people to come and sign up for the site after that. It wasn't very much, but it was great because it was our very first early launch and there were a lot of bugs we needed to resolve. It just started growing from there.

Did you see yourself starting a company while you're still in school?

I think there's a stereotype of the college kid nowadays who drops out of school to start a company. But the real value of a college education is to enable people to find their passions. I have always wanted to work on challenging engineering problems, build companies, and work for myself. I'm fortunate enough to have already found this outlet. I look back at friends who are still in school or recently graduated and have no clue what they want to do, and wonder if I would be in the same boat if I had stayed in school. Nothing wrong with that, of course, but I have already found my passion so I plan to run with it.

A lot of people start companies while they're in college just to put something on their resume or because they've convinced themself that they've got a great idea. But this felt like something I couldn't pass up. I knew the customers. I didn't need to spend three months doing market research – this was an exploding opportunity. Like my dad always says, "Never let a good crisis go to waste."

TAKEAWAYS

- If you identify an explosive opportunity, jump on it.

Josh Ho

Title: Founder & CEO, Referral Rock

Value proposition: Drives word of mouth referrals and brand awareness

Industry: Marketing

Keywords: Bootstrapping, freemium, mindset, pricing

What is Referral Rock?

We help businesses run online programs to scale word of mouth referrals and brand awareness. These are programs such as refer a friend programs, brand advocacy, and affiliate programs.

For a lot of businesses, this is an untapped resource where we can help a business generate consistent word of mouth referrals through automation instead of waiting for it to happen.

How did you identify this as a problem?

I have a background in software. I got my degree in engineering, but when I entered the workforce, I quickly adapted more to the business side, leading teams and taking on roles in product management. I went off on my own 15 years ago, and created a software called Ubernote. We actually launched our web version of a note software before Evernote. Then 2008-2009 happened. We turned on the pay switch, but consumers didn't really want to pay for things then – not as much as now.

We burned out a little. I had a few years where I took a break, did some software consulting, and got married and started having kids. But in the back of my mind, I always wanted to go back to SaaS.

If you got burned out initially on SaaS, what made you want to go back?

I always felt like I was able to see around corners. People say that entrepreneurs are risk-takers. But I always felt that it was less risky to bet on myself than to tie my wagon to other hitches. When we shut down Ubernote, I picked up software consulting gigs by word of mouth and did well. But I always asked, *What's the next challenge? How can I take my own knowledge and productize it?*

How do you get someone to actually pay for your product?

There are a couple different ways we approach paid subscriptions with Referral Rock. We learned a lot of lessons with Ubernote. We had 20,000 users. But when we switched on a paid version, we had maybe 20 people that actually paid. That barely paid for the server.

I started asking the question, *How do I tie value to the product?* I wanted Referral Rock to become a paid product quickly. Within the first three or four months, it was probably up to $1,500-$2,000 a month.

Tell me about bootstrapping.

I wanted to strictly stay on the self-funded path. It's important for me to not let timing affect the business. It doesn't mean I don't have long-term vision, or that I couldn't see the business dominating a certain segment. But I don't want to go and hire a bunch of people and burn a lot of relationships or have an investor say, *You missed a quarter and you're unfundable.*

I wouldn't do anything different if we had more money. Because we're self-funded, I get to call the shots. I get to control the destiny of the company. And that feels good.

TAKEAWAYS

- Bootstrapping your own business means you get to stay in control of the timing (and destiny) of the company.
- Don't wait too long to put up a paywall.

#81

Steve Toth

Title: Founder, SEO Notebook; Founder, Gscore

Value proposition: Wordpress plug-in that identifies critical keywords not in your content

Industry: SEO

Keywords: Customer acquisition, non-technical founder, work-life balance

What is SEO Notebook, and what is Gscore?

SEO Notebook is my newsletter, which grew to 9,000 subscribers in just two years. Now I'm launching Gscore. Gscore is a WordPress plug-in that connects to Google search console, and helps you identify keywords that you are within page one striking distance of, but that are not in your content.

To spur sales of the plug-in, I'm giving away my archives of notes over the last year. Every week I email out one strategy, but now I'm collecting everything in one place. Anybody who buys the plug in is also going to get a copy of the full archive of notes. Hopefully it'll be an irresistible offer.

How did you get into SEO?

I've been experimenting with SEO since 2010. It was always very gratifying to see my blogs on SEO rank. I was in the corporate world for a long time. I worked in-house at FreshBooks, doing some really cool work and working as a consultant. By now, I've built up the flywheel so that I don't have to work to get leads. I can choose my clients.

The SaaS thing came to me in a very roundabout way. I had an idea for a product based on a very specific insight. I didn't think very hard about it. A client of mine recommended this development agency to me. He just said, "These guys could make your product if you want." So I went for it.

What has it been like to build a product as a non-technical founder?

I'm just the guy with the idea. That's basically been my whole career. I set the project in motion and people bring my ideas to life. Gscore is just a continuation of that.

Have there been any unexpected challenges to building a SaaS product?

The budgetary scope more than doubled. But that's okay. I've worked to be in a position where I knew even if the budget ran over, I would still be okay.

To anybody who is launching a SaaS product without developing it yourself: Make sure you have lots of breathing room when it comes to budget, because it can blow up in your face really fast.

What do you think will be the most rewarding part of building a SaaS?

It could change my lifestyle. My business is very attached to me right now. I can't really go on vacation. Having my involvement in a day-to-day capacity change is something that really excites me. I would be much happier to make half as much money and own a SaaS business than make double the amount and be a consultant.

Don't get me wrong. I love SEO and I love working on my clients' accounts. But eventually I will have enough money to be comfortable. Making the extra million dollars a year is not going to matter as much. Gscore will have annual billing, but eventually it will be something that has monthly recurring revenue as well.

When you built up your fan base for SEO Notebook, did you ever imagine that it would someday be a good customer base to launch a product?

I didn't think about that in the beginning at all. I just thought that it would be a good way to get clients. But eventually, I had some insights like, *I've got something here*. I had promoted and generated a lot of business for other people through my list. I thought it was time to start doing that for me.

What advice would you give to a SaaS founder who wants to build up an audience?

Consistency is the main thing. There are so many bright people in tech, people who are a wealth of knowledge. But there are very few people who would commit to sharing that knowledge on a weekly basis. Honestly, there have been imitators of SEO Notebook. One guy imitated not just the concept, but the color palette, everything. He quit after four weeks.

I've been sending a weekly email for 2+ years and then posting once per week on LinkedIn. For me, LinkedIn has been money in the bank. That's where I get most of my leads from. I seem to be able to generate hundreds of likes on each post, which is awesome.

Any final advice for SaaS founders?

If you want to become a successful entrepreneur, you can't complain that your job is to solve problems and fix things every day. Take on the mindset of, "There are no problems, only solutions."

TAKEAWAYS

- Make sure you've got breathing room in your budget. Building your product will likely cost you more than you think.

- When you're building your audience and sharing content, consistency is key.

- Don't complain about problems. Your job as an entrepreneur is to solve problems.

Chris Spags

Title: Founder, Jetboost

Value proposition: Provides premium add-ons for Webflow without custom code

Industry: Website plugins

Keywords: Customer acquisition, MVP

What is Jetboost?

We provide add-ons for Webflow that you can add to your Webflow site without any custom code.

Webflow is a website builder that is mainly targeted at designers. Basically, you can visually design a website without knowing HTML, JavaScript, or any programming languages. It's more powerful than Wix, WordPress, or Squarespace in that you can build any type of visual website that you want. But there are certain limitations, and that's where Jetboost comes in to provide additional features like filtering and searching content directly on a page.

How did you identify this as a problem to be solved?

I learned about Webflow from Corey Haines (see page 272). He built a job board using Webflow. I was looking at it one day, and I thought it would be cool if you could quickly search the jobs. I asked him if he had thought about adding that, but he said there was no easy way to do it in Webflow. So I wrote some custom JavaScript code that he put on his site. Over the course of six months or so, he started sending more and more people to me who were using Webflow who wanted a similar search for their site.

Initially, it wasn't something I pursued as a product. I was just writing code for people's websites for this custom feature, but eventually I thought this would be super cool if anyone using Webflow could do it themselves. I thought there might be a way I could build a product on top of Webflow that would allow them to do that.

What were the biggest risks to starting Jetboost?

There were two major risks. One, not knowing if people would pay for it. Two, I wasn't sure if this type of product was even possible to build because Webflow doesn't have an official marketplace or app store.

The first thing I did was just try to see if this was even possible. I started working on the product side and in the meantime, I also put up a landing page saying, here's what's coming. Here's this search feature that I'm working on and maybe a couple of other features that might come in the future. Here's the email sign-up. But I didn't attach any sort of price to that. I built the MVP, which took about a month, and then I went through the email list and started setting up calls with people one-on-one. On the fourth call, someone was ready to purchase.

What have been some of the unexpected challenges of running a SaaS?

The amount of customer support needed. It's a very low price point, and the intention is to be self-serve. You set it up on your own, but because people can use custom JavaScript and other things, there are a lot of different ways that it may not work exactly how they want it on their site. I didn't realize the amount of support that would be involved, and I waited far too long to hire someone to help out with that.

How are you approaching customer acquisition?

In the beginning, I relied heavily on Twitter. I started following anyone that would comment on Webflow accounts, Tweets, or their CEO's Tweets. Sometimes, they would follow me back and I'd get to share about what I was working on. That got shared around a little bit and then posted in some of the other Webflow communities. I did some outreach in the different communities where people talk about Webflow. From there, it started to spread primarily through word of mouth.

What do you like about running your own SaaS?

When I was consulting, my clients would have me coming into the office a few days a week. I was very much on their schedule. Now I'm working totally on my schedule, which is really freeing. And, my income isn't tied to the number of hours I can work, which is cool.

Any final advice you'd give to other aspiring founders with technical experience?

For a solo technical founder, going the route of building for an existing platform gives you a headstart because you don't have to do so much marketing. Whether they have an app store or a website or at least an integrations page, you can be in these areas and get distribution from the main platform itself. You can focus more on making sure the product is right.

Make sure you launch as fast as possible, because it's so easy to want to tinker around with the product, and make sure you don't feel embarrassed about the MVP. Until you know if people are going to pay for it, nothing else really matters.

TAKEAWAYS

- Building a product for an existing platform means you won't have to invest as much into marketing.

- To avoid building something no one will pay for, launch your MVP as quickly as possible.

#83

Danesh Karimi

Title: Founder, Sonat

Value proposition: Simplifies the process of writing, translating, and publishing technical documents

Industry: Technical writing

Keywords: Development, freemium, mindset, MVP, side hustle

What is Sonat?

Sonat is a tool for technical writers to create online user manuals, user guides, and tutorials. It simplifies the process of writing, translating, and publishing documents.

I was working in a company in Canada as a software engineer and I had a really bad experience with a similar tool. I thought, *I can create a better one*.

Did you develop Sonat yourself?

In the beginning, I decided to outsource development. I have a full time job, and I don't have much extra time. But I wasn't happy with the output. So, I hired a few full time engineers from abroad, who I still pay to develop the product.

Would you discourage other SaaS founders from outsourcing?

Outsourcing wasn't a successful experience, even for me as a technical person. At the end of the day, it just wasn't easy to get what we wanted. We had lots of delays, and we had problems with the quality of the software. So I decided to hire people, but I hired people in a different timezone. During the day, I work my full-time job, and at night, I do a standup meeting with my engineers from Sonat.

In the beginning, one of my biggest challenges was choosing between speed vs. good infrastructure. In other words, I didn't know if I should create something fast (focusing on time to market) or I should take my time and focus on the right infrastructure and patterns.

I did some research (read a bunch of articles from other SaaS founders, listened to the related podcasts, etc.) and I decided to focus on time. As a result, I chose "simpler" technologies (ex: Microsoft SQL Server) instead of scalable technologies (ex: Scalable Cloud native database).

After a while, I realized that I was going to have problems with these technologies because a) I want to use a freemium as a marketing strategy and get attention in the market, but to be able to do that, I need a scalable platform, and b) there are similar tools in the market, and I should be differencing myself with "quality." Better infrastructure could help me get there.

So I spent a few more months developing the freemium based on a cloud-native and scalable platform.

Why did you decide to launch a freemium version?

One main reason was I wanted to let people know about my software. I knew there were other tools in the market for years, and a freemium is a good way to get some attraction between all competitors. I know that I'm not really good at marketing and sales. So I wanted to use a freemium as a way to market the software.

Another reason (which is specific to my tool) is when you create an article or publish a user manual with Sonat; there is a "Powered By" at the bottom, so it links back to my site, which helps SEO.

Sonat has a low-touch sales model, meaning that we should do some marketing and SEO, and people can get on board with the software without interacting with any sales team.

How do you balance running a business with working full time?

It's not easy. But I always wanted to create something of my own. I have experience as a product owner, as a team leader, and as a technical architect, so even though I don't know anything about marketing and sales, I'm familiar with a significant part of the product life cycle.

Managing time is a bit challenging. I get finished with work, eat something, and at 6 or 7 PM, I jump into the stand-up and design meetings with my engineers. But at the same time, it's sort of a relief for me. Creating my own business was always my plan.

What made you finally take the leap into starting a business?

I always wanted to create something, but there were delays. I'm originally from Iran, and I knew I wanted to leave. There are a lot of smart people in Iran, but unfortunately, they don't have the opportunity to create and sell things for customers outside of Iran. I eventually moved to Canada and then to the United States. When I finally settled down, I thought, *if not now, when?*

What I would say to any aspiring entrepreneur is that you should love what you do. If you don't love it, especially if it's a side hustle, you'll give up when you encounter obstacles and challenges (believe me, there are a lot), and you're going to end up wasting time and money.

TAKEAWAYS

- If you get your product to market as quickly as possible, that can come at the expense of scalability. Be strategic about speed vs. infrastructure.

- Make sure you love what you're doing. If you don't, you're going to give up when you hit roadblocks and hurdles (and there are many).

Jessica Mangona

Title: Founder, Lumii

Value proposition: Real time analytics for HR to prevent turnover and disengagement

Industry: Human resources

Keywords: Mindset, time management, validation, work-life balance

What is Lumii?

Lumii is like Google Analytics for Human Resources. We measure real time interactions between employees happening within a company through automatic data collection. That way, human resources and management can identify employees who are siloed or at risk, and they can take action to prevent turnover and disengagement.

How did you identify this as a problem to be solved?

I've been an HR executive in tech for six years. I started at an agency and then went to a San Diego startup that does sustainability analytics. I saw that every department had access to real time data that they used to make business decisions, except for human resources. We were still working with surveys that were up to a year old. With how fast business changes and companies have to adapt, there was no way to be proactive with that type of information and prevent turnover and disengagement.

How have you validated product market fit for Lumii?

Launching this product during COVID was interesting, because from March to July of 2020, HR was really busy. No one wanted to talk to us and do customer interviews. Honestly, it was an excellent way to kick off startup life, because that's how it often is; you just have to keep pushing through.

As a founder, it's so key to understand that you are not the customer. You have to talk to a ton of people and get the research that validates this is not just a problem in your own head. We conducted 40 interviews and then drew out a Balsamic wireframe, which you can do for free online. For four months, we didn't spend any money. We didn't spend anything but our time to reach out and talk to people.

How do you balance your time?

When I get to those points where I'm working 14 or 15 hour days, I stop and ask, *Am I actually being effective with my time?* People will tell you that you have to manage your time, but what does that mean tactically? For example, this morning I sat down and took an hour and a half to write out our strategy for fundraising. If I have to have 100 conversations with different investors over 10 weeks, how many do I have to reach out to each day? How many do I have to research? I build out a plan of bite-sized pieces that I can do in one or two hours every day.

Again, people might give you high level advice like, "balance your time." But you've got to figure out the technical steps to make sure you accomplish your goals and not get sucked into distractions or mindless tasks. In the B2B space, it's important to be on LinkedIn, and in the investment space, it's important to be on Twitter. Just like any social media site, it's easy to blow up your day by scrolling for three hours. You have to be really strict.

What has surprised you about the journey of starting a SaaS?

It takes a long time to find quality work. You can go to Upwork or Fiverr, but if you pick the cheapest one, it's going to require a lot of your time. You're not going to be happy with the product. It might be worth your time just spending a little bit of extra money to get something really quality. Early on, I tried to be very cost conscious, but it definitely came back to bite me. We lost a couple of months from working with a vendor that wasn't able to deliver the quality we needed and we lost a couple thousand dollars.

What's the most important advice you would give to a founder?

95% of the time you feel down about yourself. Then you have one day or one meeting – that 5% – that lifts you up. You have to see the big picture and play the long game. You've got to just take it day by day.

TAKEAWAYS

- Assess how you're using your time. Working long hours isn't proof of productivity.

- When it comes to development, don't be so cost-conscious that you pay for low-quality work.

Bill Mcglade

Title: Founder, Hyvve

Value proposition: Creates an ecosystem where all your content can be viewed, engaged, and interacted with by your subscribers and members

Industry: Multiple

Keywords: Bootstrapping, customer feedback, mindset, pricing

What is Hyvve?

Hyvve is an app creator in which you can create an ecosystem where your subscribers and members can engage and interact with your content. It acts as an extension of the live events, by blending virtual capabilities with live. We put together community features, event listing features, and virtual capabilities all within one platform that's easily customizable.

With COVID, it just so happened that the industry is moving this way. That's a good thing, but there are also a bunch of other tech companies in the space now. All of a sudden, the ocean has become quite red.

How did COVID-19 impact your business?

COVID impacted us in the sense that budgets were strapped. But my firm belief is that technology should be affordable. Our product costs around $6,000 a year. Our competitors start at around $24,000 a year. For that reason, budget becomes almost a nonexistent conversation when we're reaching new customers.

What has affected us more is that people in the association space don't really know what their strategies are going to be. These associations are kind of in limbo. Do I just stay virtual? Do I go back to full live events? Do I blend the two?

That's where we hop into the conversation and say that it doesn't matter. This technology is going to help you do whatever you decide to do. In a sense, we blend live and virtual by providing a medium in which interaction and engagement doesn't stop at the event but lives on 365 days a year.

What lessons did you carry from your previous business into Hyvve?

In the last company, we had an astronomical number of project managers. This time around, I wanted to have a SaaS that didn't require that many project managers. Right now we don't have any. I like to joke that we're a "two and a half person" team. As the CEO, I act as the sales, marketing, and operations department. In a way, I've cloned half of myself in order to complete everything.

Everything is built to be self-serve and easily configurable. Once we do the initial two-hour onboarding, the customers are able to do most everything on their own, although they can reach out to me for help.

What advice would you give to SaaS founders?

We had 95% of our knowledge doc done before the major launch in November. In October, we spent most of the time developing all of the knowledge base, so that when the launch came, onboarding was smooth and easy.

I think a lot of companies spend so much time talking to customers that they sometimes forget to build out the knowledge base. The labor is gruesome and tedious, but it really helps. You'll find bugs in the system before your customers. It also helps you understand that there are more capabilities behind your service than you even thought, and puts you in the shoes of your customers.

What are three qualities that every SaaS founder needs?

Number one is passion. If you don't believe in what you're building and what you're doing, don't do it.

Next, founders need to know how to receive feedback. I've seen so many friends that started out with a product, and the moment that they get any sort of feedback and criticism, they push back and say, "Well, it doesn't matter. Other people will buy it." The reason you're doing your soft launch is to get feedback and to fix certain things. Internalize and process feedback, and then decide whether you're going to either take action on it or say, no, I'm going to stick with the route that I'm going with.

Number three, figure out ways to keep yourself motivated. You have to constantly keep your foot on the business dev pedal, especially if you're bootstrapping. If that's the case, your number one job is business development until you can hire a full-fledged sales team – but only if you need it.

TAKEAWAYS

- Build out your knowledge base. It will help you identify bugs and really understand the capabilities of your product.

- Learn to receive and process feedback that you don't like.

- Keep focusing on business development, especially if you're bootstrapping.

#86

Curran Van Waarde

Title: Founder, CallScaler

Value proposition: Tracks call response rate for different marketing campaigns

Industry: Marketing, Communications

Keywords: Development, mindset, resources

What is CallScaler?

CallScaler is a call tracking company. For example, if you're a pest control company, a good way to track your calls for different marketing campaigns is to set up different numbers. You can use CallScaler to track how many calls each marketing campaign brought in.

How did you identify this as a problem to be solved?

I had a client who needed this. He had 20 different numbers for different campaigns. Every other solution immediately put me in the enterprise plan if I was going to be buying numbers. So, I found this API that had super cheap phone numbers. Then I thought, *If I find a lot of value from this, I'm sure other people will.*

What's your professional background?

I used to do a lot of WordPress design and development, and I freelance. But I've always wanted to do something in SaaS.

Why SaaS?

There are other businesses out there that have recurring revenue, but this one is so consistent. If you can keep churn down, SaaS is always going to grow steadily over time.

Has it met your expectations?

It's definitely tested my patience, and It's hard to move super fast without burning through a bunch of money. I work on it in sprints because I have a developer who I work with and I'll do the design. I'll put something on the product roadmap and then it takes him way longer to develop it than it does for me to come up with the idea. I'll often do design for a couple of days and then wait a couple of weeks while he executes.

Did you always know that you wanted to run your own business?

One hundred percent. When I first graduated college five years ago, I worked for a consulting firm for nine months, but quickly left that to start doing my own thing. From a very young age, I was always a builder. Even back in grade school, I was building things with Legos all the time. I like starting something from scratch and turning it into something else. I find a lot of personal satisfaction from that.

What's one lesson you've learned from building a SaaS?

I did not realize how important it is to build the right infrastructure from the start, specifically with SaaS. Now we're a year and a half down the road and there are issues with how we started it from a technical perspective. If I had to do it again, I might do things a bit differently.

I don't think there's anything wrong with using overseas developers – that's what I've done – but getting a more experienced person who's built a scalable platform can help give you the right foundation.

What would you say to a college student who wants to start their own SaaS?

If you don't have an idea right away, try freelancing. There are so many opportunities out there, and basically you get paid to learn how to do stuff. There's a lot of people who don't take that opportunity. When you freelance, you can learn the infrastructure part before you start your own thing and make a bunch of tactical mistakes.

What would you recommend for learning more about running a successful SaaS?

There are a few podcasts that I really like. One is the "Art of Product" podcast, which follows two guys on their journey of creating two different SaaS businesses. It's not a bunch of hype. It's just them talking about what they're doing.

One of the best things was going to Facebook groups and seeing the issues that people have. Almost the majority of my first customers were just from talking with people in Facebook groups and trying to figure out their problems. If you see people constantly commenting on one thing, or asking the same question over and over, you can identify the pain points.

What kind of mindset does it take to run a business?

You've got to be comfortable with risk. If you're not comfortable with risk, it's probably better to just get a full time job.

TAKEAWAYS

- Focus on infrastructure from the start. You're less likely to experience regrets later on.
- Check out Facebook groups to see what your customers are talking about, and what their problems are.
- Freelancing will give you great experience (and an income) until you have an idea for a product.
- If you don't like risk, get a regular job.

Roberto Inetti

Title: Founder & CEO, ROBOAMP

Value proposition: One line of code that increases website speed to 1 second or less on any mobile device

Industry: Internet

Keywords: Resources

What is ROBOAMP?

With just one line of code, we can make any website load in one second or less on any mobile device.

There are a trillion active websites in the world, and Google estimates that 70% of those sites take between four to eight seconds to load. You don't have to be a math whiz to realize that represents billions of lost dollars in revenue.

What's your background?

I'm a software engineer by trade. I was lucky to start my programming career extremely young. In fact, I started programming when I was seven years old, when I was growing up in Uruguay. I have no clue what inspired my mom – a woman with no formal education –to put me in studies for programming.

Very early in my career I was lucky to work in Tier 1 companies developing large scale websites. I have a true love for the web. I think it's one of the most important inventions ever created by humanity.

What has your journey been like?

I went against the grain, against the common knowledge or common advice, of pushing hard or selling right away. The first year was all heads down development. I was working on this full time. This wasn't a side gig. I focused on the long term vision and made sure the user experience was right, no sales whatsoever. Now, we're one of the three companies in all of Texas that were invited by Google to go for the Google startup program. Sometimes going against the common wisdom pays off.

Have you encountered any challenges along the way of pitching your product and reaching customers?

Yes and no. I used to be a CTO. If someone came to me three years ago and told me, "We can make your website 10 times faster with absolutely nothing to code on the front end and absolutely nothing to code on the backend, and no extra server configuration. All you have to do is to put in one line of code and that's it," I would have been the first to call BS on that. Because three or four years ago, this concept of web performance as a service wasn't developed. So in that regard, because it's kind of bleeding edge, there is an education curve. You need to explain to people how it's possible.

Because we are very data-driven, however, it's easy to show potential customers how fast their website will be, and how beautiful it can look. It's not only faster, it looks almost pixel perfect compared to your current website. So in that regard, it's very easy to demonstrate the benefit. With SEO for example, you're maybe going to see results in three months. With this, you can see results right away.

What's one of the most common mistakes that you see founders making?

I love to read and I surround myself with very good mentors. In other words, I consume a lot of information. Knowing how to filter advice is one of the most undervalued skills for a founder.

Here's a short story to demonstrate that: We were in the process of landing a very important customer–a company that generates billions of dollars a year. It was totally unexpected. It just happened serendipitously. So, I met with three of my mentors. These are people who were very business savvy, people who have sold their companies. I asked them, "How do we price this?" And all of them replied with different advice.

Be able to filter information based on your current situation, try to be in the mind of the people who are reading the content or answering your phone calls. Most advice comes from a good place. People want to help you out. But it's your job as an entrepreneur to try to say, "Okay, this is useful because of this. This is not useful because of that." Being able to parse information and advice is something that I think every founder – SaaS or not – should spend time trying to nail.

TAKEAWAYS

- Be prepared to show potential customers data on how and why your product will improve their lives.
- Filter advice that you get from other entrepreneurs.

Andrew Wynans

Title: Founder, Afire (on hold)

Value proposition: Makes it simple to manage one-to-one connections across social media platforms

Industry: Social media

Keywords: Customer discovery, mindset, validation

What is Afire?

The idea of Afire is to build a better way to manage and understand your relationships and your network across different social media platforms. The average person has between eight to 10 social media accounts. Most of us – especially marketers, investors, and founders – are communicating on a bunch of different platforms at one time.

While there are a lot of great tools for social media, there aren't a lot of great tools for one-to-one communication on social platforms. Direct messages (DM's) are wildly under-built, mostly because they don't make money. What we're finding is that our professional lives and our personal lives are being lived in DM's. Traditional CRM's don't take these things into account because they only look at the professional side of things. But our lives have sort of blended between the professional and the personal – especially during the pandemic.

How did you identify this as a problem?

My previous company, GameWisp, worked specifically in the social influencer space with gamers. So we started to learn about all of the problems that content creators face and started to dig into those problems. Gamers are often on the cutting edge of what's happening, and I knew that the problems they were facing were going to be the same problems that everyone would be facing in a couple of years.

The biggest problem that content creators have is complexity. There are so many platforms and you only have so much time, effort, and creativity that you can expend building your content. If you're a YouTuber and you want to take on Tik-Tok, that's more work. If you want to do YouTube and Instagram and Tik-Tok and promote it all on Twitter, you're at a 120 hour per week job. Then what happens when the next Tik-Tok comes along?

The bottom line is that solo content creators don't have the ability to take on all of the elements and all of the opportunities that are in front of them. When I started digging into that problem, I realized there are discrete elements that even the platforms themselves haven't started to think about. DM's for personal and professional relationships are one area where most social networks aren't spending any time, but where the users are spending a lot of time.

I realized very quickly that people were feeling burnt out and overwhelmed. They were feeling like they weren't keeping up with important relationships. They were losing opportunities.

How did you validate your idea?

Any time I have an idea, I ask, *Who's likely to have this problem?* Then I contact as many people as I can who might have the same problem. Once I get on their calendar, I sit down and have an honest conversation. My background is in law. In law, they say you never ask a question you don't know the answer to. In entrepreneurship, you never ask a question you *know* the answer to. If you're pretty sure someone's going to answer your question in a particular way, don't ask it. All that's going to do is validate something you already believed in.

Around 50% of founders identify a problem that they have themselves. Then they go and solve it. The problem is, you might end up having a market of one – yourself. Then there's about 50% of founders that actually go and do the homework. Those are the ones that tend to be super successful. They measure twice, cut once.

What do people need to know about branding for SaaS?

What people miss about branding over and over again is that brand is not colors and logos and taglines. Brand is fundamental identity. Part of the reason doing your homework is so important is that you learn the visceral motivations behind your customers' problems. The visceral motivation for Afire, for example, is FOMO.

You've got to develop empathy. Doing your homework means not just asking, "What are you doing and how does it work?" It means asking, "What does this mean to you? What does this do for you on a day-to-day basis? If this saves you an hour, what does that hour go to?" When you ask those questions, you'll start to get a sense of what this person cares about the most.

The next step is really to sit down and to craft an idea of who you are based on that emotion. If your whole identity is based around the product, that's only going to take you so far.

What's the #1 most important piece of advice you'd give to founders?

Founding a company is hard. You run into problems. You get discouraged. Imposter syndrome is a thing.

Celebrate every win, no matter how small. That might just mean you take a break and jump around a little bit. Too often we allow ourselves to get caught up in the grind. By the time we're done we realize that we didn't just miss the minor moments, we missed the major ones. If you celebrate the little wins in your own life and in your own work, you'll do it with your teams. That's going to make your teams much more excited to show up every day.

TAKEAWAYS

- Don't ask questions you already know the answer to.
- What emotional need is your product meeting? That should be a fundamental part of your branding.
- Celebrate the little wins.

Dom Zijlstra

Title: Founder, Traverse.link
Value proposition: Learning tool
Industry: Online education
Keywords: Bootstrapping, product/market fit, validation

What is Traverse.link?

It's a platform where you can create an online course and see if it works for your audience, and if so, you can make it bigger. The idea is that you can get started much quicker than with traditional course creation platforms.

How did you come up with this idea?

I had the idea when I was struggling to learn Chinese. I developed a method for myself to learn, and I wanted to teach that method to other people through a course. But it was hard to get started with existing platforms, so I decided to develop my own. It wasn't my original goal, but there seems to be a good product/market fit.

How have you seen product/market fit?

That's basically the stage I'm at right now. I'm talking to lots of people – mainly on Twitter – who are trying out the platform. I'm talking to them to see what problems they run into, what works for them, and what doesn't. Some people think they're interested, but they drop off. Apparently, that's not the right target group.

I'm also bootstrapping, and building a course about that experience.

What's your professional background?

I studied engineering physics. First, I worked for Airbus and Aerospace as a software engineer. After that I went to a London Fintech startup, where I worked as a data scientist for three years. I did that up until one month ago, when I left that job to work full-time on TraverseLink.

What did it look like for you to take the leap from leaving that job and now be full time bootstrapping a company?

It was scary at first. I was doing it on the side for a while, so I thought I'd just take the jump. But then I realized how hard it is to actually monetize what I've built. I was very excited at first, but I had to get some confidence to just get out there and talk to people and build an audience.

What has the customer development process been like?

This was another thing that I had to learn from scratch, because I've never done much social media before. I did reach out to a lot of people cold and once some of those people replied, I started connecting with them and started connecting to the circles around them.

What has been rewarding about going full time into your own product?

One of the most rewarding aspects is to realize how much there is to learn. UX design is one example. Building an audience or marketing are other examples. You see those fields from the outside and you know what they are doing – or you think you know – but then you have to do it yourself and you realize how little you actually know. For me, that's very interesting.

Any final advice for SaaS founders?

Validate the problem before you start. Find an audience and set out to solve one of their problems before starting a product. I kind of went the other way. I have to fit my product onto an audience. I think if I researched properly and validated it before starting out, that would have been much easier.

TAKEAWAYS

- Enjoy the learning process of becoming a founder.
- Find an audience, then build a product for them.

#90

Jesse Tayler

Title: Founder, TruAnon

Value proposition: TruAnon prevents identity fraud, scams and bad actors from exploiting your service

Industry: Identity Confirmation

Keywords: Mindset

How did you get involved in software?

My parents are university people. I didn't even know the word "entrepreneur," but I had the disease, as some of us do. I was going to be in a band, but that actually requires talent. The only thing that I could do that people would pay me to do was software, which I had been doing for fun since I was very young. I was a terrible student, and I didn't think of software as a vocation – even though I was exceptionally good at it.

My entrepreneur story is stumbling into it and moving to Seattle. I met my first business partner, who was probably old enough to be my mom and in a lot of ways, was kind of a mother figure to me. But we made a great team. I brought a lot of enthusiasm and an unfettered approach to building, and she brought the wisdom, the people, the players, and the money. I learned about ethics and doing business.

We got to build some interesting stuff. In fact, we built the first App Store in the early 90's. That (Steve Jobs demo) gave me the latitude to pick and choose some of the stuff that I might do in my career.

What's it like to be an entrepreneur?

I was recently watching a Ken Burns film on baseball, and there was this moment where a guy says, "In baseball, we revere the greats, the best of the best. They step up to the plate to fail seven out of every 10 times."

That's the way I view startups. You willfully step up to the plate to fail seven out of 10 times. We like to make movies about folks who hardly stepped up to the plate and achieved success that seems phenomenal. Typically, entrepreneurship involves a lot of failure. Entrepreneurs who are sometimes down on themselves or thinking that they haven't succeeded with their project are just facing a mental hurdle. They have to know that failure is part of the game.

Do you regret anything in your entrepreneurial career?

If I had anything to regret in my entrepreneurial career, it's saying that something was a failure because it was either too early, too awkward, or didn't have all the pieces yet.

When you're a startup, you're essentially inventing something. Otherwise you don't have a reason to be there. This means that you're going to be assembling parts that didn't exist before. Sometimes, you fail seven out of 10 times. I think the only regrets I've ever had are saying to myself, "Well, that code takes me time and effort to keep it running. I don't see the business need right now," or, "I've failed. The team is disbanded. It's over." Therefore, I'm going to throw it away and discard it rather than spending a little bit of time and energy keeping it around just in case.

Some of the things I've created would now be viable due to some other technology. But I've dropped my service or the code is now so far out of date that it's an insurmountable thing. I would have a message of cautious faith. Software is certainly not for the faint of heart. Give respect to the folks who were born with the disease. We would try and make our mothers proud some normal way if we were able. But I do believe that software will be humanity's great effort in this next generation.

TAKEAWAYS

- Failure is inevitable, and part of the process. Keep in mind that your product may have failed because the timing was wrong, not because it was a bad idea.

#91

Philipp Tsipman

Title: Founder, Artland

Value proposition: Premium marketplace for hiring world-class digital designers and marketing experts

Industry: Hiring, creator economy

Keywords: AI, chicken or the egg, marketplace

What is Artland?

Artland is a premium marketplace for hiring the world's best digital designers and marketing experts.

How did you get the idea for Artland?

I've worked in marketing for over 10 years. The bane of my existence has always been figuring out how to rapidly spin up new creative projects and to get the right agencies and the right help. One week you want to do a video, the next week an infographic, the next a blog post or an ad campaign. No one has enough staff to do all this. So more often than not, it's felt to me like "making do" with suboptimal options.

Fiverr and Upwork were the originals in trying to organize people into a talent pool. My biggest issue with them has been that they are very messy marketplaces with unpredictable quality, which undermines a lot of trust. My first experience with Upwork was that somebody stole money from me. And, you often see people who claim to write content, but their profile is riddled with misspellings and broken sentences – even if they're one of the "top recommendations."

For me, it's critical to have an incredible pool of both talent and clients. The two feed off each other. We have multiple creative experts on the platform who are Emmy and Cannes Lions winners. And they attract the type of clients that you won't find on other platforms.

There are a few key principles that create a marketplace that functions well and where people find a lot of joy. One is good design. One is removing as many awkward inefficiencies from the process as possible – from bookings, to project management, to tax compliance. As Web 3 technologies scale up in the future, I can see a ton of new opportunities for financing really cool creative collaborations between the talented folks on the platform.

How do you handle the "chicken or the egg" challenge of building a marketplace?

In my previous company, we did A/B testing for ads and developed a deep network of clients and talent. So, I had the connections to create a strong community out of the gate. As a founder, I'm basically running back and forth between the two sides of the marketplace and helping to facilitate each one. As Artland scales, the process becomes less manual. The more data we have on what pairings of clients, talent, projects and process steps have worked well, the more we can create useful AI-generated recommendations for how to make the next project better.

What opportunities could Web 3 technologies provide to grow your platform?

I hope Web 3 technologies allow for much easier co-operative economics. Imagine a young startup (like us!) wanting to collaborate with a top-tier creative director on a video project. It's pretty challenging to be able to pay for something like this out of pocket, or to issue stock or options outright. But, if we could drop a set of NFTs to the creator with some exclusive rights, that becomes very interesting. When Facebook first started, it paid graffiti artist David Choe $60K to paint its building, which he took in stock. This became $200M at the IPO. I hope that Web 3 allows for collaborations along these lines to become much more common – giving creative folks some real financial upside.

What would you say are three qualities that are needed for someone who is starting a business in SaaS?

The first quality is that you have to be able to nail the technology. If you're starting a restaurant, the most important thing is how awesome the food is. If it's not, it doesn't matter if you have beautiful tables or decor or music. As a restaurant owner, knowing how to make really good food is the first place to start. In tech and SaaS, the code is the core. I don't think you have to be the technical co-founder to be successful, but you have to be comfortable and fluent with it and willing to learn.

The second quality is being a good storyteller. People really have to believe in you. A founder has to be able to tell their story and enjoy it.

The third is that you have to be a people person. You don't have to be extroverted, but you still have to like people. You can't get too far in creating something new by walking alone.

TAKEAWAYS

- If you're a non-technical founder, learn enough to be comfortable with programmers.

- Be able to tell your story in compelling ways.

- You don't need to be an extrovert to be a founder. But you do have to like people.

#92

Seena Makari

Title: Founder & CEO, Ogma

Value proposition: Two-sided marketplace for tutors and students

Industry: Education

Keywords: Chicken or the egg, development, marketplace, non-technical founder

What is Ogma?

Ogma is an e-learning platform that connects students with online tutors. What differentiates ourselves from the plethora of other websites that do this is that we focus on speed, convenience, and affordability. Our goal is to get a student on a call with a qualified and affordable tutor in less than five minutes – we call ourselves the "Uber for tutors." If a student wants a session, they fill in the subject they need help with, their grade or level, and the time they want their session. They will then be given a list of tutors available at those times, and can request them with one click. We set up meetings and facilitate automatic payments to make the experience more convenient for everyone. In return, we take a 20% commission.

How did you identify this as a problem to be solved?

For whatever reason, a lot of people are graduating university and they can't find jobs. They're competing with outsourcing. They're competing with artificial intelligence. They're competing with downsizing. But these people have a commodity, and that's education. If you have a bachelor's degree in chemistry and you're having a tough time finding a job, instead of doing a gig such as Uber, you're video calling somebody from the comfort of your home. And you're going to be making a lot more money than if you were delivering food or if you were ride sharing. I'm not trying to say that these are bad choices. But there are options that can help you make more money with less effort.

Have you experienced this personally?

The University of Washington did a 2019 study and found that over half of recent college graduates are either unemployed or underemployed. I'm not trying to say that you can make loads of money from being a private tutor. But it might help you with groceries or rent.

Where are you in the process of development?

I'm doing an alpha stage and a beta stage at the same time. I have one paying customer, but we still have some bugs. We started the test about a month ago and everything's fine except for payments. When people pay, the money goes through. But they don't get access to the student list. We're working hard to fix that technical bug. Once we do that, the website is pretty much complete.

How do you plan on acquiring tutors?

Right now, I have 80 tutors. I found them mostly through Reddit and Twitter, and I believe some people found me through LinkedIn as well. I'm also planning on leveraging Instagram. Each platform is unique; you have to approach each in a different way to get people's attention.

I had a Tweet that blew up. It was pleasantly surprising because I had only 22 followers at the time. I said something like, "I got my first sixteen dollars of revenue for my startup." It got like 15,000 likes because so many people were retweeting it. After that, business just exploded. Lots of people signed up as writers and students.

What's your background?

I'm an economics and political science student, and I've just finished up my second year at the University of Ottawa. In my economics class, we talk about the economy, artificial intelligence, and technological development and how they squeeze labor out. Being able to identify trends like that allowed me to leverage this idea that education is going to be around whether we're in a recession or in a period of economic expansion. I've programmed in the past, but I still have a unique look on things because I'm not really a tech person. I work with programmers who do the coding.

What advice would you give to aspiring SaaS founders who are also students?

Leverage your network of peers. Ogma would never have worked if I was working with people who had 15 years of technical experience. One of my programmers is a good friend of mine who gave me a deal that I could actually afford. I can't pay $20k for a website. Talk to computer science students, talk to people who run student consulting firms. There are options.

TAKEAWAYS

- If you're a student that wants to start a SaaS business, leverage your network of peers to help you.

Brian Fife

Title: Founder & CEO, Local Links

Value proposition: Concierge platform that connects local businesses with tourists

Industry: Travel

Keywords: MVP, time management

What is Local Links?

Local Links connects people who are taking trips with local services. It's basically a concierge platform that connects households with services like personal chefs or tour guides.

I believe there's an opportunity for more egalitarianism in the tourism industry – similar to what Uber does, where the drivers get to be in control. Our goal is to provide a revenue channel to those that are renting out their homes. We do a percentage revenue share of all of our transaction fees with owners.

What have you learned in the process of building an MVP?

An MVP is not going to be exactly what's in your head. What's in your head is much bigger than you can possibly afford to build before you launch a business. Don't overdo it because it's easy to spin your wheels and think about all different kinds of features you might want to add. An imperfect product is better than no product at all.

How do you manage your time?

I'm a night owl, so I sleep from 4 AM to 10:00 or 11:00 AM. I don't mind it because I make my own hours. I work three hour chunks of time, and then I take a break. I do that in three to four different segments throughout the day, including from 11:00 PM to 3:00 AM.

Is there any final advice you would give to new entrepreneurs in SaaS?

I have a mentor that said that as an entrepreneur, you could go from the happiest moment to the deepest, darkest madness all in one day. Your emotion right now may not stand so tomorrow, just keep moving.

Starting a business is an emotional process. It is one of the most stressful and yet also the most exciting and wonderful parts of my life.

TAKEAWAYS

- Don't overdo your MVP – what you're imagining is probably more than you can afford to build in the beginning.
- Don't pay too much attention to emotional lows. Just keep going.

#94

Paul Williams

Title: Founder, Social Popcorn

Value proposition: Gives TV and movie watchers a channel to connect and respond to media with asynchronous communication

Industry: Media, social networking

Keywords: Mindset

Tell me about your app, and what kind of problem it solves.

The app is called Social Popcorn. The problem that it's trying to solve specifically is because of on-demand media like Netflix or Amazon Prime. They've given us a glut of content that we can watch whenever we want. There's no appointment viewing anymore, like "We're all going to watch that show on Thursday night at 9:00 PM."

That kind of convenience and glut of content has created this thing where we're watching a lot of our favorite TV shows and movies alone. For me, the biggest problem that I want to solve is when you have one of those moments when you're watching that TV show or movie and your jaw literally drops, and you can't believe what just happened. And you're sitting there looking around like, *Who can I share this with?*

Other companies have tried to solve this problem by creating these real time watch parties, which are cool. The problem is, they require you to schedule with friends or even strangers. But no one wants to wait two weeks until everyone can get their schedules together. So I'm trying to get that experience back for all of us.

I want to be able to connect people on an emotional level. But it also has to be practical. It has to work with the way we consume content.

What kind of advice would you give to another founder who is just starting out?

I read a lot of books and listen to a lot of podcasts. You don't always hear this, but the most successful business people in the world make time to read and to keep educating themselves. My goal is to avoid as many mistakes as I can because I'll make so many on my own. If I can learn from other people's mistakes first and knock out a good 20-30% of mistakes that I wouldn't have made otherwise, then that's what I'm going to do.

TAKEAWAYS

- Keep educating yourself; take advantage of resources and learn from the mistakes of others.

PART 5

NO-CODE HEROES

Founders who believe that building a SaaS doesn't have to mean coding

#95

Art West

Title: Founder, NoCodeDevs

Value proposition: Supports and empowers people to build using no-code tools

Industry: No-code

Keywords: Development, mindset, no-code

What is NoCodeDevs?

NoCodeDevs is a community of makers, founders, and business people–such as project managers and product developers – that all use a suite of no-code and low-code tools to help them be better at their job and start their businesses. Within that suite of products, we have everything from education modules to no-code test products like marketing products, email distribution products, automation tools, and a whole gamut of different digital tools to help makers.

How did you get involved in no-code?

By accident. I use no-code and automation tools in my day job to automate certain processes and to streamline the work that I do. I bumped into the no-code community down some sort of rabbit hole looking for a tool. No-code was becoming a buzzword, a more relevant term in the space. I could just see nothing but upward growth. So I dove in headfirst and immersed myself in the community. As a consequence, I've sort of emerged as a figurehead in the no-code community, so to speak. My place in the community is definitely mixed, but I touch a lot of different parts. I'm not just like back-end or front-end or marketing. I traverse through all the different channels. It's a lot of fun.

How do you help people build SaaS products specifically?

We help folks build tools to solve their problems. Maybe they don't have a technical cofounder or perhaps they don't have the budget to fully develop a tool and they just want to get to some sort of a mobile product.

What's the first thing you would tell someone wanting to build a SaaS tool with no-code?

Have a clear set of requirements of exactly what you need, because if you don't have requirements, then you really don't even know what you want. You don't want to waste your own time. You need to know what you're trying to accomplish. If that person was to work with us, we'd match you to the correct tools, because let's be honest, there are so many tools out there and so many different ways of doing something. If you're not clear on what you're trying to accomplish, you'll likely choose the wrong one and not exactly solve the problem you set out to achieve in the first place.

What's the first step in coming up with specific requirements?

Mind-mapping or whiteboarding. Then, market research, which could just be talking to people on Twitter or asking your friends or family to give some feedback. That's the first step. It sounds pretty rudimentary, but people often skip that step. You can end up going down this path of solving a problem that doesn't need to be solved or isn't worth somebody paying for.

What are you excited about right now in no-code?

What's really cool right now is some of the automation stuff that you can do, and of course, audio is super hot. We've seen that with Clubhouse and Twitter, and Facebook and Reddit are also introducing audio. So we've done some cool stuff with audio, video and transcription – all with no-code. One thing that we helped with was to take a podcast clip, transcribe it, and then convert it into a video and overlay it on top of a marketing image. That creates a shareable clip. Two years ago, you would have never been able to do that without a technical back-end.

What's one challenge that you faced in terms of helping people build SaaS platforms?

With no-code, the question that everybody brings up at the onset is scaling. Part of the scaling equation is not just scaling of users, but also scaling from the team development side of things. Can you have 10 developers or marketers all working in the same no-code tool to build a product? In a traditional dev world, you've got version control. You've got a robust suite of products that's taken 25 years to evolve. Is *not* having that track record going to be a major hurdle that's going to cause my SaaS to break as we get to scale? The space hasn't really fully matured yet. Over the next one to five years, it will be really interesting to see how both these problems get solved.

What are some of the qualities that you think are important for entrepreneurs?

Patience, persistence, and the ability to be bored. So many people say they want to be in a startup. But I always ask, *Do you really?* Because after the excitement wears off, it's a lot of experiencing the same thing day after day, like Groundhog Day. It takes a lot of consistency, a lot of hard work and constant iteration, so to speak, because if you don't evolve the product constantly, your SaaS will slowly dwindle.

Any final advice to SaaS founders?

You can have the best product in the world, but you have to consider marketing and sales. If you don't get your product in front of anyone, no one is going to buy it. It's really important to build an audience, even before you launch a product.

TAKEAWAYS

- If you want to build with no-code tools, create a clear set of requirements before building. Before creating requirements, do market research!

- Get comfortable with boredom. Starting a business can feel like Groundhog Day, every day.

Cam Bannister

Title: Co-founder & CEO, FreeByrd

Value proposition: FreeByrd helps people launch their businesses online, bringing website development, email marketing, online education sales funnels, and more into a single place

Industry: Marketing

Keywords: Bootstrapping, fundraising, iteration, mindset

What is FreeByrd?

FreeByrd is the ultimate all-in-one platform to build your business online. It's for people who are tech averse or who have never brought their business to life through digital marketing. It allows people to build websites, create online education sales funnels, and do email marketing all in one place.

How did you identify this is a problem to be solved?

I used to be a traveling hair stylist in Dallas and New York. Through that journey of learning the beauty industry, I realized that there was this gap in knowledge and resources of how to build a successful independent business. I saw so many professionals working multiple jobs, trying to work for Uber or be waitresses while I was working 48 days a year clearing six figures. I'm thinking, *Where is this great divide?* It certainly wasn't my background, because I'm from a small town. It was my passion for what I did that just drove me to keep growing.

One night, I was scrolling through Instagram, very frustrated that my industry was more concerned with the numbers on their Instagram account than they were about reaching clients and strategically marketing the work they were producing. I wanted to tell them, "You're going to miss it!" So I went into my living room and rolled out some paper and started building the first concept of FreeByrd. My husband Derek walked in, and I'm like, "I think I have an idea." As soon as I finished sketching it out, he started wireframing.

That's how FreeByrd got started. We've seen great success so far. To give context, one of our professionals who didn't even have a website four years ago has cleared $120k by bringing her services online through FreeByrd. She just did her first online class through FreeByrd and made $9,500.

What has this journey looked like as a non-technical founder?

I didn't have a computer until about two years ago. I started FreeByrd with an iPad and my iPhone. But being a non-technical person has allowed me to better understand my market. I know how to hold the space to educate a demographic of people who don't have this knowledge. I'm still learning too, as I'm running a company that looks so different than what I've done in the past. It's like learning a new language.

What has the development process looked like for you?

My technical co-founder and I have worked with multiple softwares to create our own. That's allowed us to stay agile and move quickly. We went the way of custom-built for the first year and a half. What we found is that in today's market, it's unnecessary to get hung up on creating something from scratch.

How have you tested FreeByrd?

We've been working with 10-15 groups of users, and every time we roll out a new iteration, we see how they like it and work with it. Then we move forward quickly. We don't ask too many questions; we just move. Over the last year, we've pivoted four times.

How have you funded your business?

Starting out, FreeByrd was completely funded. After concepting it in our living room, our first investment came two days later, when one of my clients came to my house and saw the sketches. I asked her to sign an NDA and she sent us a check three days later. In our first year and a half, we raised $140k in Friends and Family – all accredited investors, all my clients.

Until now, all of FreeByrd has been funded 100% by my clients. To date, we've raised $170k and we're doing another raise, but we're also bootstrapping. With bootstrapping, I would tell founders just to be mindful that money ebbs and flows drastically and you need to be prepared. You're in it for the long haul. I'm taking my family and moving into my mom's house because I want to make sure that I can still run and grow a sustainable company. In five years, I don't want to have this overhead of capital that I raised just to get to a certain point when it would have been more diligent to focus on what my customers need and expedite sales that way. I'm all about making sure my investors get their return, but I'm not about to go into debt.

Today, the company's doing better than ever. We own 100% of our company, and three years, in we're running a successful SaaS.

What would you say are three character traits that SaaS founders need?

Perseverance, patience and vision.

When you are building something that you're passionate about, don't get lost in what other people are doing. If you believe your company is not headed in the right direction, go quiet and ask yourself, *Am I headed where I want to be?* In the end, you're the one who shows up every day for your company. If you're creating something that isn't going in a direction where you can see yourself in one year, or five years, you need to hone in on your vision and mission and go back to it as much as possible. You also need to be willing to let go of everything and pivot if needed.

TAKEAWAYS

- Is your product taking a direction you can't commit to for the next five years? If so, be willing to pivot.
- Consider stitching together your MVP (or final product) with existing software tools.

#97

Corey Haines

Title: Founder, Swipe Files

Value proposition: Provides community and courses for SaaS founders & marketers

Industry: Marketing

Keywords: Customer acquisition, customer discovery, chicken or the egg, marketplace, no-code

What is Swipe Files?

If you work in marketing, your friends, your family, and even some of your coworkers don't really know exactly what you do. Same goes if you work in SaaS. So "SaaS marketing" gets really niche. A lot of founders and marketers in SaaS find themselves in a situation where they have no one else to lean on for advice, insight, or inspiration. You might be in charge of marketing without having done it yourself, be the first marketing hire with limited resources, or an emerging leader. No matter who you are, odds are you'll be making it up as you go. If you have a question, you can go to Twitter or maybe ask someone you know. But you don't want to pester people.

Swipe Files is basically a place to connect with other SaaS founders and marketers who can answer your questions, keep you accountable, and share proven strategies to grow. Swipe Files also provides three video courses and monthly "Office Hours" sessions for member Q&A. My experience is in growing SaaS companies so I leverage that to help others who want to do the same.

How did you identify this as a problem to be solved?

I am one of the rare marketers that got a degree in marketing. But even then, I didn't learn very much. The things they teach you in marketing in school are things from five or 10 years ago. It's basic high level stuff, nothing around tools or technology.

I remember setting up an affiliate program for a B2B SaaS company I worked with. I was like, *What the heck goes on a landing page to recruit partners for an affiliate program?* I had no idea. But I didn't want to reinvent the wheel and just guess my way through it. I didn't feel like I had a place where I could go and find people who could give me insight. There are other paid communities out there, but they aren't created for SaaS marketers. I finally decided to start one myself.

Can you tell me about this journey of building it with no-code tools?

It's gone through a couple of different iterations. The original concept was quite literally a swipe file, which is basically a folder where you keep inspiration and ideas for marketing. For example, you might see a good email or ad or landing page and then you save it to your folder or file. Later, you can use that for inspiration. The original concept acted like a detailed swipe file, with teardown analysis of each of those examples.

I personally built it on Webflow. It was connected to Memberstack as the content system to gate the actual member content. I used ConvertKit for the newsletter and the automations, and for keeping people in the loop.

In addition to the newsletter and the Swipe Files, I added a community, which is built up on top of Circle. Circle is a fantastic emerging community platform that has allowed me to see the community part of Swipe Files come to fruition. It's a nice medium between the chattiness of Slack and the posts and interactions of Facebook. Circle also hosts all course and workshop content as well. Now I've also built a curated Swipe Files and other pages that use Airtable and

Zapier. I also have an "open" page that shows my journey to 1,000 true fans.

When did you launch Swipe Files?

I started breaking ground on it in March of 2020. It is very much a COVID business baby. I launched to the public the last week of April 2020, and then I launched the community in October. I revamped and officially launched on Product Hunt in January of 2021 reaching the #2 Product of the Day.

What kind of advice would you give to a SaaS founder who's wanting to build a product that is centered around community?

Starting it up, I was pretty terrified because I had no idea what I was doing. I didn't have any background in community. It's this two-sided marketplace where you're just matchmaking people. How do you get people in there when the appeal is that there are supposed to be other people already there? You need this big bang event that gets people all together at once, and then you can get the ball rolling. Then there's this flywheel that happens where the community takes on a life of its own and you don't have to worry about facilitating everything one by one.

I started putting out feelers at first. By that time, I had a few thousand subscribers on the newsletter, and several thousand followers on Twitter. I also started seeding the idea to close friends to get some feedback. I would ask them, "Are you part of a community? What do you like? What do you not like about it? If you're not part of a community, why aren't you? If you are part of one, is there something that really keeps you coming back to that community?"

I started doing a lot of customer discovery and customer validation, just like you would with any other product, especially a software product. To build a product that solves the problem, you have to talk to customers to figure out what they need and what they're looking for. What I found was that a lot of people were on these free Facebook groups and Slack groups, but they wanted something that was paid and curated, where they didn't feel like they needed to check in constantly and make sure they didn't miss things.

Essentially, I got to a point where I said, *I'm just going to start it*. It's all going to be based on the idea that we all have unique experiences and perspectives we can all bring to the table. It's not going to be a very homogenous group where we all have the same job title and we're in the same industry. It's all going to be very different and it's mostly going to be asynchronous. I had a form at one point and I had a few hundred people reply. I had like 100 different Twitter DM conversations and 100 different email threads. I went back to each one of those individually and gave them an update, and asked if they wanted in.

One day, I opened the floodgates and said, "Come in, introduce yourself." I had a couple of friends come in and seed the first posts by asking a question or sharing something interesting, and that helped build momentum.

You have to kickstart things and manually push that boulder up the hill yourself. But eventually you get to the top of the hill and then you can let it roll down the other side and it takes on a life of its own. It all comes down to this: First, you have to model the behavior you want people to have. And then when people do it, you have to reward them both publicly and privately.

Any advice for SaaS founders who want to build a community-based product?

Play the long game. With a software tool, there's a very clear utility and need. This thing saves you money, it makes you more money or it saves you time. But with a content-based business, with memberships, with community, with newsletters, it's not so black and white or utilitarian. It's very emotion and connection based and it's very informational. You're building up a skill set where you don't see the immediate results. Because of that, you have to play the long game. You have to build your audience. You have to establish trust with people. You have to show that you know what you're talking about. You have to give away a lot of stuff for free. And then at some point you can start figuring out how to make money.

TAKEAWAYS

- To build a community, you need to do the work. Connect with people one at a time, and follow up.

- If you're building a community-based product, you've got to model the behavior you want to see in your users (e.g. interacting, sharing questions, and asking questions). Then, find ways to reward users for modeling the behavior you want to see.

- A content-based business means that you'll have to play the long game. You won't make money right off the bat.

#98

Catherine Weilaender

Title: Co-founder & CEO, HarmonyCB

Value proposition: Enabling companies to transform their customer experience with no code

Industry: Software development, internal business applications, enterprise applications

Keywords: Bootstrapping, co-founder, iteration, no-code, prioritization

How did you get into no-code?

I founded my first company about four years ago. It was a software company where we built business applications. We were taking the traditional software development route – developing custom applications as needed. That, of course, takes lots of time and money. In 2019, I started thinking, "There must be a better way to do this."

Because my co-founder had built declarative UI systems before, we thought we could combine this experience with custom software development. So, we started building HarmonyCB, a no-code tool for people to set up business applications – like ERP systems or CRM tools – using their own company and customer data. Our tool allows people to visually build without needing any programming knowledge.

HarmonyCB reduces a lot of time, energy, and money spent on coordinating multiple layers of people to build and approve an application. There are a lot of no-code tools out there for making mobile apps or prototypes, but our focus is on customer portals for business applications.

Are no-code tools the future of software development?

No-code tools will definitely be the future for a lot of software development. It makes technology so much more accessible to people, and enables them to experiment without spending 30k+ euros or dollars on a custom application. I think it will also counteract the lack of developers in the market. You'll be able to build things without having to spend a year looking for a developer.

Has starting a SaaS company been harder than you thought it would be?

The hardest part has been bootstrapping the company, which means things move slowly because you constantly balance income and product or business development. It's definitely a different approach than raising a round and then building the product subsequently. Because we've been bootstrapping, we've also focused on working with customers from the first day, providing value, seeing that they're willing to pay for our product, and improving our application by experiencing what customers actually need. So far the most productive way for us to do that are continuous iteraterations based on customers feedback and needs when working with HarmonyCB.

When you release a product, nobody automatically cares, right? Because nobody knows about it. You have to build up a base of customers who are really excited about finding a solution to their problem in your product.

Right now, the biggest challenge is prioritizing what will have the greatest impact on the development of HarmonyCB. We still have limited resources, so good prioritization between business development, product development, design, sales, etc. is key for getting to the next milestone.

Any advice for someone who wants to bootstrap their SaaS company?

It might sound obvious, but you do need enough money to create enough iterations to make a great product, unless you're really lucky on the first try! Plan a lot of time to talk to your customers, apply the "Mom Test" (ask questions that not even your mom could lie to you about), and narrow in on your problem before settling on a solution hypothesis.

How do you find a good co-founder?

I was lucky because the co-founder from my previous company is also my co-founder for HarmonyCB. We came up with this idea together. But it can be hard to find somebody. You can get lucky and meet someone new, and it might really click. But I think it works best when people come from your own network. Look for someone you've interacted with before and that you can get on with.

I've repeatedly seen comparisons between finding a co-founder and dating. That sounds about right to me. You'll be going to go through a lot of different phases together. So, you want to find out as quickly as possible whether you work well together, where you complement each other and where you have friction. You've got to know that you can make it through the long haul.

TAKEAWAYS

- Make sure you have enough money to iterate several times.

- Ask potential customers questions that not even your mom could lie to you about ("The Mom Test.") Don't look for compliments; look for facts.

- Before committing to a co-founder, find out as quickly as possible if you work well together.

#99
Marty Lindsay

Title: Founder, RosterBuddy.app
Value proposition: Automated chore roster
Industry: B2C
Keywords: No-code

What is RosterBuddy?

RosterBuddy is an automated chore roster allocation service that takes the hassle out of chore management for households. Our target customers are people who are sharing houses with other people—students, families, young adults, anyone else who might fall into that category.

In that scenario, there's generally one person who gets most irritated or frustrated at the mess, and has to take ownership of managing chores. Typically, that one person gets annoyed the most and has to pester others and becomes the bad cop. Then, everyone gets irritated.

I'm targeting that one person who would be happy to spend a few dollars a month to generate a roster and send out reminder emails.

How did you build this product?

I spent a couple of months using Bubble.io – a no-code tool – to build it. I spent the previous 12 months brushing up on coding, as I was a coder 15 years ago. But progress was slow because I'm working full-time as well. I pivoted to no-code about six months ago, and I've been very happy with that.

How easy has it been to use a No-Code tool?

I've got 25 years of IT experience, so it's been a bit quicker for me to get up to speed with building things. But Bubble makes it really quick to get it up and running.

The downside of Bubble is that you start with a blank slate in terms of the user interface design. You can do anything you like, but it's quite daunting. It's like starting with a blank bit of paper and you have to draw something there. I learned early on that creating a UI was not my strength because user interface stuff is easy to make ugly and it's easy to not have a responsive interface that works well on any device. So I shopped around quite early on for templates that I could use.

Is this your first business?

12 years ago, I was successful in generating a six figure amount of money over about three years, using a combination of an old thing called Google Gadgets and Google Adsense. I've done other things since then that generated a little bit of money. But mostly I've been raising a family and staying busy with my full time job.

At this point, I've been working nonstop in IT since '96, and I think I've just come to the end of the road of being an employee. Being an employee is fine for continuity of income, but I don't want to be doing this constantly. I'd like to have income that's not tied to my time. The downside of that is that it's hard to rely upon it, especially if you're still paying a mortgage and have kids to feed. I'd like to have a whole portfolio of things that generate some income. I know from experience you can try 20 things and one will work and 19 won't.

How are you reaching your target customers?

That is a bit foreign to me. I'm an engineer by inclination and that's the biggest risk, I think with engineer founders is that they like building. So I'm trying to make myself do something every other day that involves marketing.

What would you say to someone who's about to start a SaaS?

It's quite hard, not in terms of the difficulty of the task, but in terms of the amount of persistence you need. For six months, I've worked on it in almost all of my spare time.

It's very easy to get 80% through a project and realize you've still got 60% left to do because you've learned a lot more through that process. And then you get to 80% through that new list and you've still got 60% more to do. That last 20% is the hardest.

People need to have a lightning focus on their To Do list, and to not try to solve everything. I launched when all basic functionality was working, but there are still many things on the to do list. The app now has three paying subscribers and three trialling.

TAKEAWAYS

- You need persistence. When you think you're 80% through, you've still got 60% left. The last 20% is the hardest.
- Stay laser-focused on your To Do list.

PART 6

REFOUNDERS

Founders who are giving fresh starts to existing SaaS companies

#100

Karthik Manimozhi

Title: Founder & CEO, Letus by RentMoola

Value proposition: Empowers renters to make flexible payments on their terms

Industry: Fintech PropTech

Keywords: Development, distribution

What is Letus?

78% of Americans are living paycheck to paycheck and and half of them are cost burdened from spending 40-50% of their pretax income on rent. We take out expensive insurance products and credit card charges, and allow people to better balance their paychecks by giving them access to what we call "Flexible Rent powered by Rent Now, Pay Later." Letus brings the convenience of e-commerce into the world of rent, deposits, utilities, and so on.

Who are the actual customers of Letus?

We target four areas: large corporates/REITs, mid cap property managers, large cap property managers, and mom & pop small cap homeowners. It's a marketplace. A landlord can sign up for the services or a tenant can sign up for the services, regardless of the landlord being part of the platform.

How do you reach such a large audience?

I'm a big believer in distribution through partnerships. Our strategy – embedding our product into other products – allows us to work with companies who have already acquired hundreds of thousands, if not millions, of consumers.

The key thing is to take your ego out of it. So long as you're helping people, they don't necessarily have to know that you're the one helping them. Figure out who has distribution, figure out where people go for advice, and then give them the solution right there and make it easy and consumable.

Why SaaS?

No one has infinite resources. Every dollar off your revenue that you reinvest should provide actual, tangible value to the consumer. SaaS is a great way of doing that. The old way was that people would use different, local versions of software called On-Premise software. When you innovated on a platform, it wasn't generally available to all your customers the same way. People would have to upgrade a certain level before they could take advantage of customization.

I'm a big believer in multi-tenant SaaS. You give up deep customization to make sure that your features are rolled out much faster. For example, if there's a change in regulation or change in privacy law or a new opportunity in the market, you want to be in a really fast innovation cycle. Your dollars go in, you do the R&D, and next time your user logs in, they see all your latest features right away. There is no need to upgrade. There is no need to set up. There's no need to re-educate instantly. Your innovation dollars drive real impact to consumers.

This forces you to make tough choices. If you can't customize, you have to think about what the majority of your customers use. But in the long run, more people benefit because your revenue and reinvestment drive a maximum benefit cycle for your customers.

What is the biggest challenge about refounding a company?

The important thing about refounding a company is not to forget the roots. You have to reconcile the past with the future, and that should drive your present. A lot of people had trust and invested their resources in the last company. You want to make sure that you're hand-holding them and telling them, "We're going to take all the good things that you like right now and enhance that."

That's what we did with Letus, formerly Rent Moola. Rent Moola is a very reliable platform with customer loyalty. It has done billions in rent processing. Now we have this new microservices enabled platform. The key is allowing people to process why the change is good for them.

How can you earn credibility?

Credibility is earned when there are problems. If you're thinking about building customer trust, you go to the customer, apologize if it was your mistake, figure out the problem, and then help them transcend and move to the next level. I've been in enterprise software for over two decades. My largest wins have come from the customer who escalated. I love a customer who is angry or upset, not because they're angry or upset, but because that allows me to go in there, engage better with them, and win back their trust.

The one customer that I'm really scared of is a customer who doesn't care who you are or what you're offering. As long as they're engaging with you and showing emotions, it means that they're invested. Be there for them and just walk the talk. They can see through BS easily. You have to be genuine. You have to really care for the customer, understand where they're coming from, really. Then you move and build from there.

Any final advice that you would have for SaaS founders?

Don't be overwhelmed by the industry vertical. Knowledge can be empowering, but knowledge can also hold you back. Look for the problem that everyone has gotten used to and try to solve it. In this industry, that's flexibility for the renter.

There's no better way to build a billion dollar brand than by solving and making something with actual tangible value for your consumer.

TAKEAWAYS

- Don't let your ego get in the way of distribution partnerships.
- An angry customer isn't a bad thing; solving their problem can help you earn credibility.

Eli Hooten

Title: CTO, Codecov

Value proposition: Helps developers write safer, better, higher quality code

Industry: Software development

Keywords: Co-founder, hiring, metrics

What is Codecov?

We build developer tools to help software developers write safer, better, higher quality code.

How did you identify this as a problem?

I actually didn't identify this as a problem. Codecov was founded by someone else in 2014. He bootstrapped it as a solo founder for four years and eventually got tired of running the business. He was looking to exit the company, and had a relationship with the current CEO of the company, who took it over and brought me on as the CTO.

We like to refer to ourselves as "refounders" because we got a product that had been worked on for four years by one person and accumulated four years of technical debt, four years of business debt, and four years of basic customer growth. Essentially, we had to jump off a cliff and build our wings on the way down. We had to learn this business, what worked, what didn't work, learn the ins and outs of this pretty complicated product, learn about our customers, and build a team at the same time. It was daunting, and one of the hardest things I've ever done professionally. But it's been so rewarding.

What made Codecov really unique is there was tremendous potential from day one. There was already impressive traction from a one-person company and potential to grow that revenue by multiples over time.

What are some of the blindspots that a refounder might encounter?

I think that people interested in refounding might think, *This is going to be easy. I don't have to validate my product. It's just free money. It's already generating revenue.*

While that might be true, the onus is on you to do all the work to get your understanding back to where the founder left off. That founder has talked to a thousand customers. That founder has shipped features that have broken and fixed a broken system again. And the system is probably held together with duct tape and glue. To refound successfully, you need to have been a founder yourself. It's your job to step into that environment, learn as quickly as possible, and know enough to know what's wrong.

Here's my most important advice. Do not do this alone. No matter what your background is, if you're an engineer looking to buy a company, or if you're a business-minded person and you want to be a CEO of a functioning company, orchestrate a good handoff process with the founder. If there is a team, leverage them. If there's not a team, scale quickly.

Can you talk about hiring?

I do not like hiring fast, period. But refounding puts you in a position to have to do it. The way to be successful is to have a good framework and a repeatable process for hires, especially first roles.

Don't just hire for the problems you're having today. Sit down and ask, *What's this person going to do in a year? What can they do in six months?* If you don't have a clear answer, then you might just need a contractor. But if you can think three months, six months, and 12 months into the future and think *I still have work for this person*, then hire. Then, define that work as deliverables. What do they need to possess to get those things done? What questions can I ask a person to determine if they can do it?

The second part to hiring well in a small company is the concept of a unanimous "Yes." Especially if you're a small team, every single person needs to have a "yes" to the new hire. Cultural buy-in is so important. When the team is small, everyone needs to be very enthusiastic about this hire. They need to want to make that person successful. If you don't do that, you risk your culture growing incorrectly, setting the whole thing on fire.

What kind of metrics do you look at?

At day zero, you actually don't know what the metrics are like. I think what becomes important when you're that small is that everything is qualitative. I don't even think you have a need for measurement before your first 50 users. If you're building a B2B product, maybe it's like five or 10 customers. When you're that small, it's qualitative. Talk to customers constantly and get feedback constantly.

As you get bigger, KPIs become more important. This becomes a question of what moves the needle. The first question is, what is the needle? Is it adoption? Is it revenue? You have to understand what the North Star is. At the end of the day, the metric that you really want to optimize for is probably not money. Revenue is always a side effect.

How do you pick a co-founder?

Picking a co-founder is very difficult. You need to be able to be 100% honest with your co-founder. It can be really tough to have conversations about alignment, or whether someone is doing something incorrectly, or whether they just need to walk away. When it comes to picking a cofounder, don't pick a friend. Don't pick family. Pick someone who you know and who will always be 100% honest with you and with themselves. It is monumentally easy to lie to yourself as a co-founder. You need a co-founder who is going to look at you and go, "I think you're lying right now." And that's pretty hard to find.

TAKEAWAYS

- If you're hiring someone to solve an immediate problem, make sure you've got a job for them three, six, and 12 months down the line. You may just need a contractor.

- When hiring someone new, have a clear idea of the deliverables you need from them now and in the future. That can help you look for the right personality traits and skill sets.

- On a small team, everyone needs to be excited about new hires.

- Early on (before your first 50 customers), focus on qualitative, not quantitative, metrics.

- Your North Star metric probably has nothing to do with revenue.

You've reached the final interview.

Do me a favor.

Tell me what you are going to do DIFFERENTLY as a result of reading this book—at kelsey@kelseyyarnell.com.

ABOUT KELSEY

Kelsey is a SaaS content writer.

She also really likes people—especially entrepreneurs—so she decided to talk to more than 100 of them in a single year. She wanted to figure out how she could help aspiring SaaS founders reach their goals a little sooner, with fewer hiccups along the way.

Over the 15 months that it took to write this book, Kelsey talked to people in the U.S., Mexico, the Middle East, Western and Eastern Europe, Africa, India, Australia, Canada, and more. She wants to thank every one of the founders who contributed to this book for giving up time and energy for *Kicking SaaS*.

She also wants to thank her mom, Karin, for proofreading the entire book.

1194GUKWH00016B/160/J
UKHW021252180426
Ingram Content Group UK Ltd.
Pitfield, Milton Keynes, MK11 3LW, UK
www.ingramcontent.com/pod-product-compliance